The "CHILDREN OF PERESTROIKA"

The "CHILDREN

OF PERESTROIKA"

Moscow Teenagers Talk About Their Lives and the Future

DEBORAH ADELMAN

**NARRATIVES TRANSLATED BY
DEBORAH ADELMAN,
FAY GREENBAUM,
AND SHARON MCKEE**

With a Postscript from
the Summer of 1992

M.E. SHARPE INC.
ARMONK, N.Y.

Jacket photo by Igor Gnevashev

Photographs on the following pages were taken by Deborah Adelman:
2, 48, 82, 138, 202, 216
Photographs on the following pages were taken by Igor Gnevashev:
ii, 110, 158, 176, 188
Photographs on the following pages were taken by Igor Timoshenko:
26, 228

Library of Congress Cataloging-in-Publication Data

Adelman, Deborah.
The "Children of Perestroika" : Moscow teenagers talk about
their lives and the future / by Deborah Adelman.
p.   cm.
Includes index.
ISBN 1-56324-000-9 (cloth)
ISBN 1-56324-001-7 (paperback)
1. Teenagers—Russian S.F.S.R.—Moscow—Attitudes.
2. Youth—Soviet Union—Social conditions.
3. Soviet Union—Social conditions—1970– .
4. Soviet Union—Politics and government—1985– .
I. Title.
HQ799.S692M673 1991
305.2′35′0947—dc20
90-25104
CIP

Printed in the United States of America

The paper used in this publication meets the minimum
requirements of American National Standard for Information
Sciences—Permanence of Paper for Printed Library Materials,
ANSI Z39.48-1984.

MV (c)   10 9 8 7 6 5 4 3
MV (p)   10 9 8 7 6 5 4 3 2

7-19-93

*For Norm Adelman
and in memory of Gert Adelman*

Contents

Preface

The narratives in this book are taken from a series of interviews with eleven Moscow teenagers of diverse backgrounds. The conversations took place between January and June 1989 and covered a wide range of topics, from family relationships to economic and political reform. They offer a broad perspective of Soviet life as seen through the eyes of adolescents, providing an insider's view into the lifestyle and thought of typical Moscow teenagers during the current period of radical change. The narratives illustrate the ways in which *glasnost* and *perestroika** have affected the perspectives and world views of young people in the Soviet Union.

This project was carried out during the academic year 1988–89, which I spent in Moscow as a participant in the State University of New York–Moscow State University Faculty Exchange program. I went to learn more about the ways in which current changes have affected secondary-school teachers and their assessment of students' work. I was particularly interested in older students—ninth- and tenth-graders—and how teachers judge their readiness to graduate and to begin participating in adult life.

Despite warnings by other researchers about the difficulty of gaining access to Soviet schools, within a few weeks of my arrival I had been welcomed in a number of them, had met many teachers, and was able to observe a variety of classrooms. Most of these schools had had no previous experience with a foreign researcher, and it was clear that perestroika and glasnost had made it much easier for Western researchers to enter ordinary Soviet schools. In fact, many teachers and administrators were eager to meet with me and ask questions about the educational system in the United States. The changes taking place in the Soviet Union have left no aspect of life untouched, and the educational system is undergoing a period of intense scrutiny and reform. There is a growing tendency to look for possible solutions to current

*The reader will find explanations of these and other special terms in the glossary.

dilemmas in the experience of other societies, and the United States is often viewed as a model. Undoubtedly, this interest in the United States made my access to Moscow schools easier.

I met many students and spent time talking to them in classrooms, in hallways between classes, in cafeterias, and outside school entrances. They invited me to join them on field trips and day excursions, to the theater and cinema, and to musical and theatrical performances in which they participated. I heard them sing satiric medleys of "Songs from the Period of Stagnation," act in plays dedicated to the victims of Stalinist repression, play the guitar and sing Russian folk songs on rides to the woods on the *elektrichka*, the commuter train; I traveled with them to amateur competitions with other schools in the city and the small towns nearby.

I was struck by the general excitement that emanated from so many of these students. Knowing the fascination of Soviet young people with the West, I had expected a barrage of questions about the United States. To my surprise, students were far more interested in discussing what was going on in their own country than in asking me about mine. This did not exclude me from conversations; the teenagers I met seemed to delight in talking to me about what was going on in their country. They wanted to make sure that I understood the essence of glasnost and perestroika, eager to discuss and to inform me, a foreigner, of what was going on. They were proud and excited and enjoyed being in the role of helping teach an adult.

I talked to both teachers and students, most often separately. It became clear to me that I was witnessing a change in the relationships between young people and the adults around them. Teachers felt that now, more than ever, one of their major roles was to raise their students' level of awareness. They felt a responsibility to talk to their students about change, about the new revelations concerning Stalinism, about the truth of the years of Brezhnev's leadership. The young people I met were clearly interested in the process taking place around them but spoke to me of their changing feelings toward their teachers and other adults. They expressed both doubt and lack of trust. They weren't sure whether they believed their teachers or respected their opinions, considering them products of "stagnation." In the last few years they have been told that during their early years of schooling they were not hearing the truth, and certainly they were not automatically inclined to believe adults now.

I remember a literature class of tenth-graders, soon to graduate from one of Moscow's best special schools. The Russian language and literature curriculum had been expanded to include *publitsistika*, the journalism and essays that have become the backbone of glasnost. When the class began, the teacher—the school principal and a well-known and respected literary critic—listed several articles from different newspapers and magazines that would provide the material for the lesson. There was not a single student in the class who had not read most if not all of them. They knew exactly which articles the teacher had referred to, and they were eager to discuss them.

One article related the experience of a woman from a collective farm in the Ural mountains, deep in the provinces, who had been awarded a trip to East Germany for her long years of hard labor at the farm. According to the article, the woman walked into a food store in East Germany, saw that there were forty types of sausage available, and fainted. For some reason a Soviet reporter was standing nearby, and when the woman was revived outside the store, he asked her what was wrong. "Look," said the woman, "I was awarded this trip because of my hard work! Me and my colleagues work day after day, from morning to night! It's not that we're lazy. So why do we live so poorly? Why don't we have forty choices?"

The teacher retold the story with great emotion. "And that was *East* Germany!" he exclaimed. "It's a good thing they didn't send her to the other Germany, where they have not forty but *four hundred different types of sausages!*" The entire class burst into laughter, and this upset the teacher. "What are you laughing about?" he asked the students. "This is not funny! This is our tragedy! *Our tragedy!*" The students became serious, and the atmosphere grew somber as the discussion continued. At the end of the period, after the teacher had left, several students surrounded me, anxious to talk. "I don't know if you realize this or not," one of them said to me, "but there is a lot of pessimism going on around here now. The atmosphere is not great." He rolled his eyes at the door, following the path taken by the teacher. Another student waved his hand in the same direction, to dispel any doubts about whom they had in mind. This same teacher they were charging with pessimism had told me, minutes before the class began, that upperclassmen were apathetic and disbelieving. But clearly those same students worried that the pessimism they perceived in the adults around them would overwhelm me.

In another conversation, a history teacher told me that ninth- and tenth-graders are the most difficult students to work with because they were taught in their early years not to think, only to repeat. He felt that they have remained skeptical and passive in the face of change, taught in their early years to be apolitical, which makes it difficult for them to take the possibility of real changes seriously. He said that older students do not want to believe, argue with him, and ask him, "Was Stalin really that bad?" The teacher felt that a fair number of students have parents who continue to support Stalin.

His words surprised me. Just two days earlier, one of this same teacher's ninth-grade students, whose narrative appears in this book, had told me with great compassion that history teachers, more than any other teachers, had been "victims of the times" because the misinformation, distortions, and general lack of historical materials characteristic of the period of stagnation had kept them from true knowledge of their own discipline.

It was obvious that these students actively were contemplating the changes going on around them, had become engaged in reading and seeking new information, and were reassessing their relationships with adults, trying to form opinions independently of them. They understood the problems their country faced and were aware of the acute difficulties that lay ahead. Nonetheless, they were enthusiastic about glasnost, which has had no less an impact on their daily lives than have the shortages and the chaos caused by the complex process of economic restructuring.

The enormous effect on their lives of the current period in the Soviet Union had become quite clear to me. After observing their conversations for a few months, I realized that I wanted to record what these teenagers were telling me in a systematic fashion. Their increasing awareness of their country and their obvious fascination with newspapers, television, and other media impressed me. It was a year of tumultuous change in the Soviet Union, and during the months I was there, many of these teenagers became politically active for the first time in their lives. In the spring, large street demonstrations and rallies were held in Moscow, and many of my teenage acquaintances participated in them. They had become captivated by the events in their country. When I suggested that we record some of our conversations and give them some structure, they were very excited. They wanted me to hear about their lives.

The eleven teenagers whose narratives are included here are only some of the many with whom I spoke. Although these selections do not represent a scientific sampling, I took care to ensure that a variety of social backgrounds was represented, and the group contains both young men and young women. Some study in general academic schools, others in the vocational schools that prepare young workers to enter industrial production upon graduation. Others come from working-class families but do not intend to become workers themselves. Ultimately, those included were the ones most enthusiastic about the proj-

ect and most eager to share their thoughts with me. The interview
sessions involved travel across Moscow, hours in my rooms at the dormitory or in empty classrooms after school hours, or, on occasion, at the
home of one of the students.

They are ordinary Moscow teenagers. All of them either are in school
or, in the case of Maxim, work. They have plans for the future and are
not marginalized from mainstream Soviet society in any way. There are
no representatives of the "hippies" or *metallisty, rokery,* or other unofficial youth groups that have sprung up in Moscow and other cities in the
Soviet Union. I met all of these teenagers through their schools or, in
the case of some of the vocational school students, through cultural and
extracurricular groups organized by the Ministry of Vocational Education. I did have the occasion to meet members of a Soviet youth gang
and spoke with them, but I could not conduct extensive interviews with
them in the way I wanted to for this book. The eleven teenagers included here do not represent "rebellious" youth, yet all of them clearly
show critical awareness and, to varying degrees, a desire to question and
examine the existing order.

The interviews covered many topics. I was interested in issues of
general importance—family, intergenerational and male–female relationships, leisure and recreational activities, hopes and desires for the
future, and the degree to which these teenagers feel empowered to
determine what their lives will become. I was equally interested in finding out more about the specific details of *Soviet* teenagers' lives, particularly the effects of perestroika and glasnost. Although I asked the same
questions of each participant, I wanted to make sure that I allowed each
one to talk about issues that were most interesting to him or her and let
topics come up that I had not included in my list. For this reason the
narratives vary greatly in content and organization, according to each
participant's individual concerns. Each theme is represented by the
teenagers who had the most to say about it. Although I have edited
these narratives extensively and they represent only a small portion of
much lengthier interviews, I have left the topics in the order in which
they were brought up, to leave intact the narrative quality of these
adolescents' stories. I have eliminated my own questions from the narratives as they do not significantly enhance the text.

It is hard to adequately convey the warmth and caring extended to
me by these and many of the other teenagers I met in Moscow. They
were excited to meet an American researcher and pleased by the
thought that they had something to offer me and, eventually, other
American readers. They spent long hours in conversation with me and
were willing to talk about anything I asked, even though at times it was

difficult for them to speak about subjects not normally part of their discussions with adults, such as sex and sexual relations among young people.

Their warmth and openness extended far beyond the conversations. Eager to share their lives with me, they invited me to many events. I accompanied them on trips in and around Moscow. I was invited on camping trips and day trips to the woods to ski and hike. I was invited to their apartments for tea. Essentially, I was adopted.

In December, before the formal interviews began, I went with a group of ninth-grade girls to a school in a small town on the outskirts of Moscow, where they had been invited by a group of students to participate in a talent contest. The girls had prepared several skits, and we went on the commuter train late on a Saturday afternoon. Spirits were high; they laughed, giggled, took out a guitar and sang—so many of the teenagers I met knew how to play guitar and loved to sit in a group and sing sad, melodic Russian folk songs! This time they entertained me with a satiric song, "Colorado," which jokingly described cowboys and the Wild West and ended in a wry comment about the affluence of America. Later, as we walked through snowy woods in the darkness of a December afternoon, the conversation turned to the upcoming celebration of the New Year. One of the girls asked me whether I usually put up a tree in my home. I replied that I never had, as in the United States they are primarily symbols of Christmas, which I do not celebrate at home.

"You don't put up a tree, Deborah?" one of the girls asked. She fell silent for a minute, and said, with a little sigh, "How sad!"

One week later this same group of girls came to my dorm room, a one-and-a-half-hour ride on the Moscow subway, carrying with them a freshly cut pine tree, complete with ornaments and presents, cakes and cookies to have with tea, a guitar, and a lot of holiday spirit. They insisted that all adults present—two Soviet friends of mine were also there—wait in one of my two small rooms. They shut themselves in the other and proceeded to decorate the tree and walls with ornaments and decorations. They did not want me to have to celebrate the New Year alone, so far away from home, they said. They did not want me to be lonely or homesick.

I tried to imagine a group of teenagers in New York City traveling from the Upper Bronx to the heart of Brooklyn, a comparable trip in time and distance, dragging a freshly cut Christmas tree on the subway for a lonely Soviet researcher!

These were not privileged Moscow teenagers. They were ordinary students studying at ordinary schools, most of whom had never had real personal contact with a Westerner before, and certainly not with an American. Many of them continue to write to me regularly. They would like American readers, American teenagers, to know about their lives. They are active and want to do something to help their country move ahead. They are fervent supporters of glasnost, but clearly understand the difficulties of perestroika. They are in some ways ingenuous but in many others startlingly clear-headed and realistic.

The intention of this book is to let these eleven Moscow teenagers speak for themselves. With eloquence and humor, the eagerness and hopefulness of childhood as well as some strikingly adult observations and awareness, they talk about life in Moscow today.

Acknowledgments

Special thanks are due to Leonid Shkolnik of the Academy of Pedagogical Sciences in Moscow. Without his collaboration and friendship this project would not have taken place. Galina Shchevchenko of the Ministry of Vocational Education also provided invaluable assistance and enthusiasm.

The following people read sections of the manuscript in progress, and their critical commentary was important: Anne Meisenzahl, John T. Cabral, Norm Adelman, Nina Adel, Emily Filardo, Shaari Neretin, Miriam Adelman, and Amy Ruth Tobol. I would like to thank Fay Greenbaum and Sharon McKee for their work in translating sections of the manuscript.

The State University of New York's exchange with Moscow State University provided the opportunity to live and do research in Moscow. Thanks also go to Patricia Kolb, my editor at M.E. Sharpe, whose enthusiasm and insightful commentary helped me complete the book.

I would like to thank my father, Norm Adelman, for his support and encouragement during the entire project. Equally important, his example throughout the years, as both parent and professional, has taught me the value of listening carefully to what young people have to say.

The Teenagers

TANYA

Tanya, sixteen, has just finished ninth grade. When she completes her secondary education next year, she would like to study at one of Moscow's pedagogical institutes.

Tanya comes from a working-class family, but she is consciously preparing to move into the intelligentsia. She views herself as part of the "workers' intelligentsia," which she defines as a link between the working class and professionals or intellectuals.

OLYA

Olya, who is almost eighteen, has just completed vocational school, where in addition to finishing her secondary education she has been trained to work as a printer in a factory. Now she must work there on a regular shift for the next two years. This is customary for students who have gone on to vocational schools, as the State spends large sums of money for their education, which must be repaid through work in industrial production. Olya chose to leave school and the academic track after eighth grade, but three years later she regrets this decision, concluding that she made it at an age when she did not understand its implications for her future.

Olya's mother is a factory worker who moved to Moscow from a provincial city in order to marry. Olya's father is a construction worker, not steadily employed. Her parents recently divorced.

LENA

Lena, at sixteen, has completed ninth grade and has one more year of school. An avid reader, an "information maniac" in the words of a fellow classmate, Lena is quite excited about glasnost and the process of perestroika. During the past year she participated in numerous demonstrations during the electoral campaign and has experienced a political awakening. Her interest in and knowledge of Soviet history and politics are impressive.

Lena's father is a film director who works for state television producing programs for young people. Her mother, also a film director by training, has recently begun working for Soviet radio.

ILYA

Ilya has just completed his secondary education at one of Moscow's elitist special English schools. He has been preparing for the entrance exams to the Department of Russian Language and Literature at Moscow State University for a year but has become so absorbed in recent political events that he has been distracted from his work. Ilya is an avid reader and is well informed about the new developments in his country. At age seventeen, he can already be considered a "Moscow intellectual." Ilya comes from a Jewish family, notes that he has been raised in dissident circles, and prides himself on being a progressive and independent thinker. His views, which he backs up with frequent references to sources, reflect the influence of one faction of current Soviet "opposition," the reformers who would like to see the Soviet Union move toward a market economy. Curiously, within the current situation in the Soviet Union, advocates of more privatization are often referred to as "leftists."

Ilya's parents are divorced, and he lives with his mother, an economist and researcher. His older sister lives with their father, a well-known psychiatrist and poet.

MAXIM

Maxim, at fifteen, is studying to become a chef. He dropped out of secondary school after the eighth grade in order to attend culinary school at a prestigious Moscow restaurant and hotel. He feels no urgency to finish school and believes that secondary education will not be significant for him in his chosen career. Soon he will complete his training program and will be free to work as a chef in a restaurant. When he reaches age eighteen, Maxim will try to complete his required military service in the navy, where he would like to work as a cook on a ship.

Maxim comes from a working-class family. In the past his father worked as a trainer for a professional soccer team, but he now works in a neighborhood health and recreation complex that runs a cafe and Russian sauna. His mother is a hairdresser in a beauty salon. The family lives in a communal apartment, which means that Maxim, his younger sister, and his parents share one room in an apartment inhabited by two other adults who are not related to the family.

Maxim's views convey the conservative social and political thinking that many consider to be most representative of the Soviet working class, which has been less supportive of Gorbachev and of changes than have intellectuals and professionals.

YELENA

Yelena, at sixteen, has just completed ninth grade. During the past year she has become interested in political developments in the Soviet Union and has begun to participate in demonstrations.

She has become intrigued by history and would like to enter a pedagogical institute and become a history teacher. Her parents work in a factory. Yelena criticizes them for the "quietness" with which they have raised her and says that she would like to raise her own children in a different, more active manner. She has only recently begun to travel to various cities within the Soviet Union, and this has made her more eager to travel to other places, within her country and abroad. She notes that her parents "like to sit at home too much." One senses that her parents are more politically conservative than she is. It seems that the school she attends, with its politically active principal and atmosphere of open dialogue, has had a great impact on her. Unlike her parents, she believes that the discussions that are a product of glasnost are not superfluous but rather an essential catalyst for true economic reform.

DIMA

Dima, at eighteen, recently completed his secondary education at a vocational school, where he learned to repair radio and electronic equipment. He comes from a working-class family and neighborhood. He is now serving in the army and intends to work in a cooperative as a repairman when he completes his military service. He would like to join a cooperative in order to earn more money.

For Dima, as a worker, perestroika and glasnost are fundamentally related to changes at the workplace and the need to motivate and raise the productivity of Soviet workers.

LYOSHA

Lyosha, at eighteen, has just completed a vocational school where, in addition to finishing his general secondary education, he has learned how to assemble radio and electronic equipment. He would like to continue studying and become an engineer but must first complete two years of military service.

Lyosha comes from a working-class family. His parents, who moved to Moscow from a provincial town before he was born, are both factory workers. The family travels often to that town, and Lyosha notes that one of the major differences he feels between himself and his parents is that they are provincial, whereas he has been raised as a Muscovite.

ALEXEI

Alexei, seventeen, is a student at a vocational school, where he is learning carpentry. His parents are university instructors who have been teaching Russian in Burundi (Africa) for the last eight years. As a young boy, Alexei lived with them in Mali for a brief period. He did not want to attend school in a foreign country and now lives with his grandmother in Moscow.

Alexei is from an intellectual family but has chosen to become a member of the working class, an uncommon occurrence. He is confused about his future and feels that he is not yet "serious enough" to pursue a degree in higher education. When he finishes vocational school he would like to study something else, but he is not sure what. He dreams about becoming a conductor on the Moscow subway.

NATASHA

Natasha, sixteen, is in a special ninth-grade pedagogical class for students who want to become teachers. She worked in her school during the past year as an assistant to a second-grade teacher and found the work gratifying. She praises the experiment as one of the few concrete successes of perestroika and glasnost in her school but feels that adults are still scared of letting children have input into programs or have any real power. She feels that much more could be done to involve students in restructuring the school if the school administration were braver.

Natasha's mother is a nurse, and Natasha feels that she has been inspired to work with people by her mother.

KATYA

Katya, sixteen, has finished ninth grade in the same special pedagogical class as Natasha. She would like to be a teacher and work with small children.

Katya has traveled to many different republics in the last few years, from Central Asia to the Baltic, and is surprised by the diversity of her country. She is particularly concerned about the nationalities problem unfolding in the Soviet Union.

Katya's parents are engineers.

The "CHILDREN OF PERESTROIKA"

MOSCOW TEENAGERS: BECOMING THE "CHILDREN OF PERESTROIKA"

Glasnost and perestroika have brought radical changes to all spheres of Soviet society, challenging the existing economic, social, and political structures. The new structures that will replace them have only begun to emerge, and this period of transition has resulted in both uncertainty and instability. Glasnost has altered the nature of Soviet mass media, offering an overwhelming amount of new, critical, and often disturbing information to an eager public. Newspapers and magazines are in great demand, and as articles on history, politics, and social problems hit the press, they immediately become the subject of public debate. There are few, if any, examples of a society absorbed in as thorough a process of self-evaluation and self-criticism as the one currently going on in the Soviet Union.

As the process of change has unfolded, it has revealed that the difficulties facing the Soviet Union are far more complex than people imagined when the ideas of perestroika and glasnost first took hold. The future of Soviet society is unclear; the only certainty is that the country is becoming something vastly different from what it has been in the past.

These changes in Soviet society have great implications for young people. The passage into adulthood is always a difficult process; experiencing it in a time of great social upheaval adds further complications. Preceding generations are held responsible for mistakes and for complacency, and the attitudes of youth toward adult authority figures, including their own parents, have been altered by revelations about the past and the challenge to the existing order. The prestige of the Party and of the Young Communist League (Komsomol) has fallen dramatically, and many members are leaving. Teachers tell their students that what they learned previously in schools is not true, and young people witness frank discussion of issues that were formerly taboo. Revelations about the true nature of Stalinist crimes make them wonder how previous generations, their parents and grandparents, could have allowed such things to happen. Faced with important decisions about their own future, teenagers must take into consideration the changes and general uncertainty of society at large.

The process of change, although welcomed by most people, has not been easy. The "de-Stalinization" of society, an essential element of recent developments, has made public shocking facts and graphic accounts of the nature of Stalinist repression and the extent to which millions of Soviet citizens suffered. Topics previously inaccessible to public criticism, or once held as representative of the highest ideals, are now debated in the press on a daily basis. Many of these concern the very foundation of the Soviet state—the nature of the Revolution, the establishment of the dictatorship of the proletariat and the one-party state, the mass exodus of artists and intellectuals after the Civil War, the fate of the peasant class during War Communism and the forced collectivization of the 1930s. Public discussion has cast doubt upon fundamental aspects of contemporary Soviet life formerly taken for granted—state ownership of industry, production, and land, free medical care, obligatory military service, and the content and quality of universal compulsory secondary education.

Social conflict and internal contradictions have intensified. Perestroika advocates new forms of economic organization, but initiatives are met with stubborn resistance by bureaucratic structures and a large sector of middle-level managers whose positions are threatened by change. There is increasing crime, racketeering, and interethnic violence. Rising nationalism has given voice to independence movements in various republics, challenging the basic structure of the Soviet Union.

Do Soviet citizens support the process of change? Are they willing to participate in it? The success of perestroika and glasnost depends upon grass-roots activity, for although reform may have started from "above," its implementation requires the engagement of all Soviet citizens in the restructuring process. Indeed, the basic premise of perestroika and glasnost is that only the participation of broad sectors of the population can rebuild a country that has inherited the economic, social, and political legacy of the command-administrative system of the Stalin and Brezhnev eras.

I first visited the Soviet Union in 1978, in the middle of the period of "stagnation," the Brezhnev years in which economic growth ground to a halt and public discussion of social and economic problems was virtually nonexistent. I traveled to the Soviet Union several times during the next ten years and had a brief glimpse of the first years of perestroika, but neither these visits nor reading about developments in the Soviet Union in the Western press prepared me for the fundamental changes that were apparent from the first week of my stay there in September 1988.

The intensity of public debate was overwhelming. In order to buy certain newspapers and magazines that people barely read before, one now had to stand in line at a news kiosk. To get a copy of *Moscow News* in the dormitory at Moscow State University, I had to go downstairs at 6 A.M. on Wednesdays, the day the paper comes out, and wait in a line that first began moving when the kiosk opened at 7 A.M. Television and radio were full of reports on an extremely diverse set of topics—Soviet history and Stalinist repression, the possibilities of introducing market mechanisms into the Soviet economy, electoral reform, critiques of Soviet education, and the state of health care. It was difficult to sort through the quantities of new information available; friends and acquaintances, wanting to ensure that I was able to share the excitement, bombarded me with newspapers and magazines, recommending the latest articles, curious to know my reactions.

At the same time, it was getting more and more difficult to obtain basic household goods and food products. Discussing what items were *defitsit*, in short supply, and in what neighborhood or store one might be lucky enough to find them was an activity almost as engaging to people as discussing the latest news report on Stalinism. In my department at Moscow State University, faculty meetings were held on the same day as the arrival of the *zakaz*, the special food order of *defitsit* items delivered weekly to many Soviet workplaces. It always surprised to me to see a group of very serious researchers run upstairs after a meeting and anxiously pull apart boxes to see what items they would find in the *zakaz*, which varied from week to week and was never known in advance.

Thus intense, candid, public debate coexists with the increasing frustration of Soviet consumers, whose already difficult lives have become even harder. Recent news reports from the Soviet Union now focus on the disillusionment and dissatisfaction of people whose lives have grown more complex. Soviet public opinion is becoming polarized; the forces that support and oppose perestroika and glasnost are consolidating and engaging in an ever-increasing struggle.

As I began my research and met people involved in many facets of Soviet education—teachers, administrators, researchers in scientific institutes—I was struck by the pervasive negative nature of their remarks. I heard barely one word of praise for anything Soviet education had achieved. The general mood was one of urgency, at times even semi-hysteria. People everywhere seemed determined to leave no stone unturned in the quest for restructuring and building a better society. No facet of life in the Soviet Union has been spared the critical scrutiny of glasnost, and the overwhelming challenge to even the most basic aspects of daily life has left people both angry and excited, hopeful and confused.

The task of restructuring is monumental, and knowing where and how to begin is difficult. Many people look for solutions in the experience of other countries, particularly the United States and Japan, and the growing tendency to glorify the experience of others is often unrealistic and lacks deep analysis, awareness, or real information. I witnessed a strong desire to disbelieve critical discussion of the United States, due in part to the fact that for too long criticism of the United States has been a part of official propaganda. More importantly, Soviets, overwhelmed by criticism of their own society, are anxious to find solutions, and they view the United States and Western Europe as affluent, stable societies with a standard of living of which, in the words of one delegate to the Congress of People's Deputies in late May 1989, Soviets "can only dream." Most Soviets have heard of American unemployment and homelessness through the Soviet media, but they have come to doubt that the problems of our society are as grave as the problems they face.

The narratives in this book must be read within this context. Most of these teenagers feel positively about the changes occurring in their country, although they approach current events with no small amount of criticism, doubt, and sometimes even skepticism. Perhaps the most significant effect recent developments have had is simply to have transformed these adolescents into avid and eager seekers of information. They follow the media closely, read and exchange articles, watch television programs, and in general have a heightened awareness of and curiosity about their country and the world.

Glasnost has had a remarkable impact on these teenagers. I interviewed them during a year in which great changes took place in their lives. They experienced a political awakening, participating in demonstrations for the first time, observing the electoral process, debating whether or not Yeltsin's candidacy should be supported, and watching the entire broadcast of the Congress of People's Deputies. They read newspapers and journals with extreme interest, watched political television programs, and in general followed events in their country closely and intently. Frequently between interview sessions, one of the teenagers would read an article on an issue we had already discussed, and before the next interview could begin she or he would insist on going back to the previous topic, wanting to add more or make a correction. Ilya, commenting on his changing relationship to Soviet sources of information, noted that they have become much more interesting to him than the once forbidden fruit of Western media:

> I used to listen to Voice of America and other Western radio stations
> all the time. . . . I've had a chance to read a lot of books published in the

West . . . we had that kind of literature in our house. . . . But now a curious thing has happened. . . . It's much more interesting to watch our television and read our newspapers. We live here, and we simply have more interesting information. "Your own shirt is closest to your skin," as they say here.

Although these teenagers are excited about the events taking place around them, they understand that the changes are replete with contradictions. For them, glasnost is noteworthy, but perestroika—economic restructuring—has thus far brought no real improvements in the standard of living and has probably made material circumstances even more difficult.

Clearly there will be no quick solutions, and the process of change will be long and complex, evolving over a period of many years. Thus, the success of reform and the ultimate outcome depend in large part upon upcoming generations. For this reason it is of particular importance to hear the voices of these adolescents. As they enter adulthood, they face important decisions about their future. To what extent have the changes taking place in the Soviet Union affected them? Do they support them? Do they feel that they have a role to play in change? The decisions they make depend upon the kind of society they live in, but if perestroika is to succeed, the society they live in will be equally dependent upon the kinds of choices their generation makes. Listening to these teenagers reveals much about the ways in which the processes in the Soviet Union will continue to unfold.

The purpose of this book is to offer an insiders' perspective on life in Moscow during this period of tumultuous change. While it would be impossible to give a thorough portrayal of Moscow teenagers in eleven narratives, the group is diverse, and through their differences as well as their similarities, patterns emerge that tell us much about life in Moscow today, not only for adolescents, but for people of all ages.

SCHOOLING AND SOCIAL CLASS

Several important factors distinguish the members of the group from one another. A crucial difference is that some of them study in academic high schools whereas others have entered vocational schools.

In the Soviet educational system, children pursue either an academic or a vocational-technical track. The decision is made after the eighth grade, when students have three options: remain in school to complete the ninth and tenth grades,* leave school to go to a techni-

---

*Soviet schools currently go through the tenth grade. The eleventh grade is being added as a result of school reforms.

cal school, or leave school to enter a vocational school.

Vocational and technical schools train students to enter the work force upon graduation. Technical schools are the more prestigious of the two, and graduates become professionals, working as medical technicians or as day-care or primary-school teachers. Vocational schools train young workers for jobs in production. These students graduate with low-level skills that enable them to work on assembly lines in factories, repair electronic equipment, or do work such as basic carpentry and plumbing. The schools vary in the quality of their training; some graduates leave with marketable skills but others do not.

The mandate of the vocational school is directly linked to urgent needs of the Soviet economy: to graduate young workers who will immediately enter industrial production, particularly in areas where there is a chronic labor shortage. Criticism of vocational schools points out that young people do not choose to attend them out of commitment to a particular area of industry: although job placements for vocational school graduates are part of the centralized planning of production, approximately one-fifth of all vocational school graduates do not begin work in the field for which they have received training. Of those who do begin to work in their skill area, many leave after a year or two of work and go on to some other type of production or continue studying.[1] None of the vocational school students in this study chose their school because of the specific training offered there but rather because of its convenient location or because they had heard that the teachers were good.

Other aspects of vocational schools give reason for concern. In vocational schools, students finish the mandatory universal secondary education, but their curriculum is officially "simplified," and it is generally recognized that its inferior quality will make it much more difficult for graduates to pursue a degree in higher education. Vocational schools are stigmatized in the Soviet Union, and students there have the reputation of being either less intelligent or too street-wise and tough to excel or care about their studies.

The decision to enter a vocational school is an important one in the life of a Soviet schoolchild and has significant ramifications for the future. Although graduates of vocational schools can continue to study and receive degrees in higher education, the choice between an academic high school and a vocational school is quite often a step toward consolidating their position within a particular social class.

The atmosphere in vocational schools, as several teenagers in this book describe in detail, often is not conducive to learning. Teachers assume that students are not interested in their studies and make few academic demands of them. The students are aware of how much easier studying became once they entered a vocational school, and the generally lowered expectations lead to a downward spiraling in which they themselves assume they will not receive thorough academic preparation or expend energy to achieve success in their studies.

Vocational education has also been criticized as a way of dealing with children who are experiencing social or emotional difficulties. In early grades, students are regularly threatened with being sent off to a vocational school, with the implicit warning that they will receive a poor education and be exposed to an atmosphere of fighting, smoking, alcohol, and freer sexual behavior. The Soviet Union in general has a lower incidence of teenage crime, substance abuse, and pregnancy than the United States; entering a social milieu that offers exposure to these problems is a particularly ominous threat in Soviet society, where many parents still feel it can be avoided by keeping their children out of vocational schools.

For Olya, this "threat" has had some positive aspects. Although to a certain extent she laments her decision to attend a vocational school, she feels she has gained in life experience:

> I went into a vocational school and ended up in a completely different environment. I didn't know that we had young people who take drugs, that young girls could smoke. I had heard about that but I didn't believe it. . . . I'm glad that I ended up in that vocational school, that I had a chance to see that kind of crowd, found out how people live, what kind of views they have, what they think about life. . . . If I had gone ahead and finished academic high school I wouldn't have found out about all of this.

The decision to attend vocational school has its greatest ramifications for Olya now that she has graduated. The government invests large sums of money in vocational schools, and graduates are required to work for two years at the same enterprise where they received their training, in order to pay back part of this investment. At age eighteen, Olya must now work in a factory for two years, whereas her friends who stayed in the academic track are free to continue studying if they so desire. A full-time job in production combined with night school seems impossible for her to manage, so she must postpone pursuing another career for two years. She feels that she has given up her freedom and, in a sense, her youth.

There is, however, a growing trend for some students to choose vocational schools rather than be pushed into them. Recently, the general ten-year school has become the object of severe criticism and its prestige has fallen. A diploma from an academic high school, once held in high regard, no longer carries the same weight. As a result, some teenagers are opting for vocational or technical schools because

they feel that they will at least have employable skills when they graduate.* Lyosha's attitude is illustrative of this trend. Although he comes
from an intellectual background and it is not typical for intellectuals to
join the working class, he feels that a general degree in secondary
education from a ten-year school has little practical worth. He does not
consider himself ready to pursue higher education and wants to take
some time off from schooling in order to work. The skills he is now
learning will allow him to do that, whereas a ten-year general academic
diploma would leave him without acceptable employment opportunities.

The growth of small, private cooperative enterprises, a major compo-
nent of the economic reforms going on in the Soviet Union, has also
made vocational schools a more desirable option. The cooperatives, in
large part designed to fill gaps in the state-run economy by providing
services the government has been unable to supply, offer salaries much
higher than state-run enterprises can. Many vocational school graduates possess marketable skills that can be extremely lucrative if they
join a cooperative.

There is a clear difference between the vocational school and academic high school students in terms of their general interest and
knowledge of society and politics. The teens who study in academic
schools, no matter what their family background, show much greater
interest and awareness of the world. This difference is even more
marked in elite special schools like Ilya's where the level of discussion
and awareness is the highest.

Special schools offer intense work in specific subjects in the arts,
sciences, or humanities, beginning in the third or fourth grade. The
better special schools are difficult to enter and often are accessible
only to students whose families have connections or the resources
available to help them complete additional studies with tutors in order to
pass competitive entrance examinations. Ilya makes it clear that he, his
schoolmates, and his teachers take pride in their general level of culture
and education as well as their interest in the changes going on around
them.

The stereotype that vocational school students are street-wise and
have more active social lives than those who remain in the academic

---

*It must be noted here that the major incentive for choosing to remain in an academic
high school rather than opting for a technical education is not monetary. In the Soviet
Union the average salary of a worker is higher than that of a professional or intellectual. A
diploma from an academic high school is more prestigious, although less practical, and it
is unusual for the children of intellectual and professional families to attend a vocational
school.

high school is supported by the narratives. In addition to their greater interest in socializing and entertainment, these students also already have experience as workers. For them, perestroika's goals of increasing productivity through active worker participation in the organization and structure of economic life are tangible issues they experience first-hand at their factory. As young workers, Dima and Maxim are aware that in order for real, concrete change to take place in the Soviet Union, workers must produce more, feel invested in the results of their labor, and develop more responsible attitudes toward work. Whether or not new generations of workers find ways to participate meaningfully in economic production throughout their work lives is an important issue for those interested in ensuring permanent change in the Soviet Union.

Attendance at either an academic or a vocational school is an important aspect of the reproduction of class structure in the USSR. Although many working-class children complete academic high schools and pursue a degree in higher education, the majority of students who do attend vocational schools are from working-class families. The descriptions of vocational schools by Dima, Olya, and Lyosha are illustrative of the attitude toward the education of future workers. Low expectations, indifference, and apathy are all part of the vocational school experience. At Dima's school in particular it is clear that the passivity, lack of concern, and low productivity characteristic of Soviet workers are encouraged through the educational system.

These teenagers are aware of the existence of classes and of their own place within a specific sector of society. This issue is of particular concern for Olya, Maxim, and Tanya, all of whom are from working-class families. Olya feels that workers are not respected in Soviet society and wonders how this has happened in a society that claims to have been built in the interest of the working class. Nonetheless, she herself has chosen to attend a vocational school and thus remain a worker. She wonders whether a decision made several years earlier, at the end of the eighth grade, when she was very young and unclear about her future, will have unfortunate consequences for her.

Maxim already has significant work experience. He feels that through work he will develop his character and mature; he advocates trade unions and, at age sixteen, has already clearly defined himself, with pride, as a member of the working class.

Tanya is preparing to become, in her own words, a member of the intelligentsia. She looks forward to studying and having an intellectual career and expresses a desire to become an educational researcher in the future, which would require graduate work and writing a dissertation. Yet she identifies herself with pride as a member of a working-class family and feels that as a member of the "workers' intelligentsia" she will be a valuable member of society, performing a role that socialist society needs—a link between workers and intellectuals, someone who understands and represents the needs of both classes.

Ilya, at seventeen, describes himself as an intellectual from a highly educated family and makes it clear that he has very little contact with workers. He further claims that "simple" people, that is, those with less formal education, are more concerned with what is available in the stores than with the fruits of glasnost. This attitude, common among intellectuals in Soviet society, where there is a clear distinction and feeling of separation between the intelligentsia and workers, is perhaps a stereotype. Nevertheless, the claim that workers are less concerned about glasnost and therefore less impressed with the developments in the Soviet Union finds some support in the narratives of vocational school students, who, more than their counterparts in academic high schools, express a preoccupation with material goods and the shortages that plague Soviet society.* They also are less impressed with glasnost due to the fact that their interest in ideas and becoming involved in the production of ideas is significantly lower than that of students in academic high schools, and thus the connection between glasnost and their future is less apparent. For them, the increased difficulties and decline in the standard of living that many identify with perestroika accounts for their more reserved, though still basically enthusiastic, assessment of the process of change in the Soviet Union.

GENDER ROLES AND SEXUALITY

Another significant distinction in the world view of the teenagers is found on the basis of gender, as seen in their discussions of male–female relationships and gender roles in the family.

Without exception, the boys' image of male–female relations and their future family is patriarchal. Alexei, Dima, and Maxim do not want their wives to work and believe that a wife's primary duty is to take care of the home and raise children. The other boys express a willingness to

---

*Although workers do earn more money than intellectuals in the Soviet Union, they do not necessarily enjoy a higher standard of living. One of the great problems of the Soviet economy is that people have more money than there are actual goods available for purchase. Thus, having access to highly coveted goods, through institutional or personal connections or through the well-developed underground economy, is as important as having a high income. In the last few years, the disparity between money and available goods has actually increased.

have a wife who works and has a career but feel that it is not the most important aspect of a woman's life and are prepared to take on the role of breadwinner if their future wife wants to stay home. They are aware of the problems women face, but they do not accept that these problems are of as great concern to men as they are to women. Lyosha sometimes feels sorry for his mother when he sees how hard she works at her job and then comes home at night laden with bags of food she has spent hours looking for in many different stores. Watching her he sometimes thinks about his own future, resolving to be a more helpful husband than his father, but he views his role as one of a helper, not as an equal partner in maintaining a household. Even Ilya, who prides himself on being progressive, if not radical, on every other issue we discussed, believes a woman is responsible for keeping the family together and the home in order. He is unwilling to discuss his own parents' divorce but does note that, in cases of an unsuccessful marriage, he blames the woman more than the man for failing in her primary duty. He does not believe that a woman should work, although he does feel that modern women for the most part are not willing to stay home. "I guess you would have to say that my views on this subject are patriarchal," he concludes, without hesitation, at the end of our conversation.

The girls' perspective differs greatly. All of them intend to work, and having an interesting profession is very important to them. They are not prepared to stay home and raise families. Nonetheless, without exception they do believe that maintaining a home and raising children are primarily women's duties, whereas a husband, if he is a good man, should be willing to "help" his wife with doing household tasks. They do not want to do all of the housework but are prepared to do the major portion.

"I don't want the kind of husband who comes home in the evening, lounges around on the sofa, and doesn't do anything else," says Katya. And Natasha, when asked how she will deal with a man who doesn't do much around the house, responds: "Well, I will re-educate my husband. Or maybe by the time I am a bit older, the consciousness of men will be higher."

Clearly the girls have understood the double burden Soviet women face on the job and at home and, to some extent, anticipate that they will have to accept it. They want a nuclear family, but there is already doubt in their words. They, too, will be faced by the dilemma of Soviet women, as described by Natasha:

> They say around here that there's nothing a woman, a Russian woman, can't do, and I think that's true. . . . She can split wood or stand in a line in a store for three hours. Look at the huge bags they

carry around—not just any man could lift those bags . . . and she still
manages to look more or less attractive!

The contrast between male and female perspectives suggests that as
these teenagers begin to form their own families there will be great differences in expectations between husbands and wives, and probably no small
amount of conflict—a conclusion not surprising in a country where the
divorce rate is one of the highest in the world. It seems that the great
differences in attitudes between Russian men and women are already
firmly in place by age fifteen or sixteen. The girls express a willingness to
compromise before they have even seriously begun to look for a spouse,
and their words carry with them a tone of resignation. Interestingly, however, it is more than simple resignation. They expect to engage in struggle,
to pursue their own desires, as indicated by Natasha's intention to re-
educate her husband, or Olya, who told me that she wants to have a
husband and baby within the next five years and at the same time to
continue her studies right after her two years at the factory.

Several of the girls talk about sexual attitudes among Soviet teenagers. They note the taboo that has surrounded the topic, recalling
their embarrassment when viewing a "television bridge" in which they
observed much greater frankness and openness among American youth
as compared to the Soviet participants.

Soviet teenagers have almost no access to factual information
about sexuality. There has been no sex education in Soviet schools
and virtually nothing is available in print, although recently, as a
result of glasnost, materials—basically reprints of foreign sources—
have become available on a limited basis. In 1984, after considerable
debate, the need for basic sex education was recognized and a course
was added to the eighth-grade curriculum. Entitled "Ethics and Psychology of Family Life," the course contains very little about sexuality
and focuses instead on building family relationships, raising children,
and maintaining a household. There are no trained specialists in sex
education, and in most schools the course has been assigned to any
teacher willing to take on extra responsibilities.

I met a teacher of Russian language and literature who had agreed to
teach the ethics course in his school the year before. He related to me
what he considered to be his greatest achievement in the class: a private
conversation in which he convinced one of his male students that he
must try to "sublimate his sexual instincts." He told the boy that this was
one of the major lessons to be learned from the work of Freud (Freud's
writings are available on an extremely limited basis in the Soviet Union,
and this teacher felt that mentioning Freud to one of his students was in

and of itself a progressive and enlightened act) and advised him to concentrate on sports! Several months later, the boy proudly told him that he had, after much struggle, managed to overcome his sexual desire. The year I spoke with this teacher, he had declined to take responsibility for the course a second time because his schedule was crowded, so it simply had not been offered again.

The teachers' and administrators' disinterested and distorted view of sex education was obvious to students. I spoke with several who told me that they felt the course was a waste of time and they had learned little that was of real value to them. They complained that the adults around them were embarrassed and full of complexes, and as a result students were denied access to information that was important to them.

In conducting the interviews, I learned that most of the teenagers had never had a single serious, factual discussion about sex with any adult, including parents. Tanya, who expresses great warmth toward her mother and describes a friendly, open relationship, says:

> I think Mom will advise me on this in the future. Now she probably thinks that I'm still too young. . . . I think that true friendship, if it's really strong, can get by without that. Without sex. I read about that somewhere—platonic love. That's on the highest level, when you don't need that.

Olya's mother, when pregnant with her second child, told nine-year-old Olya that children come from cabbage patches, and the reason why her stomach was so large was that she had drunk too much water.

The lack of information on sexuality and the poor state of medical care in the area of reproductive health have become public issues during the years of glasnost. Soviet women and men have very little access to contraceptives and are poorly educated in their use. At the same time, conservative public morals and attitudes toward sexuality inhibit open discussion of reproductive issues and women's health.

The results of poor education, ignorance, and conservative ideas about sexuality have been appalling. Most Soviet women use abortion, available on demand, as the primary form of birth control, and it is not uncommon for a woman in her mid-twenties to have had at least four or five abortions. The Soviet Union has the highest abortion rate in the world: an estimated 25 percent of all abortions performed take place in the Soviet Union.[2] According to a Soviet estimate, for every birth in the Soviet Union, there are between five and eight abortions.[3]

The girls I spoke with are aware of these issues. Most of them frown upon premarital sex, and one of the major reasons for their negative stance toward sex at an early age is concern about pregnancy. When I reminded them that women can be involved in sexual relationships without getting pregnant, they dismissed this possibility as unrealistic. They know about the frequency of abortion in their country and the poor quality and general lack of contraceptives, and this knowledge has become part of their attitudes: avoid sex to avoid getting pregnant.

Certainly another important reason for their disapproval of premarital sex is on moral grounds. They are concerned about young women preserving their "honor." They worry that a young woman may lose the respect of a young man if she has a sexual relationship with him, and this would ruin her prospects for marriage.

Conservative moral values are characteristic of Soviet society, which encourages early marriage and nuclear families, with little tolerance for alternative lifestyles. The average age at which Soviets marry, already earlier than most people in the West, has continued to decrease over the years. One Soviet survey found that one in four women were only eighteen when they married, and men nineteen or twenty.[4] A large number of couples have children within their first nine months of marriage,[5] suggesting that pregnancy may have been a factor in the decision to get married. At the same time, single mothers are not uncommon, although this often occurs at a later age among educated women who, for various reasons, have not gotten married.

In these narratives, there is no thought of alternative living situations. Without exception, the teenagers intend to marry and form a nuclear family unit. They hope that they will be lucky enough to get their own apartment in order to live separately from their parents.

It is interesting to note here how important group and collective activities seem to be for them. Although several—particularly vocational school students—have had relationships with a girlfriend or boyfriend, almost unanimously they express the importance of spending their free time not in pairs, but in larger groups. Dating does not yet seem to play a significant role in their lives, even though it is very important to them to find a spouse and start a family in the future, and, according to statistics, at age sixteen they are not that far from the time when young people in the Soviet Union often do get married.

GENERAL TRENDS

Increased social and political awareness

Despite class and gender distinctions, common threads unite these narratives. Concern about the processes taking place within their country is extremely high among all of these teenagers, and they are all aware of the important issues facing Soviet society today. They express a remarkable interest in history and use examples from the past to help explain the events they observe around them in the present. Lena talks at length about the philosophy of revolutionary change, discussing the Russian Revolution and Lenin's thought, mentioning the example of the French Revolution to support her assertion that it is not possible to bring about real change through violence. Even Maxim, who shows the least interest in formal education, discusses Peter the Great and his role in Russian history with great enthusiasm and exhibits a general interest in history as a subject.

Heightened political awareness, particularly concerning the Soviet Union, abounds in these narratives. Constant references to articles, books, films, and television programs are indicative of an impressive level of knowledge and consciousness.

This heightened political awareness, with its fundamental preoccupation with *change*, contrasts with the teens' relative social conservatism, particularly around issues of lifestyle.

Standard of living

The preoccupation with material conditions and standard of living found in these narratives is striking. During my year in Moscow, I was repeatedly surprised by the number of times the term "light industry" came up in conversations with young people, and although American teenagers are certainly no less interested in consumerism, they are probably not as aware that the goods they purchase are fundamentally linked to the process and problems of industrial production. Not only are Soviet teenagers concerned about how and where things are produced, and where they are available, they also care about helping light industry produce more efficiently and abundantly.

This is not surprising in a society as plagued by shortages and deficits as the Soviet Union, where most adults are as concerned about these matters as teenagers. The availability of sausage, a staple in the Russian diet, has become the barometer by which the Soviet economy is measured in popular conversation. Knowing that I was surprised by the frequent mention of sausage in talking with people, Yelena tried to explain the Soviet obsession with that word: Can an American possibly understand what it means for a man engaged in heavy physical labor to have a ration of only a half-kilo of sausage per month? (I don't think many people really believed me when I pointed out that there is a lot of hunger and malnutrition in the United States.)

The cooperatives

This concern with the availability of goods and with shortages and deficits makes it clear that the teenagers are acutely aware of the need for
perestroika and are counting on it to change the conditions of their
own lives. Thus it is not surprising that the teenagers discuss the development of cooperatives.

The purpose of the cooperatives, one of the fundamental components of economic reform, is to allow and encourage small private
business. This private sector, which has grown rapidly since a 1988 law
made group enterprise legal, is expected to help fill in holes in the
economy by offering services and goods that the government and state-
run enterprises have not been able to provide. In their brief existence,
the cooperatives have actually been quite successful. In early 1990, they
employed close to five million people.[6]

At the same time, the cooperatives have been extremely controversial and have become the object of considerable popular resentment.
People in cooperatives often earn many times more than wage earn-
ers in state-run enterprises, and prices in cooperatives are considerably higher. Although everybody acknowledges that these goods and
services must be provided, the cooperatives run counter to some
fundamental notions highly valued by Soviet citizens. Many people
object to private ownership of production. Even more problematic is
the growing economic polarization, as it runs counter to the social
equality that is an ideal to many Soviets. In fact, much of the popular
wrath that has unseated Communist Party members in elections
across the country has centered around the privilege and extrava-
gant lifestyles enjoyed by some Party members. People view cooperatives in a similar fashion: If people in cooperatives are making such
exorbitant profits, it is not through honest work but rather through
speculation. Furthermore, it is believed, cooperatives procure goods
in scarce supply, making life more difficult for people who can only
afford to buy at state-run stores, where prices are cheaper but goods
increasingly scarce.

The attitudes toward cooperatives expressed by these teenagers reflect this controversy. Some of them support the cooperatives, whereas
others view them with caution and suspicion and object to the high
prices and shoddy quality of goods. Only Ilya gives unreserved support
to the cooperatives and feels that the problems are not the fault of the
cooperatives themselves. Throughout their development, the cooperatives have been controversial, and laws restricting their scope and activity have prevented many people from forming them.

The ideals of social justice and equality

Ilya, who aligns himself with forces in the Soviet Union that refer to themselves as radical and "leftist," is also the only teenager here who says that he does not support the ideal of social justice and that he is not concerned with disparity in income and distribution of wealth. The other teenagers, while criticizing much of the historical development of their country, have not rejected the ideals of social equality and redistribution of wealth that were rallying cries of the October Revolution and the attempt to build a workers' state.

Social justice and equality remain an ideal to these teenagers, despite the fact that most of the basic tenets of official Soviet ideology have been challenged. Recent events in Eastern Europe have taken the world by surprise, and the dismantling of most of the governments led by Communist parties has led many people to conclude that socialism has no future in these countries. The situation in the Soviet Union, however, is far from clear. Whether socialism will remain a "viable option" in the Soviet Union is an open question. There are forces that strongly support socialism as well as others that favor the complete privatization of industry and the economy. There are also forces that represent many gradations of thought between these two positions. The will of the Soviet people either to rebuild socialism or to build another kind of system will play a crucial role in the process of change. At the present moment, nobody can predict the future of Soviet society, but these interviews suggest that socialism, as an ideal among young people, survives. Whether or not socialism has potential as a system that can allow people to take charge of their own lives as well as provide them with a decent standard of living and a humane lifestyle is a question of importance for these teenagers, although most of them have not yet answered it for themselves.

Admiration for the United States;
pride in the Soviet Union

Many people in the Soviet Union today express great admiration for the United States and for Americans. These teenagers are no exception. They view the United States as an affluent society, and although they acknowledge that there are great social problems in the United States, they believe they are not as acute as the problems and basic questions of survival facing their own country.

Ilya, responding to my comment during an interview that Americans are not known for a high level of political involvement and that many Americans do not participate in elections, states: "I think that that is indicative of a certain level of well-being because people tend to get involved in politics when they have a lot of troubles."

Tanya, comparing Russians and Americans, believes that Russians will "zigzag" if left to their own devices, whereas Americans are active and self-motivated. To the teens, the United States is a country where everything is available, a consumer's paradise. Their relationship to our country, however, is complex and also has a competitive edge, evident in the frequent comparisons. At times their comments suggest feelings of inferiority, but at other moments they take great pride in their country and culture.

During my first weeks in Moscow I disappointed a group of students when, in response to their questions, I revealed that I own neither a VCR nor an automobile, spend almost half of my income to pay for an apartment in New York, and have no prospects for owning my own home anytime soon. Several days after this conversation took place, I stood with a group of the same students in a station, waiting to take a commuter train to Vladimir, one of the beautiful ancient cities several hours from Moscow. One member of the group, Volodya, apologized profusely for the state of the train station, adding that he was sure Grand Central Station must be in much better condition. I began to describe the state Grand Central had been in when I left New York several weeks earlier—specifically the highly publicized tension and conflict between the large numbers of homeless people who sleep there and the police who are supposed to remove them.

I tried to convey this to Volodya, but he simply did not want to listen to my words, surprised to hear, from the mouth of an American, something that he had suspected was only official Soviet propaganda. Suddenly he asked, as if I were confusing him, "Say, aren't you supposed to be a bourgeois element?" There was irony in his voice, suggesting that the term "bourgeois element" was not really a valid concept to him. Yet at the same time I felt that he was testing me to see whether I was indeed different, a representative of the "bourgeois" ideology he had been taught to repudiate, yet clearly found fascinating. I saw in his question a struggle to sort out which aspects of official Soviet ideology he accepts and which he rejects.

"Well, what is a bourgeois element?" I asked him, taking my time in order to think of an appropriate answer. He looked at me with irritation for what must have seemed to him to be a typical teacher's trick, impatient with my evasiveness. "Look," he said, "I'm sure that word means something else to you than it does to us. We Soviet people don't use that word in a very nice way. Around here it doesn't mean anything positive."

Earlier, the teacher who had invited me to observe Volodya's class laughed with me about how the students would no doubt consider me an "American of inferior quality" if I continued to dress in jeans and sweaters when I visited their classrooms. I was sure that Volodya would have found me more interesting if I had resembled what he considers to be a typical "bourgeois" American, fancy and wealthy. Yet at the same time he defended his own "Soviet" understanding, letting me know that my "bourgeois" view was not the only legitimate one.

It seemed like a minor incident at the time, but during the ten-month period I spent in Moscow, I realized that it actually revealed quite a bit about the complex attitude Moscow teenagers have toward the United States. This attitude contains elements of admiration, envy, and defensiveness, but at the same time these teens are not ready to accept condescension toward their country and culture. Soviet youth's fascination with the West is well known, but it conceals other elements of equal importance. Their pride in their country and culture was apparent to me in the pleasure with which they sing Russian and Soviet songs, insisting that I really *listen* to them, explaining the words and nuances with tremendous patience. They told me countless specifically Soviet jokes, also accompanied by careful explanation.

Although they are quite critical of their country, they can be sensitive about the opinions others express. Once, having tea at Lena's home, a group of girls talked to me about the unofficial rationing of meat in their district. At that time in Moscow, sugar had just become a rationed item, but everything else was supposed to be available in unrestricted amounts to anybody. Buying sugar with ration cards was bad enough to Muscovites, who prided themselves on living in the only city in the Soviet Union that still had no rationing, and they were even more indignant about the unofficial rationing that had begun in many stores. Signs had been posted stating what quantity of each available item each shopper could buy. In a long, humorous anecdote, one of the girls related the efforts she had to go through in order to purchase two kilos of meat, twice the allotment of the unofficial rationing. The other girls laughed and I did as well, for her storytelling was quite funny. But when they noticed that I, too, was laughing, the tone changed. They grew serious and remarked that it really wasn't that funny after all and asked me whether I could imagine having to do that—stand in those kinds of lines, all of your life.

"Our poor people," one of them said.

Collectivism

Soviet teenagers spend a good deal of their time in group activities, and collectivism is an important value to them. Consistently articulating their need to be part of a group in school activities as well as during their leisure time, they see a sense of collectivism as an important element in their future, both at work and in their personal lives. Dima talked to me at length about the need for a good work collective, and Tanya expresses the importance of group activities for her group of friends: "I want my friends and me to continue to be close, always. We are always together now, and imagine if when we have families we can continue to be together, as families. That will be simply wonderful!"

The collective is an important part of life in the Soviet Union, and it is clear that for these teenagers, it has already become a significant value.

The Komsomol and the organization of young people

The significance of the Komsomol in several of the narratives may not be apparent to the American reader. The ideal of a political and ideological youth organization devoted to the development of future generations of socialist-oriented youth has been an integral part of Soviet policy. The Komsomol, known in the past for its active role in building a new society, defending the Soviet Union during World War II, and so on, became a formality during the period of stagnation, and membership in it was almost automatic. Most young people who wanted to enter institutes of higher education or advance their careers joined the Komsomol for those reasons. Until recently, in public discussion, the Komsomol was a prestigious, highly revered institution. It has now come under attack. The teenagers I spoke with were, to varying degrees, aware of the changing public attitudes toward the Komsomol. Most of them belong to the Komsomol, but their opinions of it differ, as do their reasons for joining.

Ilya believes that the Komsomol is merely a formality that will help him enroll in the university and feels that it will never become anything more than that. He believes that the "informal" youth groups that have developed in the last few years offer new opportunities to organize young people, although he himself has not participated in any. Most of the other participants feel that these "informal" groups are composed of shiftless delinquents who show no initiative or creativity in disposing of their time.

The growth of the "informal" youth organizations has become a topic of great public concern in the Soviet Union and a particular cause for worry among adults who were traditionally involved in youth work. These adults must now search for new ways to approach young people, having realized that old solutions will not prepare them for a new society. The growth of the "informal" groups indicates that youth are taking their own initiatives, often in ways that do not meet with adult approval. It is hard for adults to point to examples they feel are more appropriate, however, as some of the most important institutions of socialization in the USSR—the school, Komsomol, mass media—have been greatly discredited or are undergoing drastic change, leaving few models. In these narratives, teenagers frequently criticize existing institutions and deny their value as examples.

Until recent times, working with young people was primarily the responsibility of the Komsomol and teachers. Problem intervention was not a facet of youth work. Issues such as substance abuse, crime, early sexual relationships, and teen pregnancy were simply not part of public discussion. Glasnost has allowed for far more open and realistic dialogue about the problems young people face in Soviet society. The diminishing role of the Komsomol as well as the ascendance of informal youth groups are part of this new discussion. Still, as these narratives suggest, many young people, now alienated from the Komsomol, are not well informed about the informal groups—or particularly attracted to them. Although encouraged to find new ways of viewing the world, they have remained without specific orientation, despite the fact that they desire to find a place for themselves within the changing society.

The "children of perestroika"?

Young people's need to find a place for themselves has a parallel in the basic question Soviet society as a whole faces at present: Although almost everyone agrees that the old structures have not worked, it is not yet clear what new solutions will help people build a better life and improve their society. Young people are at an age of transition, and they happen to be living in a society that is experiencing tremendous general change as well. Maxim talks about how he has been caught between the old and the new:

> . . . I'm neither a Nazi* nor an activist in the Communist Party. Not a Komsomol member. I'm not interested in either one. . . . None of them has managed to interest me, not those who are against Soviet power who stand around shouting, and not those who go around saying, "Long Live the Komsomol!" I'm just an average guy.

---

*Maxim is using the neo-Nazis, one of the youth groups formed recently, as representative of the new kinds of informal organizations. Of course, not all of these groups represent the extreme that the neo-Nazis do, and some informal groups are decidedly progressive, having nothing in common with the neo-Nazis. The important point here is that all of these groups represent a way of allowing youth to organize themselves in some way other than traditionally, through the Komsomol.

I once heard a college student, the son of a friend of mine, refer to himself and his peers as the children of stagnation. I heard this expression many times, a humorous reference to *Children of the Arbat*, Anatoly Rybakov's popular novel about the effect of Stalinist repression on a group of young intellectuals in Moscow in the 1930s. I was surprised by his implication that his was a lost generation, mired in complacency and indifference. I asked my friend's son if he felt that his generation was being shaped at all by the new thinking advocated by glasnost. He replied that the generation after his, people five years younger, the age of the teenagers whose narratives are found in this book, could be called the children of perestroika. I repeated this question to all of the teenagers I interviewed: Has your generation been affected by the changes taking place around you?

I had assumed that the answer would be a resounding "yes," thinking that teenagers anywhere would be quick to distinguish themselves from their parents and even more so in a country so intent on critically evaluating the past. Generational change is part of all societies, and in times of general accelerated change, these differences intensify.

To my surprise, the teenagers I spoke to responded with caution. They viewed change as a process that would take time to come to fruition, and they viewed their generation as only one link in this process. In response to my question, Ilya distinguished his generation from his parents', but he was careful to limit himself in his generalizations:

> Without a doubt, what distinguishes my generation . . . [is that] we aren't afraid of anything. I'm not saying that we're ready to go out there and fight, but basically we haven't become scared. . . . Without a doubt we are becoming more responsible and freer. We have been freed of the fears that the previous generation had, and we are able to talk more openly. . . . You couldn't really call us the children of perestroika. But on the other hand there are differences between us and our parents. They're still afraid of something—sometimes even *my* parents tell me to watch what I say over the telephone. But I don't have any fear inside of me. I'm not afraid. I *want* not to be afraid.

The major topics repeated throughout the narratives, of such importance to these teenagers, are part of daily discussion in the Soviet Union. Not surprisingly, much of what these adolescents say is a reflection of what they read and hear in the adult world around them. Nonetheless, they are able to talk about these issues with knowledge and detail and offer their own opinions, revealing the extent to which they have become socially and politically aware. They have clearly become active seekers of information. They read papers, watch television programs, and discuss these issues among themselves.

True, most of them are not actively participating in change, although several began to attend political demonstrations during the year I met them. (After the events in Tbilisi in April 1989, in which protestors were brutally killed by soldiers, several of the girls told me their parents had forbidden them to participate in any more demonstrations.) It is significant, however, that becoming an active member of society in and of itself has become an ideal to them; they want to become committed citizens, whether through political participation, scientific research, or active participation in their work in industrial production. They do feel that their generation is different from preceding ones, and they hope that people will continue to grow and change. Tanya expresses her hopes for perestroika and glasnost in terms of the ability of each generation to improve upon the preceding one:

> Our generation, it seems to me, if it continues along the present path, will raise a different kind of children, even better than we ourselves are. And this is the essence of perestroika. They will be more honest and they will be responsible people, as soon as all of this turmoil of Stalin and Brezhnev is over. Maybe they will be more active, which is to say that they will have enthusiasm. . . . And things will be more cheerful. There won't always be this constant, heavy memory. People will be better—that's the way it seems to me.

Showing both knowledge of and interest in current events and their own history, critical of the past and present, hopeful for the future, the words of these teenagers suggest that the great change in the public awareness of Soviet citizens has affected people of all ages and social statuses.

NOTES

1. "The Country's Public Education on the Eve of Radical Changes," *Soviet Education*, July 1989, pp. 35–43 (translated from *Vestnik statistiki*, 1988, no. 3).

2. Irina Kuznetsova, "Tretii pol: kontseptsiya zhenskogo schastya," *Novoe vremya*, October 1988, pp. 46–47.

3. Conversation with Dr. Archil Khomassuridze, as quoted by Francine du Plessix Gray in *Soviet Women: Walking the Tightrope* (New York: Doubleday, 1989), pp. 14–20. Dr. Khomassuridze's figure is an estimate that takes into consideration the number of illegal abortions performed. The official statistic of the Soviet Ministry of Health does not include illegal abortions and is lower, claiming two or three abortions for every birth.

4. As reported by Nancy Traver in *Kife: The Lives and Dreams of Soviet Youth* (New York: St. Martin's Press, 1989), p. 56.

5. Ibid., p. 59.

6. Richard Parker, "Inside the 'Collapsing' Soviet Economy," *Atlantic Monthly*, June 1990, pp. 68–80.

TANYA

THE WORKERS' INTELLIGENTSIA

TANYA
Sixteen years old, ninth-grade student

Tanya is slim and athletic. She wears her long blond hair in a braid down her back and seems unaware of her striking features. She wears no makeup and, when not in her school uniform, dresses in casual, sporty clothing. She is both talkative and shy: she tends to blush a little at the beginning of each of our interviews, pulls frequently on the end of her braid when searching for the right words, but once she warms up she loves to talk at length and with great conviction. If something she says strikes her as funny or embarrassing, she laughs, turns her head to the side, and hides it for a moment before going on.

There are three people in my family: Dad, Mom, and me. Dad is a foreman at a factory. He works in the construction and maintenance department, with the electrical equipment. Mom works in an office half-time, and she really likes that schedule—from eight in the morning until one thirty. Of course, she gets less money than she should, but she likes it because she can be at home almost the entire day. She comes home at one thirty and can spend the whole afternoon and evening with Dad and me. Dad comes home around 6 P.M. One grandmother lives in Moscow and the other lives in the countryside, with my grandfather.

My parents don't talk much about their work, probably because their professions are completely opposite and don't have anything to do with each other. I think my Dad loves his profession; he says that he knows people need him, and he sees the results of his work. Not Mom. The only thing she's happy about there is that she has a lot of time to spend at home, with the family. But she doesn't like what she does at work. Her job doesn't bring her any satisfaction. She can't see the results of her work.

Mom works at an enterprise where sometimes they have work and

sometimes they don't. And when they don't, they still have to sit at work
all day; they sit there the whole time and don't do anything. But they're
not allowed to do anything else either. So they knit, for example, and a
boss comes around, and they hide everything under their desks. If the
boss notices, then they get scolded. There are lots of places like that.
Even when there is no work for them to do, they get paid. My mom
knits, reads the newspapers, sits around talking. Why should she go?
She'd be better off at home doing something else.

I'm still very dependent on my parents, but not in my own affairs, in
school. I'm not saying that my parents don't care about my school life,
but they try not to interfere with my solving my own issues. Of course
materially I'm still dependent on them, but in all the rest I'm basically
free. I decide things for myself, and they don't help me very often with
that because they have their own little problems that come up. My dad
says, "Look, perestroika and glasnost are going on here now, and you
don't need anybody's instructions or orders, decide for yourself. Do
what feels the best for you." It seems to me that the most important
thing is for a person to be independent.

I don't think my parents are independent because so much depends on
their bosses. I suppose on some level you could call it discipline, but where
my mother works you could say that it's going way beyond discipline. Now
some kind of terror has started there. She can't take one step on her own
at work. If she wants to do something she always has to pass on the word
that she's done this or that, and it will be better that way, but they tell her,
"That's not the way it's done here." And she says, "What can I do? By myself?
Nobody supports me because they don't want to ruin their relationship
with the bosses or among themselves." And so it seems to me that as soon
as a person starts working, he's no longer independent. But in school, life
is so full, and you're only studying there, you're not dependent on your
teachers and certainly not on the principal. When children are still small,
in first to third grade, they're still dependent, and the teachers really
pressure them. "That's right. That's not right. That's allowed. That's not."
But when students get older they already think about the teacher, "Ah, who
is he anyhow? Nobody. I'll do as I please," and if they try to scare you and
say they'll call your parents, that doesn't work anymore. Because a person
has become independent, and his psyche is already different. He thinks
that the teacher is nothing to him, and he'll do as he pleases.

In the future, I will have a profession that I love, I hope. And if I have
the chance, I would like to become a teacher-researcher. If that doesn't
work out, I'll be a primary school teacher. I really like little children. I
love them a lot. They're so cute. And they don't have any complexes
yet. They have their own way of seeing things, even though it's a child's

way. I can imagine that if a person came to me with an almost empty head, but when he left he knew something, well, I would be proud that I was able to explain something. So I want a profession that I love, and a husband, too, also beloved.

I can't really imagine this husband. I haven't really thought about this yet. Everybody says that a husband should be well off, but I don't think that's the most important thing. Because if you have the chance to dedicate more time to raising your children, even if you're from the working class, then you will be raising the workers' intelligentsia. The way they want to do it here now. Not just the intelligentsia but the workers' intelligentsia.

A person who works in a plant or a factory is from the working class. And from this working class a sector should emerge to be the connecting layer between the working class and the intelligentsia. Because the intelligentsia looks down on the working class somewhat, they have more time, they read more, they see more, they travel more, and maybe they know more as well. And a person who works never has enough time, even though he might have money. And so this workers' intelligentsia should serve the purpose of connecting the intelligentsia, which plays such an important role in the life of a society, and workers, many of whom are passive. The workers' intelligentsia should be closely connected to workers, and at the same time should be a little bit higher, so that it's able to come up with solutions to problems itself. So that there will be one whole, and not, as they say, "Well, these are the strata that we have, this one and that one." I think that we should all be one whole entity.

I'm from a working-class family. But I'm going to be an intellectual—a teacher. They say here, "Where are you headed? To the intelligentsia! Then your level has to be higher!" But I think basically anybody can become an intellectual. Depending upon the way he has been raised, even a worker can be an intellectual, in the way he relates to his work, to the people around him, even though officially he is not an intellectual. But in terms of how he thinks he can be a very educated and cultured person.

I myself would like to learn—without any kinds of institutions, without any bureaucratic obstacles—foreign languages for myself, and for my future children, and I think that if I learn English, I will teach it to my children from an early age. The way they did it before in tsarist Russia. I think that any educated and intellectual person then knew three languages: French, English, and German. I study music. I love to sing, but to tell the truth, I don't do it very well. I love folk songs, but not Russian folk songs—I love Estonian and Lithuanian folk songs. Their language is so nice, so rich. I like Moldavian songs too—I think that's from the Romance language group. I play the piano well. I like classical music a lot. Bach is my favorite composer. His works are very complex; you need good technique. I like the preludes and fugues; I can play some of them. They're really beautiful.

I would also like to at least visit the most important cities of our country. I've been in Leningrad, Riga, Vilnius, and we have so many more! I love Asian cities—Bukhara, Samarkand—I have postcards of them, and when I look at those mosques, I get this feeling. . . . And I would also like to go to Australia someday. I really like kangaroos. I've never seen one live. They're so cute—I saw them on television. And I think everything in Australia seems to be interesting.

I would also like to go to the jungle, just get at least a little glance. I'd like to see so much—and probably nothing will work out. Because it's a problem.

When I was very little my mother sometimes said to me, "You know, Tanechka, maybe one day we'll be living without any borders at all. The way it used to be, a long time ago, in history." Countries will have the same kinds of relations between themselves that neighbors living along the same stairwell do. There are exchanges now, and international relations have changed so much that it seems to me everything is going to be all right because people will get together on their own initiative, to see another country and somehow share their experiences and learn from the experiences of others. Everything will be done much more freely. The language barrier of course is a problem, but politics are already changing so much that it will be possible to teach the languages in school in America and here. There won't be only summit meetings but meetings between ordinary people as well. People shouldn't have the feeling that it's someplace far away. It's close—what is it, six hours to fly there on an airplane? When we take the train to visit grandmother we ride for six hours. What difference does it make what direction you travel in? Look, we have to change that psychology, people have to learn to relate to one another person to person. It seems to me that in any case things are going to be better. Those Cold War times are a thing of the past! Sometimes I remember them, and it seems like a long time ago.

PERESTROIKA: "NOBODY CAN GUESS HOW LONG IT WILL TAKE"

I can see perestroika only by looking at what they're writing in the newspapers because so far there is nothing in the shops.

It took us half a year to buy an ordinary cupboard. We were on a waiting list in the furniture store and waited for the postcard that the store was supposed to send us when the cupboards arrived from the factory. We waited until our turn to receive one came up, and then we were faced with the problem of how to bring it home. But the biggest problem was the half year we waited for the postcard from the store. That is really outrageous! In order to buy any kind of furniture, any kind of clothing, you have to waste so much time. You have money but you can't manage to buy anything.

The only thing they're doing is publishing good books; that's the most important thing. For example, Rybakov's *Children of the Arbat.** They're publishing a lot in journals as well. Perestroika—new plants, factories, land-leasing to farmers—that kind of perestroika will happen when people themselves start to care about it, but it seems to me that to try to restructure ministries is useless. To restructure them, everything would have to be changed, all the way down to the secretaries, the big bosses who have become accustomed to getting their little pittance from those same ministries.

If they are going to change, then change them completely. And it seems to me that in order to really restructure those ministries, young people should take on those positions, like Ryzhkov.† Because a lot of those who are there now lived and governed during Brezhnev's time, during Khrushchev's. They remember all that, and of course it rubbed them the wrong way when Gorbachev came along. And perhaps they'll do something when it's actually demanded of them, but what they really think is that they already had a time when things were better for them, and now they're not going to let anybody have a quiet life, not the young people who want to live in a new way.

Look, I didn't live in that period, I almost didn't see any of it at all; I was in second grade, but now I live in this age and I like it. You can learn more. But my father says that he was around for Stalin and for Khrushchev and all of those people, and because of this he is rather skeptical about anything new. It's true that when Gorbachev gives a speech on television my father approves, but he always takes the position that people are going to want to see things immediately; soon people are going to want to see visible results. And that will never happen, because if we are going to really make perestroika work, it will

---

*Anatoly Rybakov's novel portrays the persecution and exile of an innocent young man during the Stalinist repression. Its publication in 1987, after more than twenty years of censorship, was one of the first major literary openings of glasnost.

†Nikolai Ryzhkov: a close associate of Mikhail Gorbachev and until late 1990 the Soviet prime minister. Toward the end of his tenure Ryzhkov became a target for those frustrated by the lagging pace of reform.

have to be done gradually, very gradually, and nobody can guess how long it will take. In the last three years I haven't really felt perestroika. But of course I want all of this to turn out for the best. If we are going to have democracy here, when I grow up I will be able to speak my mind, and not just get up and go to work and take care of my home, but I'll really be able to participate in the life of this society. I think that will be very interesting. I have a friend whose mother is the secretary of our district government office. I really find that interesting because she gets to see the life of our district from the inside. When you go into a store, you're not really seeing anything, but if you see things on the level of the whole city, that's fantastic! And she travels all over the city, compares things. She is a very progressive person who has accomplished a lot. Her daughter—my girlfriend—is the same kind of person. She doesn't do anything in a sloppy way, just the opposite, if she takes on any responsibility, she won't let anything that goes against her principles slip through her fingers.

Perestroika will take hold only among those who are under forty. Look, my father is simply an honest person, but his friends and comrades at work, they all have the kind of job that they do at a factory where they fill out papers and get paid on the basis of the percentage on the paper. This is how they relate to that work: they just sign the paper without doing anything. My father can't. That's just the kind of person he is. But his friends are unable to live differently, they have become so accustomed to that kind of bad work, and they steal a lot. And our generation, it seems to me, if it continues along the present path, will raise a different kind of children, even better than we ourselves are. And this is the essence of perestroika. They will be more honest and they will be very responsible people, as soon as all of this turmoil of Stalin and Brezhnev is over. Maybe they will be more active, which is to say that they will have enthusiasm. Before we used to have false enthusiasm, for show, but now a different kind of enthusiasm is beginning, the kind where people's activeness comes out of their own will, not what somebody up above wants to see. And things will be more cheerful. There won't always be this constant, heavy memory. People will be better—that's the way it seems to me. But in the meantime there is nothing in the shops, even though they are writing about leasing land to farmers, which is supposed to increase the amount of food available.

I do like the cooperatives. But I don't think that forming a cooperative is perestroika. I can understand cooperatives that lease land, produce goods, produce machine tools at a factory, organize construction work. We really need those kinds of cooperatives. But those cooperatives that produce shoes, sweaters, clothing—in the first place they're very expensive and secondly you look at the things they make and you wonder whether come tomorrow you're still going to like them. Because this is how these cooperatives produce: their things are arranged prettily, the first couple of items you see are quality-made, but then they start making things in a hurry, probably to get people to buy more. Cooperatives should be formed at the factories that produce clothing, right there at the factory so that they have good equipment and good materials to work with. Everybody's saying that the cooperatives are buying out all of the materials, and I don't like that. And look at those scarves, dresses in the cooperatives! A dress there costs two hundred rubles, and it looks more like a robe with some buttons stuck on it!

I think that those who lived through the period of stagnation are more afraid than those who stayed alive through Stalin. In the period of stagnation the government fell to pieces, and people stole, particularly those involved in trade.

When my father used to see Brezhnev getting ready to go away on a trip he would say, "Oh, there he goes again, off to collect pins!"* My mother remembers when she was eight years old and Stalin died, she was on her way to her grandmother's, walking with her mother, and she says there was a sea of people in the street. Everyone was crying. She says she was standing there wondering whether she should be crying too. Everybody was crying and saying, "What are we going to do? How are we going to go on living? Without Stalin?" But our history teacher told us about an old woman who was walking around collecting empty bottles saying, "It can't get any worse than it's already been." That's the way people related to what happened.

I feel good about our current leadership, and it's good that there's been this kind of movement in our relationships with the United States and other countries. And they're going to get even better! It's not right to have strained relations, or no relations at all. We all live together on one planet. Different countries should have the same kind of friendship as different people have between themselves. Not just trade, business transactions, economic cooperation, but people should also be able to travel to visit each other without encountering any obstacles or making the kind of effort one has to make now.

And of course it's gotten better inside the country as well. But Gorbachev has a very hard time. My mother's afraid that something's

---

Znachki, the decorative plastic or metal pins that Soviet children love to collect and exchange.

going to happen to him because there are a lot of people in the Soviet Union who oppose what he's doing. Above all, people involved in trade are against him. There are very few honest people in trade, and they get swallowed up among all the dishonest ones who are used to sticking their hands into the government's pocket as if it were their own. Also those who held high positions under Brezhnev and who have retained their high positions under Gorbachev are against what's going on. Maybe on the outside it seems that they have undergone a process of restructuring, but really they have remained the way they were.

If workers and peasants see that things can be better, they'll be able to restructure themselves very quickly. But it's still not easy for workers to accept perestroika. Perestroika has happened very quickly, and a lot of people have lost some of their wages. My father lost one hundred rubles from his monthly salary from his job in construction. He used to get paid automatically. Now he gets paid only for as much as he gets done. Before, sometimes he would leave work a little early, but now, leaving work even half an hour early isn't allowed. All of that would come out of his salary. People used to steal a lot from work, but now there is strict control over everything there.

My father says that he lost a lot of money, but it wasn't because of him. He says that he always worked to the best of his ability and says that sometimes the bosses covered up for the workers, or they themselves stole. He likes Gorbachev a lot. All of his trips. My mother also likes Gorbachev a lot, particularly how he relates to the people. She likes his wife, too, and says that she's a wise woman who approves of her husband having started these kinds of policies. She probably even tells him when he needs to be more careful about things. Together I think they form one whole.

People simply have to think a little now, because if we don't succeed in disarming ourselves, some weapons are going to remain. From the beginning, when humans began to transform themselves from the apes, they already had some type of weapons. They fought among themselves, and there have always been wars, from ancient times to modern. In today's era it seems to me that we shouldn't be ready to fight so automatically, out of some kind of inertia, but rather we have to think about this much more seriously. Gorbachev limited the number of weapons we produce, and the reductions are already taking place. All countries should disarm, the big ones and the little ones as well.

There have been a lot of changes in the press; it's become much more interesting. Everybody is saying that the limitations placed on newspaper subscriptions are related to the fact that newspapers have gotten so much more interesting to read.*

Then there's been interesting cinema—all these films about the life of the ordinary Soviet family. *Little Vera. All Costs Covered*—that's quite a film. Before they wouldn't have shown films like that for anything. I remember the kind of films they made before, always good relations between workers and bosses, everything was always so good. In this one there are a lot of conflicts, and they get rid of the boss because of it.

I love to watch television. There's so much material. It's impossible to show so many photographs in a magazine, and on television you can just sit and watch them all. I really like the news program *Vremya* now. Everything has become quite exact and concise. Before, they would go on and on. Sometimes for fifty-five minutes, nothing but news. Suddenly you look and see that it's already ten o'clock, and you wonder how it's possible for a person to talk so much! And now they've started showing short clips at the beginning of the program, and you know what's going to be interesting and what's not. So at least you can figure out your time and for those fifteen, twenty minutes you can do something else. Otherwise you sit there and watch and wait to see whether it's going to get any more interesting. Now you know from the beginning whether it's going to be or not. And now you get the impression that they've started showing the news program *Novosti* the way they do in your country, they show things quickly, one-two-three, la la la. She talks, smiles. You see the announcers, and oh, they're smiling! You get the feeling that they're sitting right next to you on the couch and talking to you. It's much more pleasant to watch television when you're not looking at someone who's sitting there with this kind of glare that says, "Keep watching and don't you dare turn this off!" They're doing this in a totally different way now. They're saying that television is replacing books, but I don't think that's the way it is. I love to read. Before I didn't watch television, I only read books, but now it seems that I will also be able to watch television with pleasure. That's perestroika!

YOUNG PEOPLE: GOING OUT INTO REAL LIFE

After finishing our schools it's impossible to get into an institute of higher education without taking additional courses or working with a tutor. You

---

*This refers to a period of several months in the autumn of 1988 when limits were placed on the number of subscriptions available for various popular newspapers and magazines. The official explanation was a nationwide paper shortage. The measure was highly unpopular and was revoked after a short time.

have to be some kind of genius. Without extra classes you'd need two years to know enough physics and enough English. We're scattered all over the place, and they demand exactly the same from everybody. Each teacher thinks that his subject is the most important one. Right now we're all really busy with literature. We have to memorize all these poems—our teacher gave us a long list to write down. That's a complete waste of time. Ninety-six pages in a notebook; we've been writing for half a year, and I have a whole notebook full! I've already started a second one! All they're doing is getting us ready for exams. But what are exams? A real mess! Nobody needs those exams! We had an exam in geometry in sixth grade, eighth grade, why do we need it again? Exams are necessary, but not the way they do them. We finish the tenth grade, we get our little piece of paper, and finally we go out into real life. And we don't know anything! We don't know how to communicate with people. There are very few people who graduate from school here and know how to handle themselves in real life.

One of our teachers, Nina Alexandrovna, hasn't really "restructured" herself yet. She stifles kids' initiative, and I think at the same time she herself is afraid. She really has a lot of fear of doing something that isn't right. She's scared that something a kid might do could have negative consequences, that is, she thinks that she can do it better than he can. So then she takes a lot of responsibility on herself. But I think things have to be done as if they were an experiment, whether it works out or not.

They're always saying, oh, young people, those young people! Even when you read *Children of the Arbat*, and it's 1934, it's that same thing, "Oh those young people, they're a mess, they're terrible, who knows what they want, what a generation." And that lack of understanding has an effect. But most of that depends on the parents and how they raise their child. Sometimes they say, well, he has everything, we didn't refuse him anything, so why did he turn out this way? Well, that means he shouldn't have been given everything. That means he should have had to struggle for something himself, he should have learned how to work, so that he could earn his own money and buy something with it! For example we go to a work camp in the summer,* and we already know what it means to earn money. My parents earn a decent amount of money, but I don't have any tape recorders, video players, or things like that. We live just fine. I don't need anything special. That's how my parents have raised me.

Of course, finding a job is a problem for young people. I wanted to work in a kindergarten last summer. But it didn't work out. And univer-

*Tanya and her classmates spend summers in a "camp for work and recreation." The camp is located on a state farm in the Ukraine. They help with harvesting and other agricultural work and receive a small sum of money. They also engage in summer camp activities—nature hikes, games, campfires, and so forth.

sity students get a thirty- or forty-ruble stipend. Can you really call that money? You can hardly live on it for a month, especially if you live in one city and your parents in another!

Schoolchildren and university students should have a certain amount of money in order to take care of their needs. One hundred rubles for a month or two. I don't know where these district and city leaders are looking, because if they used young people they could fill the ranks of postal carriers, cleaning women, school janitors, even nurses since anyone can learn basic medical care without much difficulty. They could collect tickets on buses, because I'm sure that even honest citizens have gone on a bus at least once without paying for a ticket.* And so I think they really have an obligation to get young people work for seventy rubles a month.

Then we also have the problem of organizing our free time. It's impossible to get tickets to the best central theaters. We can't pay twenty rubles a ticket to scalpers either because we don't have money.† And so instead we compensate at discos. And discos are really something dreadful, they're really nothing, and you don't get anything out of them outside of jumping around there and sweating off a few extra ounces! If there were good equipment, a real place to dance, that would be good, but the way they're organized now, they take you to some neighborhood House of Culture that's just barely standing, you jump around and exhaust yourself, run around, and then leave—well, that's hardly a way to spend leisure time. I think the most important thing is to get kids access to theater. We were in the Operetta Theater, and in the first five rows most of the people were elderly, but come on, let's be honest, operetta isn't really for them. It's youthful, modern! But getting tickets for the first rows isn't possible, so you have to buy them in the balcony, far away where you can't see anything. So of course your desire to go evaporates. You think you'll get there, you'll look, and you won't be able to see a thing, and young people try to go where you can hear well, see well, and where they won't bother you.

So those are the most important problems young people are faced with: free time, getting a job, and personal contacts.

When I was little, I was an Oktobrist,‡ and I really envied the Pioneers and really wanted to become one too, to give that Pioneer salute.

---

*There are no ticket collectors on buses and trolleys. Tickets are purchased from a small dispenser in the back of the bus and paid for on the honor system. Occasionally an inspector boards a bus or trolley to check that passengers have paid and impose a fine on those who have not.

†The average price of a theater or concert ticket would range from one to four rubles.

‡The official political youth organization for children from six to nine years of age. Membership is almost automatic and considered to be the first step toward becoming a Young Pioneer, at age nine, and eventually a member of the Young Communist League, or Komsomol, at age fourteen.

That was my biggest dream. I was a Pioneer five or six years. And then that got tiring, those endless salutes, the same missions and assignments every year. Then I once ended up at a Komsomol meeting where they were voting with their Komsomol membership cards, and as soon as I saw that, I wanted to be able to vote with a Komsomol card, too. It occurred to me that things would be more interesting in the Komsomol, and so I joined at the end of the seventh grade. I went to a Komsomol meeting at school and I saw that that was it—the only people talking were the teachers and the secretary of the Komsomol organization, and all the rest were just sitting there voting with little scraps of paper, sometimes they didn't even have their membership cards there, just one book where they kept track of everything. I didn't really feel like myself there. And during those years I didn't do anything in the Komsomol—I had my membership card, my Komsomol pin, and that was all. And then when perestroika began in our school, they began pestering the Komsomol members to do something. Before the ordinary Komsomol members didn't do anything, only the leaders did what they called work. Now they make the members do something.

I don't think that they should completely do away with the organization, because if there were no Komsomol, that void would have to be filled by something. That would probably be those informal youth groups.* And I think that those informal groups are simply young people who really want to show off, so they fight with chains and are constantly involved in rowdiness, and I think they could develop in a completely different direction. I don't understand people who say, "We don't have anything to do. We have a lot of free time, but we don't know what to do." That's absurd! What do you mean, you have a lot of time? Where are you working? Of course I don't mean in the full sense of the word, in production, but going someplace, helping someone, helping old women, old men, and then there won't be any free time at all. And they say they have nothing to do! How can they have nothing to do, when the Charitable Society has been organized, and all kinds of other organizations, for the preservation of nature, for example. I think those informal groups just don't want to use their heads and think about what they might do. They get together and just waste their time. I am against all those informal organizations, especially violent ones. The violent ones have to be lured someplace else.

---

*Tanya, like many of the young people I spoke with, didn't know many details about the informal groups and seemed to associate them with groups such as the *rokery* (rockers) and *metallisty* (heavy metal fans), which are named for their identification with certain trends within Western music, or the *lyubertsy,* a violent gang whose name is derived from the tough Moscow neighborhood of their origin.

TWO SYSTEMS, TWO COUNTRIES

I don't know any definitions of capitalism and socialism. We studied that topic this year in school, but I didn't understand a thing. If you want to compare the two, according to what I know, we have it written on paper that we have all our rights and freedom. Here, till now, that hasn't really been fulfilled. And it hasn't been in your country either. The only thing we have here is that in socialism every person has hot water for their tea, and it's more or less guaranteed that he will be able to work. Actually that's certain—no matter who he is, even if he hasn't finished studying anything, no matter how poor his qualifications are, he will be able to work. Basically he will have his apartment, even if it's only a room in a communal apartment,* and most importantly he will have free medical care and free education.

In capitalism things are a little foggy. Education and medical care have to be paid for, and the apartment as well, and it's not clear whether a person will have one. But I don't know how to compare those two words more concretely. Our history teacher is just beginning that topic now. That is, he still hasn't started to talk about the capitalist structure yet. Right now we are talking about the [1917] socialist revolution, and when we covered America it seemed as if he didn't really go into great detail about capitalism. So it's hard for me to talk about this. In fourth grade they told us, "Capitalism is bad and socialism is good."

In socialism at least a person will always have the basics. Education is free. It doesn't matter if you are a worker, or a collective farmer, no matter who you are you will have a chance to participate in the life of your country. I think a person feels freer, has some kind of moral support, knowing that the government will intercede for him. There is a kind of feeling that if something happens, for example, an accident on the job—and there seem to be a lot of them—or something happens in the family, you won't be left without help.

Socialism is supposed to be a society of equal people. I am for socialism, and even if I had the opportunity to live in capitalism, I wouldn't exchange socialism for it, not even if I lived just as an average person, and I know that materially the average citizen has a higher standard of living in capitalism. Still, I would choose to live in socialism.

I saw New York on television, a very pretty city, and in our textbooks we have photographs. The cities there are all very different. Chicago,

---

*The continued existence of communal apartments is indicative of the severe housing shortage in the Soviet Union. Communal apartments house two or more families, each one residing in a separate room, sharing kitchen and bathroom facilities. Communal apartments are generally found in old, run-down, unrenovated buildings and are one of the least desirable forms of housing in the Soviet Union.

with all those skyscrapers, and then some city, I don't remember where, with all of these two- and three-story houses. And I saw some modern cowboys in Texas. Of course everything for them has changed, before they used to round up all those mustangs. Now they raise animals, they have special farms, factories, on the steppes, and there are all those horses, bulls, and a woman there was working right alongside the man, a husband and wife. She does all the men's work; I was so surprised to see that, she was doing the branding and rounding up the bulls on horseback. I really liked that. Of course it must be very hard. And then there was a program about an unemployed man who came to the Soviet Union, I don't remember his name, but they showed a lot of New York in it. They didn't just show one side, unemployment; they also showed the life of official people, who are working, the way our ministers go to their offices and sit there; it's also difficult work. And then I saw the magazine *Paris Match*, some friends of mine get a hold of it sometimes, and there are a lot of interesting photos in it, the life of these American engineers. . . . It doesn't seem fair for them to show only the unemployed, because there is such a great contrast and one has to compare—it's like night and day. In any case it's interesting, not the way it is here in the Soviet Union, we have a kind of middle level here, not those who are higher and those who are lower. Here everything is just painted over, as if there were no problems, and there, even in the official press they talk about it, about both the unemployed *and* the millionaires. That just seems interesting to me.

If an American works and earns well, then I think he has only one problem—how to keep from losing his job. Not to get fired. I think he has everything else. I've met Americans. Some American doctors once came to our school. We were little, of course, but we still got a look at them. Solid people, men, women; it seems to me that you really are the same kind of people we are, although I've read that Americans are a peculiar people, and, for example, if Russians don't follow some very strict rules, then they lose their way a little bit, two steps to the left, to the right, they zigzag a little; I don't think that Americans are this way. If an American decides he wants to live a minimum of eighty years, then every morning he'll get up and go to the tennis court, take his vitamins every day, and eat fruit and vegetables. But really I think Americans are the same as we are. Their language and customs are different, but I think we all have the same psychology.

MEN AND WOMEN

Men and women often have disagreements. A lot depends upon how a person is brought up in the family. Sometimes, when the child is small, he's already taught a lack of respect toward women; he's told that the other half is weak. In the case of a girl, you are taught that boys are stronger than you, and you have to accept that . . . those are the kinds of things they tell you. But why men and women have disagreements— well, I don't know.

The modern woman is active and practical, of course. But she is still the same as women have always been—in other words, she has her family and all the constant worries of trying to keep family life going. And if that woman has some kind of administrative or supervisory position, no matter what, the work affects her. That post dictates what she does. If there are men under her command, she probably thinks it should be the same way at home. She'll say something and she'll want her husband to agree with it, but I imagine there must be contradictions in all this. If you're a commander at work, at home you should try to behave in a soft, tender way, because what men can't stand more than anything else is for someone to boss them around. He probably thinks that he's stronger and always right about everything—about family matters as well as all the rest.

This is hard to understand. I don't know. It seems to me that a woman has to be capable of everything—she has to know how to give orders, on the job at any rate, and also how to be a wife at home. She has to be ready to take over for men, for everybody. That's a modern woman for you. She has to know how to do everything and still have that female nature. And perhaps have some kind of male qualities as well.

In the Metro you see a lot of men in suits and ties, all clean and polished, it seems that they're all some kind of bosses, or at least have some kind of position of importance. I read someplace about the modern male who comes home in the evening and lies down on the couch and reads a newspaper. He doesn't help with anything and doesn't find anything but his work interesting. But my father, for example, is interested in everything—he even has an almost sports-like interest in rock groups and he follows them closely.

I think that what they write about the modern man is not a man but something more resembling a woman—with their inertia and their passivity and their "I don't care about anything, I don't know anything." Women are supposed to be interested only in their family. That's how it used to be, but now it seems that the opposite has occurred.

It seems impossible to me that women wouldn't work. You need some kind of variety, no matter what. All of that laundry, cooking, rooms with dust everywhere, washing floors, vacuuming rugs—in my opinion all that is unbearable. How is a woman going to do all that by herself? Only if she doesn't work. But in her case it's always plus the work. And anyway she wants something more for herself than just to be in that apartment all the time.

No matter what, I would have to work. Because it wouldn't be at all interesting to live; everything would be so one-sided. When a woman is on her way to work, she thinks, "Good, I'm going to work and I'll do something there," and when she is on her way home, she thinks, "Oy, how fed up I am with that job, I'll go home and I'll do something else." When all you do is stay at home, and you're surrounded by all those things, with those kids underfoot who you can't take your eyes off of all day long, well, you need work; it's a kind of catalyst for family life. Even if I had the opportunity to stay at home, I would work. It's boring to spend the day at home doing nothing but housework. I want to have people to relate to.

I remember when my mother didn't work for a half-year—she enjoyed herself at first, but then she wanted to get back to work because she got fed up with being at home. Most importantly, one needs to interact with other people. But probably there have to be arrangements for a freer work schedule, for half-time work, so there's a little more time to be at home.

Maternity leave is now one and a half years, and it seems like too little to me. A child should be at home for three years so his education can start right and he can learn something.

It wouldn't work to give men a leave to take care of a child because in the first place men are the main breadwinners, and secondly, a man wouldn't agree to stay at home. My father isn't the type to sit at home, and even though of course he does help at home, even when he's ill he'll go running off to work. He says he can't stand sitting at home. Staying at home is a rather limited kind of life.

I think women's problems need to be solved by taking women out of those kinds of heavy jobs where men could work, for example, working in railyards, using a crowbar, lifting all of those rails—how strong one has to be!! Look, you see a woman with that same crowbar breaking up ice that's twenty centimeters thick. That's like a rock—and you have to hit it with enough strength to split it. Then you have to take that crowbar and haul it off somewhere, and in factories . . .

My grandmother's sister works at a cement factory. It's just horrible. She's gotten so many illnesses there and she always has to haul around all kinds of heavy things. She says that sometimes on that job they don't give out gloves or tools and they have to do everything with their bare hands, mix cement with their hands, pour out bags of dry cement—and making cement slabs is really hard work. So women could be motor mechanics, fur dressers, shoemakers—no, shoemaking is men's work because strength is required there as well—women could work sewing bags and clothing; those are the kinds of work a woman can do without damaging herself. It's really bad that women have to work where men could be working. I think a woman could both work and take care of the home, but things have to be done differently so she wouldn't have to go run off somewhere and stand in lines in the stores. There are enterprises now that have stores right on their own territory, so a woman doesn't waste her time trying to find the store that has what she needs. Everything is right there. But so far there aren't many of those kinds of stores.

In medical care as well. A lot of time gets spent on neighborhood clinics. If you end up there you have to wait for three hours until they take your child, and then you still have to go to see all the different doctors to get prescriptions and certificates. That has to be simplified and made more readily available so that a woman doesn't have to spend her work day going around with her child from doctor to doctor.

DATING AND SEX: "I DON'T INTEND TO GET MARRIED EARLY"

The group that's gotten together now at school, well, I can't be taken away from it. I didn't expect that this kind of friendship between young men and women could exist. I don't understand how some girls can talk to the same boy over and over again two hours every night. After two evenings like that all of my imagination is drained, and I need a break for two or three days so that I can get my thoughts together again. I guess they get used to each other. But I don't want that, because the kids in our group are more than enough for me. I absolutely don't want to tear myself away from them on account of one particular person. When you're in a group, at least there's something to talk about.

I can't imagine how young kids can have intimate relations. A man and wife are close to each other. But being in bed with a person you're not close to? I think that true friendship, if it's really strong, can get by without that. Without sex. I read about that somewhere—platonic love. That is on the highest level, when you don't need that.

It seems to me that if people really respect each other and love each other, they'll get by without it. Everybody says that's not possible, but I think it is. Purely friendly relations. But I guess if you have the idea of a family you are going to create, well, then, you'll have to. It's your obligation. I don't know. They say that two people who have become very close to each other, well, there are some functions they will have to fulfill. I only know about this from newspapers and magazines.

I haven't really talked about this with my girlfriends. Of course it's an interesting topic, but, well, it's not *that* interesting. Sometimes they talk about it on the radio, but not very much. Something about a young girl not losing her honor, not getting involved in those kinds of relations. Somehow a person has to keep her relations under control. I guess if it's gotten to that point with someone, well . . . what can you do? But everything has to be done within certain limits, and not with every Tom, Dick, and Harry you come across. Whether you like it or not.

I think Mom will advise me on this in the future. Now she probably thinks that I'm still too young. I haven't spoken to anybody yet about sex. Maybe it's come up in conversation somehow, but not in the way that we've gotten together and sat down and talked about it. That doesn't happen.

There's more information about it now and they've begun to write about these things, using medical terms of course. Not long ago in *Komsomolka** I read an article, the kind of thing you could cut out. About the functions of men and women, in bed. And then there was *Interdevochka*, mainly about prostitutes. They're writing about that now in some magazines. Our teacher Nina Arkadyevna tells us that at our age we should know about these things even if we're not involved in them yet. Well, not absolutely *everything*. She's a good teacher, a good woman too. She says, "I am in favor of it," meaning that she thinks that they should start writing about all of these things here, and not just kind of whisper about these things to each other on the sly. But I'm against them printing these things in the newspapers. That's such an open method of propaganda. But I think it makes sense to print it in magazines, especially specialized ones like *Woman Worker* and *Peasant Woman*. And not just in bits and pieces, but more detailed.

We have a class "Ethics and Psychology of Family Life."† It doesn't cover things dealing with sex, but it's about the relationships between man and wife, parents and children. Decent relationships between young men and women. But when it comes to sex, or what they've written about it in the newspapers, well, groups of girls get together to discuss it separately, and groups of boys, because we haven't grown up

---

The Moscow Komsomol, official newspaper of the Moscow Young Communist League (Komsomol).

†This course was introduced into the official high school curriculum several years ago as an attempt to begin addressing the need for sex education. The course, however, contains very little that could be considered sex education, and it is taught by teachers of any discipline willing to assume the responsibility, regardless of their qualifications to teach that topic.

enough to get to the point where we could sit around and talk about it together. This is the first year we've even had that course in our school. Before, they put it in the schedule, but they replaced it with something else. Now it's an official subject. They think it's about time we talked about it. Things have gotten freer now. But they are guarded about what they say, they're adjusting their psychology. That same teacher won't talk to his own children about it! Some can talk about it freely, but the older people get, the more they get embarrassed. They are terribly full of complexes. I remember three or four years ago, if somebody suddenly took it into his head to write the word "sex" in Latin letters on a wall in a public place, that was considered something really awful; they'd try to wash it off, paint over it, in short, a tragedy on a global scale. Even in the bathroom here in our school. That's just a sign of ignorance, to write that word and think that whoever saw it suddenly in the midst of a generally pleasant vocabulary . . . well, that's just complete mediocrity or something, a complete lack of culture in these areas.

I remember one of those television bridges where there were only schoolchildren.* No adults. Only the moderator. They talked about all kinds of problems, and toward the end, when there were only fifteen minutes left, somebody suddenly started talking about sexual relations. And our kids suddenly clammed up, they just sat there, and they were told, "Go ahead, ask questions, they'll answer you," but I don't think even one hand was raised in that group. They just sat there; a real swamp!! I don't think they didn't want to ask questions, they probably had a lot of questions, but they were so embarrassed. What is there to get embarrassed about, if this is something completely natural? And from your side, the American side, there was a whole sea of hands, they asked a lot of questions. Our kids just sat there with such faces—you could see they were just wishing the time would pass as quickly as possible, because what a subject! That contrast was really great. But in other questions people were just as active, yours and ours. They talked about all kinds of questions and issues. But when it comes to real life, the problems closest to you, well, what a fog!

My mom says not to get married early. She thinks eighteen years old is just not the right age. From twenty to twenty-five. Well, at twenty-five of course they're already the most hard-to-please kinds of brides. And she says that a future husband should know how to do everything, has

*Television programs that use satellite link-ups between cities in the Soviet Union and the United States are extremely popular in the Soviet Union. Many teenagers I spoke with had viewed several of them and noted with particular interest those that involved young people from both countries.

to be kind and respect me. She thinks that a person has to be careful in making a choice, a girl shouldn't listen to the advice of her girlfriends. It turned out that when she was my age she was already friends with one particular boy who had entered a military academy and was going to become a military man. And her closest girlfriend, the person she was the closest to on earth, somehow managed to come between them and got them into a big fight. And my mom says that if she hadn't listened to her girlfriend, they would still be together. She says that when she met my dad she kept on comparing them, one to the advantage of the other, but seeing as it was already over with Yuri—that was the other one—my father was the one who won out, because a bird in the hand is worth two in the bush! But I guess she doesn't really believe in that early love, at fourteen or fifteen, sixteen, it's not real, or natural. And after school you forget each other, it's just a lot useless nerves. But she's sorry that she left the first one. She says that when she was younger she didn't think about it, but now that she's forty, she's sorry. She doesn't say why, she just says that it wasn't that he was so exceptional in any one thing, he was just very kind, sort of shy, and she says she was surprised that a young man could be so kind and so shy. She says it wasn't the same way a girl could be kind, it was completely different. But she's satisfied with my dad. He's an active man, he knows how to do everything, he knows everything. I guess she remembers her youth, but when she comes back from her reminiscing she feels that everything between them (my parents) is good. They haven't had any major fights, and they're not about to separate, they live together peacefully, in a friendly way. She was twenty-six when she got married. Relatively late. They lived two years without me, and then in 1972 I was born.

I don't intend to get married early. First of all, I have to finish my studies. They say now that a young man, a future husband, considers two things above all: looks and social status. So in any case, I'll have to finish studying.

"GOING STRAIGHT TO WORK MEANS GIVING UP A PART OF YOUR FREEDOM"

OLYA

Seventeen years old, vocational school student

Olya arrives at my dorm room a little breathless, smiling; she seems cautious. She looks around my room, politely but thoroughly, and sits down in the chair I pull out for her. Tall, blond, she wears a colorful print dress, heels, and brightly colored rouge and eye shadow. Her lipstick and bag match her clothing. She is poised and confident and appears to be in her early twenties, although I know she is younger.

She turns down my offer of tea and cakes. She asks me a few questions about the United States, about my life, about my family. After a few minutes her caution disappears, and she begins to tell me about herself. As she moves into the flow of her story, I find myself asking very little. She is a natural storyteller, and a few occasional words from me are all that is needed to direct the conversation.

The first day we talk for several hours. By the end of that conversation, we are friendly and relaxed with each other, we laugh together, and she has begun to use the familiar form of "you" with me. After I shut off the cassette recorder, we have a cup of tea. Once or twice she uses the diminutive when addressing me: "Deborochka."

By the end of the second conversation, we have definitely become friends. She asks about the lives of women in the United States. She sits with one arm propped up on the table, resting her chin against her hand, listening with great curiosity. At one point she sighs a bit and says, "Ah, life is a difficult kind of thing, isn't it?" I feel that I am talking to another adult woman.

During the next few months, when I call Olya, her mother answers the phone and we talk. Both of them invite me to come to the house and have tea. On one of my last days in Moscow I go to visit them. They live in a

OLYA

*two-room apartment near Kolomenskoye Park, a lovely expanse of grassy
hills along the banks of the Moscow River in the southeast of the city, the
site of several ancient churches and a former residence of the tsar.*

*Olya's mother has prepared a meal: soup, appetizers, and chicken. They
send Olya's younger brother out to play, and the three of us sit around the
table and talk. The apartment is bright and cheerful, decorated simply but
carefully. A samovar sits in one corner of the living room, which serves as a
bedroom for three people at night. After we eat, they bring the samovar to the
table and we drink tea, Russian-style, accompanied by large pieces of cake and
chocolate candies, in scarce supply these days. Olya's mother tells me about her
life, much of which I have also heard from Olya. It hasn't been easy. She seems
tired but not worn down.*

*After the meal we take photos, and the three of us walk to the bus stop.
Olya's mother invites me back to her home the next time I am in Moscow. In a
few hours, she will go to work, to her second job. We hug. Olya rides the bus
with me back to the Metro station; we take a few more pictures. I won't see her
again before I go. It's hard to say goodbye to her; her openness and warmth
have moved me. I find myself wondering what the next five years will bring her.*

I will be eighteen this year. I finished studying in a vocational school,
and now I'm doing my practicum, before I get my diploma. We're
working now in production, together with the adults, getting experience from them. My school is a polygraphic institute; I'm going to work
as a printer. We print various products—passes for public transportation, different documents, passports, money. We work in a "regi-
mented" factory. That's a closed factory;* we have secret departments.

We'll work together with the adults who taught us for two or three
months. If we like the work we'll stay there, but after all, life is life, a girl
might go and get married, start a family, and a lot of the guys go to the
army. I like it; it's a good job. The people there are kind and we have a
good collective.† They treat us well, because after all we don't know
everything yet, they show us and explain.

---

*Not open to the general public for reasons of state security.

†The *kollektiv*, or collective, is an essential element in the life of Soviets. Collectivism is
encouraged from earliest childhood, in day-care centers and throughout schooling. Many
teenagers I spoke with used the words "our collective" to refer to their classmates. On the
job, people speak of their co-workers as the "work collective." Recently, collectivism has
been criticized for ignoring the role of the individual and overlooking individual potential. Nonetheless, it remains an important value in Soviet public life, and many people I
spoke with in the Soviet Union stressed the importance of having a good collective in
building a meaningful life. The collective undoubtedly remains an important concept for
the teenagers I met in Moscow.

Even though the work is interesting, it's hard to get up early every day. I like to sleep in a little. Still, I think a person should work. If you didn't work for a year you'd get fed up; there wouldn't be anything for you to do. A person who isn't working might come up with all kinds of strange ideas. Life would simply be uninteresting.

My parents are workers. My mother is a worker; she finished a technical high school for trade, and now she works in a factory. She says she likes it a lot. They produce medicines, penicillin and things like that. I've never been there, though; it's a closed factory because there's hazardous production going on, the preparations they make and use are expensive, so they won't let just anybody go in there. They have showers, and she takes one before work and after work. She has to—there's a lot of dust there and it has some kind of effect on the body. There have to be good hygienic standards there. After all, if a person works in that factory for fifteen or twenty years, who knows what the consequences might be? And that's about all she's told me about her job. She's been working there about five years.

At first she worked in one factory, then she worked in another, then I was born, then she went on to another place, and I think she even worked in a store; my father hardly helped us at all, so she had to take me to the day-care center early in the morning in order to get to work on time. Then she lost her seniority when my little brother was born, so she ended up back at the kind of job where she earned very little. Now that we're grown, she's gone on to a steady job, where she really likes her work.

When I was little she just couldn't get work where she wanted to because she was practically on her own with two children. She had to take us to kindergarten, then pick us up from school, and still have enough time to feed us. There was never enough money. Her parents didn't help us either because they have thirteen children. I think that now only six of them are still in touch. My mother is really the only one of them who helps her mother; she loves her a lot. Sometimes it surprises even me—she does everything for her; she'd give her the shirt off her back. The things that we bring them from Moscow her other children take away—my mother finds it amazing that a person could even think of taking things from one's parents. We've never really expected any help from them. They live very far from here, near Lake Balkhash in Kazakhstan; it takes six hours to fly there by plane and three and a half days by train.

My mother was born in the Orlovsky Region. Her mother didn't work all her life because she had a lot of children, and they had to raise them, and my mother's father was a geologist, so they were always moving from place to place. My grandfather doesn't work any more; he's on his pension.

My mother traveled a lot. She didn't just sit in any one place. She was a cook by profession, a chef, actually, so she went to work for the River Fleet, and after technical school she ended up on a ship, sailing from one city to the next. She worked as a cook, preparing food. She was in Alma-Ata, then in the Krasnoyarsk Region, and then in Krasnodar, then . . . I don't even know where else; for some reason we haven't talked much about this. Then I'm not sure, she worked in some ministry, someplace in Alma-Ata, or in Togliatti. She went to visit her girlfriend and completely coincidentally she met my father. My father lived in Moscow and had gone to Togliatti on a trip for his job. They wrote to each other for a long time, and then my mother went to him in Moscow and they got married. At first they lived in the dormitory where he had been living. Even though he had a regular Moscow registration,* he lived in a dormitory because that was in the 1970s, and if now, almost in the 1990s, we don't have enough housing . . . well, you can imagine that then there was really nothing.

When I was born they were given a room in a communal apartment. We lived there eight years. After that my father worked for five years at one place in order to get an apartment.† He earned very little, about 120 rubles a month in all. And my mother worked too. In order to take me back and forth to school, she worked at the kind of job where she earned nothing more than pennies, really. Now we live in a two-room apartment, and when

---

*Every Soviet citizen is supposed to register to live in a specific place (village, city, farm, etc.). This entitles him or her to the right to obtain housing, employment, and so on in that place. If a person moves to another part of the country, she or he re-registers. It is quite difficult to obtain a registration, or *propiska,* in cities considered the most desirable. A Moscow or Leningrad registration, for anyone not raised there, is almost impossible to obtain. Considerable speculation goes on by people who wish to obtain a *propiska* to live in either of these cities, the two most important cultural centers in the country. Recently the registration system has come under severe criticism in the press and from reformers, but it has not yet undergone revision. In this instance, Olya notes that even though her father was a legal resident of Moscow, with a legitimate *propiska,* he was still unable to obtain an apartment due to the housing shortage and had to live in a dormitory instead, even after he married.

†There are several ways to obtain an apartment in the Soviet Union. Olya's family, in their first move, was able to exchange a dormitory room for a room in a communal apartment (a considerable improvement) through the central exchange bureau. In the second move, her father worked at an enterprise that was building apartments for its own workers. People often receive apartments through their place of employment, which may have housing for its workers. Indeed, this is often an incentive for choosing a particular place of work. People may keep the apartment even if they no longer work at that enterprise. This was the case with Olya's father, who worked five years at a low-paying job specifically because he was on its waiting list for housing. Once he obtained the apartment, he was able to look for another job that would pay him a higher salary. The five years he waited for an apartment was considerably less than the average ten years most people in Moscow wait for new apartments.

we moved to this apartment another child was born in our family—my brother. His name is Alyosha. I was eight or nine. There's a difference of nine years between us, and he's already nine years old. At first my mother didn't want to have another baby; she kept saying that she was old already—she was almost forty. But then somehow she decided to do it. And then there were continuous arguments in our family, always some kind of conflict. My father hardly gave us anything in life; he was mainly concerned just about himself. My mother was the one who took care of us. My father came home, read the newspapers, watched television, but didn't do anything at home, and he didn't manage to bring home any money either. He didn't want to do anything, and my mother would tell him that we couldn't live like that, that even the children helped her, but he would say, "If you need that done, go ahead and do it yourself." So when the situation with him became too conflictive, she divorced him, two years ago. He suffered from it, of course, but I think that basically he's the one to blame. After all he's a man, and seeing as he created a family, he should worry about how to provide for it.

My brother and I were still little then, and we needed our father, especially my brother; he's a boy after all, and my father was closer to him or something. My brother was close to my mother too, but somehow a boy wants to be with his father more than with his mother. Of course, when boys grow up they understand that there is nothing more precious than a mother—and that's really the truth—but when they are little they want to be with their father. When my parents divorced, my mother found a second job, because we could hardly survive on what we had, and here it is the second year already that they've been divorced and she's working two jobs. Right now we can't really complain; we bought furniture, and now everything's going okay for us. Before we really had nothing; we were just going around in circles.

My mother works a lot, she gets very tired so I have to cook and clean . . . all of that ends up on my shoulders. And of course I don't say anything. I would simply be ashamed—my mother works alone for the three of us, and at two jobs no less. She comes back from one job and has to go to the other . . . and she's working alternate shifts at her main job—from eight until one, and from four until eleven, and from twelve on she works the night shift until seven in the morning. I don't even know when she sleeps. Especially since she comes in late, sleeps three or four hours, and then goes to her second job. After that job she comes home and she has to do the night shift again. Her other job is in a store. She gets about eighty rubles there, no more. Basically she doesn't get any days off. At least she went on vacation with Alyosha (my brother) not too long ago. She's on vacation now. I hope she gets some rest.

My mother talked to me about the divorce. I think she was right, because it really was impossible to go on living that way. I would have gotten divorced a long time before she did! They're completely different people. My mother is a very active, vital person, interested in a lot of things. She goes to art exhibits, to the theater, to the movies. She has a variety of interests and you can talk to her about any subject. My friends come to her for advice, but my father—he drinks, lies down, goes to sleep, and doesn't care about anything else. So of course it's not interesting for my mother to be with him. Other men somehow manage to take care of their wives, they help out, do something. There are few men who don't do anything at all and don't bring home any money. Basically, I can't imagine how one can live like that; I don't know how we managed, how in our times we were able to live on that kind of money. . . .

We were poor. I was always ashamed because we didn't have anything in our apartment, only the bare necessities, and I was ashamed because others were better dressed, because they had something. Before first grade I was better dressed, things were cheaper, but then everything got more expensive, and I had only the most basic things. My parents just couldn't allow themselves to get me anything that wasn't really needed. Of course my mother tried to dress us, to get us shoes, and didn't buy certain things for herself in order to buy for us. I don't know how she managed to live. When they divorced, my mother owed a lot of money, but by now we've paid it back so we don't owe anybody anything and we live well. So I'm happy that she got divorced. . . . If a woman is working two jobs and the man isn't doing anything to help his family . . .

Actually my father is an intelligent man; he could have become a skilled worker but he didn't want to study. He's a fitter, a construction worker. I don't know where he's working now. We don't talk much.

He still lives with us. We live in a two-room apartment, and he doesn't even want to let us keep it.* He says that we should exchange

---

*The situation Olya is describing is quite common and illustrates one way in which the housing shortage puts strains on family life. For example, if a family has a two-room apartment and there is a divorce, its members maintain only the same amount of living space—two rooms (excluding kitchen and bathroom). To separate the household, they must exchange the two-room apartment for two one-room apartments. In Olya's family, the situation is complicated by the fact that three people—Olya, her mother, and her brother—would have to live in a one-room apartment, using the same one room as both a living room and bedroom for all three. Her father, on the other hand, would receive a one-room apartment for himself. Olya's mother feels that arrangement is unfair and impossible. Olya's father could take a room in a communal apartment but doesn't want to. Not only divorce causes such problems. If a grown child marries, she often must bring her spouse to live in the same apartment she has been sharing with her parents. In some cases, in order to let a young couple begin an independent life, parents will agree to give up a larger apartment they have spent years in for two smaller ones.

the apartment. In other words, my mother, brother, and I should go live in a one-room apartment, and he would get a one-room apartment by himself. I've confronted him about that a lot. "Why don't you let us keep the apartment?"

My mother was able to get all the way through to see Yeltsin about it, she even got to Raisa Maximovna.* They offered him a room in a three-room communal apartment but he refused it, he said that he didn't like it. He didn't want to live in a communal apartment; he would have had to live with neighbors. They offered him a room three different times, but he wouldn't agree to it. Now I have no idea what they are going to do. I have told him many times, "What have you given us in life, absolutely nothing! The only thing we have at all is this apartment, and now you want us to divide it up!" He tells me, "Well, you have a mother, let her buy you shoes and clothing, and take care of you, after all what's a mother for?" And I tell him, "But you're our father, aren't you the man of the house?" But he doesn't listen to anything. I really don't respect my father at all. I used to love him, when I was a little girl, but I don't now. I can't imagine how my mother was able to live with him for sixteen years. I guess once she did love him.

When my parents met in Togliatti, my mother was very pretty. She was almost thirty when she got married. There were thirteen people in her family, and she was the second oldest child. Aunt Lyuda, her older sister, was more clever than my mother because my mother was the one to sit at home and take care of all the children. My mother was very good to her parents; they had eleven children and she loves them and really cares for them. Her sister Lyuda went wherever she wanted to go, stayed out, played, went to school. . . . They had one pair of boots for the two of them, and they went out one at a time; they took turns with the boots. They told me about how they had to eat wild swans after the war. To make a long story short, she says that she didn't even want to get married. She had a lot of young men interested in her—she was pretty, and she had a nice personality.

She used to say to my father, "I've gone through fire and water for you and ended up staring the devil in the face!" She didn't pay any attention to the nice young men who were interested in her, and what she saw in him she herself doesn't know. She was so unhappy in her life with him; he didn't give her anything. She regrets that she married him.

Of course we eat separately, we do everything separately; he pays 80 rubles a month alimony for two children, and my mother works two jobs. We have enough. She gets 200 rubles at one job, and 80 at the

---

*Raisa Gorbacheva. In Russian it is common to refer to public figures by their first name and patronymic.

other: 280 rubles. And those 80 rubles of alimony: 360 rubles total. Around 400. Also my mother has a brother who works in the North,* and sometimes he sends us money; he sent me 50 rubles and my mother 100 rubles on her birthday.

My mother hardly ever rests. At the factory they have a rotating schedule, and her days off hardly ever come on Saturdays and Sundays, so she rarely gets two days off in a row. She has a very hard life. I really feel bad for her. But soon I'll start working, and of course I'll help her. My brother is growing up fast, not long ago we bought him a bike, and one of these days he's going to ask for a motorcycle, and then he is going to want a cassette recorder. We buy him a pair of jeans almost every month, he wears them out so quickly! But all in all, I don't think he dresses any worse than anyone else. He has really expensive toys, cars that cost fifteen to twenty rubles. We hardly refuse him anything. We think of him as the baby and we give him everything. "Alyosha, Alyosha!" Sometimes I quarrel with my mother, "Why do you spoil him so much?" And really, he's become so demanding because he knows that whatever he asks for he'll get. That's not right either. What will happen to him later on? When he's grown? Of course she agrees with me, but still she loves him a lot.

When I was little my mother loved me a lot too, but now she thinks that I'm grown, an independent person, and soon I'm going to start working. So she worries more about him than she does about me. He's so restless, mischievous . . . and I was a very even-tempered girl, everything went well in school. And then I went into a PTU† and ended up in a completely different environment. I didn't know that we had young people who take drugs, that young girls could smoke. I had heard about that but I didn't believe it. On the one hand I'm glad that I ended up in that vocational school, that I had a chance to see that kind of crowd, found out how people live, what kind of views they have of things, what they think about life. I think if I had gone ahead and finished general school [academic high school]‡ I wouldn't have found out about all of this. I think that a person should experience everything.

BECOMING A WORKER

At first I had decided to enroll in a technical high school,§ but then, I don't know why, I took my papers back and went into a PTU to the polygraphic department, where I've just graduated.

---

*As an incentive to attract workers to the harsh but economically important northern regions, salaries there are well above the average salary in the rest of the country.

†The Russian acronym for a vocational school, or *politekhnicheskoye uchilishche*.

‡Refer to the introductory material explaining the tracking system in Soviet education.

§A technical school is more prestigious than a vocational school.

They had accepted me into the ninth grade in school.* I could have kept on studying. I had done all right in school. I had some C's, but they still accepted me into the ninth grade. But I chose not to go on to ninth grade, I don't know why, maybe I just didn't feel like studying any more.

In general I wanted to learn a trade as soon as possible, so I could start to work and help my family. I had those thoughts then. I thought that if I finished general school, I would have to keep on studying, start something new, and even more time would go by. And if I went to the vocational school, I could be finished with studying in three years and I'd have a trade and a secondary education. And if I had only finished tenth grade, then I'd just have a secondary education, no trade.

I don't really know why I chose the Polygraphic Institute. I guess I didn't really know what vocational institute to go into. When I was doing the course work it was one thing. We used to take excursions to different factories, to publishing houses—"Malysh" (children's books) and "Kniga"—and that was all very interesting, seeing how they make books, how they put them together. But when I went to work at the factory, that was something else. Printing a book is one thing, and printing money, all those tiny little sheets of paper, that's another, and it's hard. Completely different.

At first I didn't know which area to study. I ended up a printer even though it's really a totally male profession. There were only five girls there in all. And there were twenty-five boys! At first we really liked that—a male collective! But then we decided that it really is a job for men. There are a few women, but they are all elderly. Young girls don't work there because it's really hard, and a young girl wants to be beautiful; she wants to have a nice hairstyle, and a manicure, and come out of work clean and neat, but when you come out of there you're full of ink and dirt, and your head's covered with a scarf. One of my girlfriends complains because she sleeps at night with rollers in her hair, goes off to work, puts that scarf on her head, and, well, you can imagine what happens to her hairdo! The uniform they wear is always dirty, always full of oil and grease, ink, everything imaginable. And you're always carrying those papers around, lifting heavy boxes, putting them into a machine, taking them out of the machine, carrying them over to be counted, storing them someplace else. Of course it's hard. For a young girl, it's really hard.

On the one hand I don't regret having gone there to study; I think

---

*Olya chose to leave school and go into the vocational school. Her grades were actually good enough to have stayed in the academic track.

that in order to work one has to start from the very bottom. Even when someone says, "Oh, I've finished an institute (of higher education); I know everything," what does that really mean? Every supervisor should go through it all. From worker to supervisor. I think that anyone who becomes a boss from the very beginning won't be able to understand the people that have to work with him. And if he himself is from the working class then he will always want to help the working class. And people will relate to him differently. There is a common attitude that only stupid people enter PTU's, but I don't agree with that. Even our own teachers at the institute tell us, "Look, you're stupid, you don't know anything, and that's why you ended up in a vocational school." That's the way they treat people who want to be part of the working class! Of course I'm not saying that everyone in the institute is an angel; we have different kinds of kids there, there are stupid ones who already have a police record, but even so, no matter how poorly they may have done in school they are wonderful workers, lots of them are already in the fourth ranking. And the masters* and the managers are satisfied with them. They are good kids; they know how to work, even though people are always telling them they're stupid, idiots. And that's the kind of attitude that exists about PTU's; they threaten kids, "If you do poorly in school, we're going to send you to a PTU!" But there's nothing wrong with going to a PTU. After graduation, a person can go to a technical college, or an institute [of higher education], or wherever he wants.† *If* he wants. And if he doesn't, so let him go out and work!

My mother told me that she could give me advice about where to go but that it would be better for me to decide for myself, so I thought about it a lot. She said, "Think for yourself, so that later on you don't blame me for your decision. Choose your own road, because if I tell you to go on to the ninth grade, you'll go, and, if you regret it, later on you'll blame me for having given you that advice. You're already a grown person, you'll get your passport soon,‡ and I have confidence in you, so decide for yourself." In general she's always had confidence in me. She never ran after me; she didn't do what other parents do. She always

---

*Skilled workers who teach technical subjects related to the trade. There are two sets of teachers in vocational schools, academic and technical.

†The working class of the Soviet Union is highly educated; approximately 40 percent of workers have some kind of degree in higher education. There are many colleges and technical institutes workers attend after completing their secondary education or at some point during their work life in industrial production.

‡At age sixteen every Soviet citizen receives a domestic passport, which serves as identification and is needed in many aspects of life. It contains the *propiska,* or registration of residency, as well as other kinds of basic information. Receiving a passport represents an official rite of passage into adulthood.

said to me, "I trust you, and you should always know that." She never
undermined my faith in myself, and that's why she and I have such a
good relationship. Of course, we do have our disagreements, but very
rarely.

She did have her opinion, but she just said to me, "You should act
according to your own wishes." My father didn't say anything at all, he
really didn't care one way or another. So I decided to go to that vocational school.

In school I was kind of quiet, not shy, but somehow quiet, although I
was friendly with everybody. And then I came to the PTU, and the
relationships were so different, a completely different atmosphere in
the school, a different kind of collective. They used to tell us that we
already have work responsibilities; we were already workers, and they
didn't go after us like the teachers in school did. They already considered us independent people. And they used the formal *vy* with us,
which was new.* So there was a big difference from school. I knew
before, of course, that young girls smoked, but I hadn't actually seen it
up close, next to me, let alone in school, and I couldn't really believe
they smoked right there. In school nobody would smoke in the bath-
rooms, but there in the PTU you'd see one kid smoking, another one
was already in trouble with the police. . . . If somebody came to the PTU
who wasn't able to defend himself, they might just beat him up and
leave him out in the gutter. That happened once. They'd make fun of
him however they pleased.

The teachers think that what one finds in a vocational school is the
lowest level compared to general schools, technical institutes, and so
on, but I think that a person can see things in a PTU that he won't find
anywhere else. I just don't believe that only stupid kids study in vocational schools.

When I started vocational school it was really easy for me to do the
work because they made the program easier in the vocational school.
They teach everything superficially, just the very basics. I think it's really
easy to study there. Maybe it's because the teachers think that the people who study in a PTU are slow and so they teach the easiest, most
accessible material. In history and literature they don't teach anything
difficult, just the most superficial knowledge. I don't think that's right. I
think that we could be given the same kind of knowledge that they get
in schools. They don't ask questions in the same strict way they do in
schools. In a school, for example, they make you go up to the board

---

*Russian, like many languages, has two forms of direct address: the formal *vy* (like the
French *vous*) and the informal *ty* (like the French *tu*).

and then they ask you questions, and in the PTU they do everything in a much easier way.

You know now it's possible for someone who doesn't want to study to finish the eighth grade, do one more year after that, and then go to work. They've made it possible now for us to work at age sixteen. So if someone doesn't want to finish his secondary education, he can very easily just go off to work.

We do get a diploma that states we've finished our secondary education, and we get a transcript with our grades from both our general academic courses and the technical subjects as well. But there's still some kind of difference between our degree and what they get in schools. I guess it's a bit of a paradox. On the one hand they act as if we were adults, and on the other, they think we're some kind of idiots. You know, the teachers tell us, "Stand up, sit down," like in a prison. So the guys say, "Who do you take us for?" There were very serious problems. Especially with the chemistry teacher. She had worked at Moscow State University, so she learned some new things, and she really demanded a lot from us. But at the vocational school we were used to things being easy, and she was used to the university and the schools, where things are very serious, so she gave up and finally said to us, "Why should I drive myself crazy?" But of course she was right. Some teachers don't really take things seriously, but she really loved her profession and would say, "I want you to know something about my subject!" And because of this there were always conflicts with her.

CLASS STRUCTURE: "CONCERN ABOUT THE WORKING CLASS HAS DROPPED OFF"

Not that many of my friends are workers. When I tell them that I'm going to work in a factory, for some reason they don't believe it and say that I don't seem like a worker, that I'm not very capable of lifting heavy things. I ask, "Why do you think that?" And they say I don't seem like a person from the working class, they think that somehow I stand higher than that. They're surprised. Some people consider the working class to be something rather low. I'm an engineer and you're a worker—you're not worth anything.

I think very highly of workers, perhaps because I myself am from a working-class family and I have known difficulties. I mean, you can't get along without workers; you couldn't just have bosses. I don't know why people have such bad attitudes toward workers. After all, workers are supposed to be the basic work force, they do all of the basic labor. Here bosses just sit in armchairs and give orders. And if there were no workers, what would they do without them? They couldn't go and do those things by themselves, they couldn't go and dig with a shovel, for instance! No, that's not for them, and I don't know why they act that way to workers, because if there were no workers what would they do?

Concern about the working class has dropped off, and it seems to me that workers have fewer opportunities, because everything here is done through connections. Workers have fewer acquaintances of the sort who can get things done, fewer connections and things like that. Of course a worker can't do something that an engineer can do, or a boss, or somebody like that. He can't really get anything for himself through connections; he goes to a store and there is nothing there, he leaves, comes back again. You can't buy anything here. But engineers and bosses have connections.

My mother could have sent me to a special school, an English school for example, or a musical school, but we didn't have the right material circumstances to do that. And it seems to me that everything is done according to material circumstances. It wasn't a real possibility. In order to go there you have to bring your kid to someone who can study with him, and I don't know any English, or German, and in order to get into a place like that you have to find a tutor.* And in order to find a tutor, well, that costs money. As it was we were living from one month to the next, and borrowing money, so we couldn't even think about finding a tutor. It was impossible. Of course I wanted to! But around here everybody says that the kids who study in special schools are the children of the big bosses who hold high positions. And I think that's the case.

Working people don't know anything outside of their work and their families. I don't feel that I am living in a country made for the working class. Just the opposite. Working people have less access to things. It's harder for workers to live in this country, in every way. It's harder to get things, get a hold of things, get an apartment. My father worked at one job for five years to get an apartment. He was paid 120 rubles a month, he worked on contract to get that apartment. A person could work forty or fifty years here and still live in a communal apartment! I don't think that's right. Don't tell me he hasn't earned a state apartment! In his whole life? I think the government should give him an apartment!

They say that by the year 2000 every family will have its own apartment, but I don't know ... we have such a big problem with apart-

---

*Students may enter a special school from the first grade. It is also possible to enter a special school in high school (ninth and tenth grade), in which case there is usually a competitive exam, particularly for the better special schools. This exam requires a considerable amount of extra studying for a student who has not attended a special school from the first grade.

ments. It's not right that my father doesn't have another apartment to move into. They keep offering him rooms in communal apartments but he keeps turning them down; of course I can understand him. He's worked all his life, and he's fifty years old, and now in his old age he's going to live in a room, in a communal apartment. He worked for that apartment, and now they (my mother) are making him move out, go into a communal apartment. Of course you can understand his situation. It's painful. He worked all his life and doesn't have an apartment. He doesn't have an apartment, and he doesn't have a family either— he's no better off than he was at the beginning. It's a tough situation.

YOUNG PEOPLE: "THE ERA OF IBM"

A lot of young people complain that we don't have any place where we can spend our time, no place to go out. I don't know what has to be done to solve that, but it's really true that a young person doesn't have any place to just hang around. Let's say he's back from work and is tired, and he wants to go someplace to relax, sit down for a bit, but everywhere he goes there are lines, and he has to wait a long time. Why can't there be places where you can just go to relax, sit for a bit, meet friends? We just don't have any places like that. If you want to get in anywhere, you have to wait in a line.

Everyone says "Moscow—this is the capital," but still there is no place to go. I think that's the biggest problem facing young people in Moscow—no place to spend our free time. We're faced with this problem constantly.

We go to exhibits, the theater, the movies, bars, and cafes. That's where young people are. But it's hard to get into one of those bars or cafes; you have to run around to ten of them to find just one you can get into. Either it's full, or everything's reserved, and making a reservation is practically impossible as well because when you call on the phone they say it's too early to make a reservation. It's always something.

Everybody tries to manage as best as he can, by any means. Some people know the right person. Others have foreign friends. I have friends from Yugoslavia. I met them when I was with a girlfriend of mine, and yesterday we went to the Sevastopol* and went to the restaurant. They have a special pass. We went up to the third floor; it was nice. There was a wedding going on, and we sat with them an hour and a half and went home.

---

*An Intourist hotel for foreign tourists and visitors.

It's easier to get in with foreigners because in hotels there are cafes and bars, and seeing as they're the only ones who can get in there, there are fewer people than in other cafes and restaurants. Sometimes the Komsomol gives out special invitations to parties and discos in the Intourist hotels.

Usually we go out looking for a place by car because there aren't many cafes that are near each other. Just yesterday we tried to get into the Arbat cafe on Kalininsky Prospect. We couldn't get in so we tried the Angara and couldn't get in, and then went to the Valdai, but there are too many people there on the weekends. They should build more cafes for young people—not like some places where there are people over forty who don't dance. They go to sit, not to meet people; they just talk about business.

When we go to bars, we eat a sandwich, get a drink; we don't need anything else. We dance a little, talk to someone, meet somebody, and that's what we like. There are new people, interesting people, each one with his own way of looking at the world. I think that every person can offer something new, depending upon the way he lives, his views on life, what he thinks, where he works. It's just wonderful when people talk to each other.

I just met some people from Yugoslavia. We talked with them—they say they've been everywhere, but they came here because the girls are pretty. We said to them, "What, you came here for girls?" I think they came here to earn money, because they get paid well. They're renovating the Hotel Berlin, and they get 306 rubles (per month) for food, and they get $1,500 in U.S. dollars per month as pay. They live alone, and work from 8 A.M. until 6:30 P.M. They don't have much free time to go anywhere or take a look around; they work Saturdays as well. They say they're enjoying it, but they want to go home. They've been in a lot of different countries, and they're surprised by how many problems we have.

I used to go to the Tretyakov Gallery,* but it's closed for repairs, and we go often to the Pushkin Museum. We go to exhibits at the VDNKh,† usually there's technology or clothing there. But sometimes there are the kinds of exhibits you can't get into. There was an exhibit of decorative arts at the Pushkin Museum, and my father was doing construction work there, and he said people started standing in line at 6 A.M. to get

---

*A famous Moscow gallery that contains an extensive collection of historical and contemporary Russian paintings.

†The Economic Achievements Exhibit, a large park in northern Moscow that houses permanent and rotating scientific and technological exhibits, and sponsors social and cultural events.

in. There's a great demand for exhibits here; they need to have them more often. We go to the movies. It's easier to get in because we have a lot of movie theaters.

I think that the Komsomol above all should deal with our not having anywhere to hang out. I do think the Komsomol is needed because the Komsomol is where young people are brought together. I don't know, perhaps it's our generation or something . . . in the 1930s and 1940s Komsomol members were completely different. They stood the entire country on its feet, and the whole country really depended upon them. Who knows, maybe after our generation there will again be people like those who existed before us, as they say, our predecessors or whatever we're supposed to call them. So I do think after all that the Komsomol is needed. That youth organization could really do quite a bit if it wanted to. I don't know, perhaps it's the times we live in or perhaps it's just not possible and nobody really cares about anything anymore.

People of my generation are better off materially, and we've seen more in life, and there isn't any war. We have enough things. If a young person takes drugs or gets high I think it's because he doesn't have anything else to do, so he shoots up or just hangs around. . . . In general they say around here that all of that comes from the West.

A lot of people are envious and they think the West has everything and we don't have anything. That's how these black marketeers appeared. They're no secret. They don't work anywhere, and they buy things from foreigners and then sell them to us at high prices. I think that perhaps it's because we haven't seen any suffering or anything terrible. Of course we are for peace and we fight for it. But I think that we don't really acknowledge what might happen. During the war there wasn't any time to think about taking drugs, and after all that destruction they had to rebuild the country. There were so many other kinds of problems. I don't know why young people are the way they are now.

The *metallisty* don't want to hear about the Komsomol. The *rokery*, the "punks"—there are lots of groups—none of them want to hear about the Komsomol.

Our parents had one kind of life experience, and we've had another. They tell us, "Look how we used to live, and what has become of you? We weren't like that." We live much better than they did and we've seen more. Because the more there is, the more you want. They're surprised, they say, "Look, they're spoiled, they hang around and do nothing," they're always criticizing young people. Yes, it's true that they don't understand us. This is a different era, we're in the twentieth century, the era of IBM! They didn't have any of that! To them it's strange, the twenty-first century, the century of the future, but we still have a lot ahead of us, living in it. They can't imagine any of this because our parents have really seen nothing during their lives.

My mother and I have different views of life. She doesn't really understand modern youth, why we wear so much makeup, why we go to bars and cafes. What are we supposed to do sitting around at home? She doesn't understand, and she says that in her day it wasn't like that, a girl didn't call a boy, and they were very proud. She can't understand modern youth. We live in a new century, a new life, a new atmosphere.

There's a lot my mother doesn't understand. She says, "Look at the way you live, how can you live like that?" She doesn't understand punks or *metallisty;* she's always complaining about them. There's a big difference between us—we are going forward all the time, and they are going backward. We have more opportunities than they do. We know more at our age than they did when they were our age. That's how I see it. They had families with a lot of children, they lived in little villages, they had their own gardens, and then the war began, and all the destruction, hunger, and so their characters were . . . well, a different kind of people developed, with their own outlook on life. They wanted to start living better, and they did, but now they criticize youth for being that same way. We live in that kind of a time . . . noisy, unsettled. . . .

They haven't seen anything. They wanted to live better, and they overfed us, or something like that. We have everything, but we want to live even better because the more there is, the more you want. Why do people live like they do in the West and we live the way we do? They have their villas, and we have our little dachas.* We want villas too!

EAST AND WEST

Our parents know very little about the West. Nowadays everything here comes to us from there, styles and everything else. Our youth follow it all closely and imitate it. Nobody here knows how to wear makeup, how to dress. They can't do anything. We have one designer, Zaitsev, only one good designer for the whole Soviet Union!! We grab like monkeys for everything we can from the West, from Italy, from France—cosmetics, fashion, stockings, music, heavy metal, rock. We ourselves aren't capable of inventing anything. It's even embarrassing. Don't tell me

---

*The country homes commonly owned by Soviet urban families. For ordinary families they can be quite simple, not more than a small house or shack with a garden plot. The dacha provides an opportunity to leave the city on the weekend, breathe better air, and do some gardening. Many families supplement their diet with produce grown at their dacha.

that people here are really so uninventive? We buy makeup from black marketeers, who buy everything from foreigners—almost all our cosmetics come that way. To get a set of Italian cosmetics we pay fifty, a hundred rubles! If there's no makeup, we use regular pencil to outline our eyes. But I personally haven't experienced a lack of makeup. I always manage to have it. Everybody has a different way of getting the money for it. Some people get it from their parents, others work. Mainly from parents.

My mother tells me, "You'll start to work and then you can go deck yourself out," because I spend a lot of money now on gel for my hair, which you can't find anywhere in the stores. I bought boots at a cooperative for 130 rubles; my mother gave me the money. If a person only earns 120 rubles and boots cost 170, 180, how can she buy boots at a cooperative? A pretty thing, but if she buys them for 180 rubles it means that for one and a half months she can't eat, drink, buy anything to wear or for her feet, just to save money for those boots!

I'm very interested in the way people live in the West. A lot of foreigners come here, and a lot of them are amazed by this country and say that there is nothing to do here, that this is a godforsaken hole and they can't imagine how anyone can live here. That's the opinion of foreigners. They don't say that to just anybody, but once we've spent time talking with them it turns out that there are very few who would stay to live in the Soviet Union. There are very few possibilities to live here in the way people live in the West. In the West there are greater opportunities in spite of the unemployment and the fact that those are capitalist countries. They themselves think that they live better over there than we do here. That's their opinion. Some of them don't understand how it's possible to go to a store and stand in line and still not buy anything. Always some kind of problems. A friend of my mother's has a daughter who married a Czech and they live in Czechoslovakia. Not long ago, in September, they came here to visit and she said to me, "Olya, I'm amazed." She and I went everywhere in Moscow, to Red Square, to the movies, the theater, everywhere. "Olya, I'm amazed at how many problems you have here! We live in a socialist country but at least we've learned how to solve these problems. We are much better off materially than you are."

Why does everybody here chase after imported goods, imported things? Because they really are of a much better quality in every way! My friend said she couldn't even get a ticket back to Czechoslovakia; she had to go back three times to the travel agency. She said, "In Czechoslovakia you go into the store, buy what you want, anywhere you want. I don't regret having gone to live in Czechoslovakia at all because the social and cultural levels are higher." We Russians suffer because we have a low level of public behavior. We yell at each other a lot; if somebody bumps into you, he doesn't excuse himself. In the West people are more polite and they treat each other in a friendlier way.

Here, on public transportation, or if someone is standing on line, they are always shouting at each other. Perhaps it's because we don't have enough goods here, we don't have enough things, and that's why it's this way.

I have a girlfriend who works in GUM,* in the leather goods department. People are always saying to her, "Young lady, why is this bag like this?" And she says, "I don't *make* them, I only *sell* them! It's not my problem!" Of course people should be polite to each other. They should understand each other and not think, "Oh, you owe me that or I owe you that." People should respect each other, try to stand in the other person's shoes. They say to her, "Look at this purse, take it back and give me another." And she says, "But I'm not the one who makes them!" And then they start to yell at her as if it were the salesgirl's fault, as if the store were the source of the problem. The quality of the things produced is questionable, but it's the salesgirl who has to answer for everything. I don't understand it. People forget that they are buying from the government, so they go up to the salespeople and take their complaints out on them. The clerk is also not the smartest and starts to shout back. But it should be possible to resolve things calmly. I think it's just that people here might be too nervous and irritated. They have such a busy life running everywhere, always with thousands of things to do at home or with the family. They always have worries.

I myself know foreigners from Hungary, France, Italy, and Madagascar. They say that the same foreigners who smile to our faces badmouth the Soviet Union among themselves. They say that their standard of living is higher and that they get yelled at in lines in stores here, and we have a lot of problems of that sort. When foreigners come here they get put in luxury hotels because they couldn't stand living in our regular hotels. They get everything—everything is for them. Why can't one of our people stay in those kinds of hotels? Perhaps it's true that we have very few of those kinds of hotels, but why should we live worse than the guests who come to visit us? They have great hotels and bars and everything, and we ourselves don't have anything like the things we have for our guests. Perhaps that's like an advertisement that things in the Soviet Union are as great as things they have at home. That's why when they

---

*The largest department store in Moscow, located on Red Square opposite the Kremlin.

enter the flow of our ordinary lives they encounter these problems and when they meet their Soviet counterparts and begin to talk, they understand that things are a far cry from what they've seen in the hotels.

We know how to treat our guests! We want them to have better conditions than even we ourselves have, which is why we do all of this for them.

LOVE

I had a boyfriend about a year ago. I knew him for three years. He lived in another city, and I used to go and visit him there; my mother let me go, and she and his parents agreed to let him come and visit us sometimes. They all thought that we would get married. But then things ended quite suddenly, that is, on my birthday he came to visit me and I went to greet him. It seems that he took a liking to my girlfriend. Our tape player had broken—we had a Japanese one. I got very upset—I thought that I would have to celebrate my birthday without a tape recorder, with no music, and I almost cried. It could be that he got annoyed about that, I guess I don't really know. And then my girlfriends began to arrive, first one, then a second and a third. At first one of them gave him her phone number and then another one did, and then later on they told me about it. So I spoke to him about this and he said, "I'm leaving tomorrow." I said, "Go ahead, leave."

I cried a lot and was very upset because I was used to having him, being near him, being together. His parents are wonderful people and they treated me as if I were their own daughter. I used to visit them in the summer—they grow berries, fruit. They have a car and we used to drive to the woods, to their dacha, to his grandmother's. His grandmother treated me very well. She's an excellent cook. He introduced me to his friends. One of his friends had this car, one of the old Pobeda models they had before 1917. It was a lot of fun. We would go to cafes and dances. When I returned home I was always full of impressions.

I used to tell my mother about it, and she said, "Olya, thank God at least *you* will be happy." Of course she wants me to be happy. And then everything ended so abruptly, he left and didn't call any more. I used to send holiday greetings to his parents for New Year's. His mother is a wonderful person. People like that turn up rarely. She understood everything, could explain everything. Such a lively woman!

And then everything disappeared. I knew all of his friends and they all liked me; I have a lot of personality in groups. Whenever they traveled south through Moscow we got together. If I didn't have any time, I would go directly to them at the railway station or they met me someplace. But I didn't see hide nor hair of him. And then just two weeks ago he called me. I was really surprised and I asked him, "What do you want?" And he said, "I just want to know how you're doing." I said, "Everything's fine." And somebody told me that he had another girl-friend over there and she had just told him that she had another boy-friend, so he "unglued himself" from her, as they say. And I asked him, "Did you get married?" And he said, "No." He's working as a chauffeur, driving some boss around. I asked him, "What are you doing with your-self?" He asked me if I had gotten married. I told him no, that every-thing was fine with me. I asked about his parents. He said that they were inviting me to visit them. He said that he had tried to call before but I hadn't been home, and now he was calling me from a booth. I got a little worried and told him, "Talk faster, your time is running out." And he said, "Before you never used to notice that time was passing." Before we used to call each other all the time; we used to talk for an hour and a half on an intercity phone. My mother used to yell at me because I was spending so much money on phone calls. "Olya," she would say, "perhaps you could speak for less time, because now you speak for an hour and a half and we pay thirty rubles or more." And I told him, "When you used to call before there was never enough time." And he said, "Well there's enough now." So we talked to each other about life, what's new with each of us. And then he excused himself and said that he had to drive the boss somewhere and promised to call again. So far he hasn't. But they just reconnected our phone—it was disconnected for a week. I don't know if he's going to call or not.

Even if we remain friends, my relationship with him will be different than it was. I don't know how things will be for him. I do things com-pletely differently. I trusted him, but he was capable of betraying me in that way. Who knows, perhaps he regrets it. His friends say that he regrets it and maybe he didn't really think things out. I got used to him. That's one of my characteristics. I get used to people very easily and very quickly. I find a common language with people quickly—la la la. It's easy for me to communicate with people at get-togethers, every-where. If I see that somebody cares about me, from the soul, and is interested in what I'm studying, where I work, I'll always respond; I'll tell him about myself, and there will always be things to talk about. I now have friends that I've known for three or four years, since I was in the eighth grade. And there are friends I've just gotten to know. People ask me, "Olya, where do you get to know these guys?" And I say, "I don't know, just like that, at the movies, on the street, standing around a drinking fountain, in the subway, anywhere." People talk to me and I talk to them. If you see that a person is interesting and has a lot to tell you, it might be that you will never again get the chance to hear just what it is he has to say. Every person has his own personality, his own character, his own psychology. It's interesting to talk to people. I'm satisfied with my life—I've had many friends with different professions, from circus performers to artists. People say that artists are not serious people, and maybe it's true, but it's very interesting to spend time with them. I've gotten to know film directors and in general a lot of interesting people, physicists and mathematicians from Moscow State University, some guys from the Agricultural Institute. Friends are friends. I've had a lot of friends who study in a lot of different places.

I met Tolik (my former boyfriend) when a friend of mine introduced us. She called me and invited me to Izmailovsky Park.* I wasn't ready— she called on a Sunday and it was already three o'clock in the afternoon. By the time I could have gotten myself ready, washed up, and dried my hair, four hours would have gone by. So she said to me, "All right, I'll come and get you." She came over. She said to me, "I met a very good, attractive young man. He's coming over with another friend of his. He asked me to bring along a girlfriend." I said to her, "Why did you bother to call me?" "Oh come on, let's get going," she said. I don't like it when people try to introduce me to someone. This was the only time I did it. Tolik, the man my girlfriend had gotten to know, came with his friend, Oleg. Oleg liked me and started to call, and then all of a sudden Tolik started to call me. I asked him, "And Oleg?" He said, "I don't know where he is." I said, "Everything's clear." Then Oleg seemed quite sad. Tolik called and suggested we meet. So I said, "And Galya (my girlfriend)?" Tolik: "Galya isn't at home." I thought, well, it doesn't mean anything, after all, we are friends, so we'll meet, talk for a bit. We met. After that he started calling more often. I liked him, too. Then I found out that he had already apologized to Galya and told her that I was the one he liked. I was very upset because I didn't know that he would say that to her. I felt guilty. Oleg kept calling me as well. It turned out that both Oleg and Tolik were calling me. I told Oleg that I liked Tolik. Later on Tolik told me that Oleg had been offended. But Oleg said that it was all right because I had told him myself.

When people have been going out for a while, they get attached. Having lost my boyfriend, the person closest to me ... when I lost Tolik, I was in a state of shock. I couldn't do anything. When I took him to the train station and his train left, I was in tears. When I remember

---

*A large park that has undergone a radical transformation in the last few years. It has become a gathering place where artisans and painters sell their work and people congregate on weekends to discuss social, political, and cultural events.

that now, it strikes me as funny. But then I was in a bad state. . . . My mother talked to me, my girlfriends gave me a lot of support, and I even had the idea to go and visit him, grab him and shake him, really give him a piece of my mind, talk to his parents. He had told his parents that he was going to Moscow for a week, and he came for only one day. I called his parents. They said, "Oh, Olya, he is so bad, a scoundrel, how he offended you, how badly he behaved toward you!" So I had the idea to go and visit him but I didn't. Nobody would have let me anyhow. I thought about it all for a long time, but then I forgot about it. Then I met another young man, and then another. At the moment I don't have a boyfriend. I have close friends, but we're just friends.

WOMEN

If a woman likes her field, if she lives to work, that's wonderful. But if she doesn't like it and if she is working only in order to earn money, then she shouldn't have to work.

I have a job that I like and I will work as long as I should be helping my family and my mother. And later on, if my family has enough . . . I don't think a woman should work. But I simply cannot sit around in one spot. I think I want to work. I might be willing to let my husband support me. I don't know if I'm going to work or not—for the moment I don't have a husband!

In marriage, if a man always treats a woman well, she will always treat him well, too. A woman has a more delicate soul, and she gets attached to a man more quickly than he does to her. It seems to me that every-thing depends upon the man. If he doesn't let her down then she will treat him in the same way. Why should a woman humiliate herself in front of a man—she's not a human being or something? A woman should have her pride. She *does have* her pride! A woman gets attached more quickly; she wants to be with a man sooner than he wants to be with her. There are families where the husband, even though he has a wife and children, has a lover as well, and he can't give her up, he had her even before he married his wife and has gotten attached to her, perhaps he loves her even more than his wife. And the wife, as many men think, is the mother of his children. But all of his troubles, his bitterness, is shared with that woman that he has in addition to his wife. Many spend more time with their lovers than with their wives. Maybe wives become uninteresting to some men; they get tired of their wives and they want variety. Some people think that every family man should have a lover—of course, it's men who talk that way. They say, "What kind of a man is he if he doesn't have a lover?" I find that disgusting.

There are cases where the husband is a good man and does everything for his wife and for the children and she's the one to go wandering off somewhere ... in life everything happens. But men cheat much more often. A woman is more likely to want to keep the family going because if she has children she has to raise them and educate them, and that is really hard to do alone. A woman always wants to be happy, have a family, have the children of a good husband. It's hard for her to be alone.

Men also say that they would like to have a family and children, but they want their wife to cook, do laundry, raise the children, and they'll bring home their salary and do nothing more. But everybody thinks in his own way. We say that men often run around on their wives, and they say that we ourselves are to blame because we don't know how to behave, that the woman is always to blame. And women accept everything. Women take the kinds of things from men that men would never take from women!!

She's always crying into her pillow—they show this in the movies— and *he* doesn't care a bit, just turns his back and walks out. Women have to stand for separations. When the husband walks out on his wife, she tries to stop him, and says, "Think what you're doing! We have children! How can you walk out on them?" And he walks out as if it were nothing. Some men regret this later. But each one has his own reasons for behaving like that.

Some men start to beat their wives. I have an uncle, my mother's brother, it doesn't matter how much you talk to him about it, he beats his wife. She's always covered with bruises. And she says she feels sorry for him. He grabs a bottle and goes out somewhere to drink. I don't understand how a person can stand that!

My mother often says to him, "How can you do that?" They have small children, one in second grade, the other four years old. It's useless. He's such a hefty guy, tall, he's got fists like shovels. She keeps running to us, on weekends, comes to live with us two days at a time. Then he begs her to return. She says, "I'm not going back; you'll kill me." Then he says that he's forgiven her, but I don't understand what it is he's forgiven her for. *She's* the one who should be doing the forgiving! She goes back to him, they live all right for two weeks, and then it starts all over again. I don't understand men like that, I think they're just showing their weaknesses, that they can't deal with a woman with words, and start throwing punches. If my husband hits me, I'll leave him. That's my character; I couldn't stand it. A woman shouldn't allow that to happen. She should hit him with a frying pan, or whatever she can get her hands on, so that the next time he'll think twice about whether or not it's worth it to him to hit her. It's important to give it back to him the first time he does it, and then maybe he won't try it again. My mother says that women are the weaker sex, but men are cowardly, and they are afraid of everything. It's important to defend yourself the first time, and then maybe the next time he'll have second thoughts about hitting you.

Like all young women, I want to marry a good person, someone who isn't like my father who doesn't care about anything. I want to have support in the family, someone to lean on, fall back on, someone to discuss things with and get advice. Men have always been men—the heads of the household. I'll raise my children, help my parents, and if my mother remains single, I'll take her to live with me. I'd never leave her alone.

I'd like my husband to be able to support the family fully so we would lack nothing, and I would like him to come to the family for advice. I'd like it to be cozy and warm at home, and I'd like for us all to understand each other. He would live my life and I would live his. We would help each other with our work. There should be mutual under-standing and respect between people. Without respect nothing can exist. He should be interested in my life and I should be interested in his.

I'll work of course, but in the home things basically depend upon the head of the family, on the husband. A man should do what a woman is unable to do. First of all, a man is physically more developed and is a strong being. But the fact is that women do everything here, because our men basically don't seem to be capable of anything. Here our men don't do a thing. Women have to run from store to store; they give birth, raise children, and do all the housework, arrange vacations, and so forth.

Men expect everything to be done for them. They are used to ex-ploiting women, in the kitchen, at home, with the children, and in the gardens. And they've gotten used to women cooking; men are too lazy to cook. They can only boil a piece of meat or fry an egg.

I would like to have a decent person for a husband. Why should a woman have to do everything for her man? She's human too! Here a lot of people think that men have now become the weaker sex and women the stronger. Perhaps it's because men have somehow lost interest in life? I don't know. Or perhaps women have taken on so many responsi-bilities? Men say that we ourselves are to blame because we've achieved equal rights. The only conclusion I can come to is that women have continued to grow and advance, while men have become stuck in the same place. Women are wiser, study more, and at the same time the home and the family are closer to them; a woman is a mother; she is more sensitive to things and puts more care into them. And these are things that might not be too close to a man—he's a bit removed from it all. Sometimes a man isn't able to do something for his children, but a woman, a mother, can do everything. But then a man thinks that if his wife can do that for her children, she can do things for him as well. A man gets accustomed to having a wife do everything for him. My girlfriends say, "Oh, you've found a treasure if he does anything at all, if he even brings his salary home!"

We women say that men are to blame, and men say that women are to blame because we've achieved equal rights. Women have taken a seat on the tractors, sat down behind the wheel of the combines, so then men say, "Well, excuse me! If you're sitting on a tractor, why do you consider yourself the weaker sex?" Everybody's talking about that at all the factories nowadays. Wherever men don't want to work, you'll find women. Women have a heavier load and more work than men. Men sit around and either don't do anything or don't push themselves too much. And women strive to work more, in order to provide for their children and for themselves. A woman is a mother so she wants her children to be happy, and if the father doesn't want that or isn't able to make it happen, then the mother does it.

I don't think that there should be divisions in a family. If she cooks then why shouldn't he do the cleaning, or take the kid out for a walk, or do something at home, make some shelves, or do something else like that? How can it be that she cooks, washes the floors, feeds the kids, does the laundry, the cleaning—and what is he going to do? Then why live together? Why bother getting married in that case? I don't understand! If you have a husband you should have confidence in him, be sure that you can depend on him, that he will help you, and honestly, if he has no idea that he should help out, why bother getting married? Only to have children? In that case there is no reason to get married.

I would like to get married, though, and I hope that I will meet a decent person. I don't know if I will, but I hope so. I hope he will be very wise, just a modern young man, a well-rounded person with many interests, so that there will be a lot to talk about with him on any subject, and he will understand people, and above all respect them. But I don't know if I will find a person like that.

Women have to solve their own problems. Maybe if women were in leadership, everything would be different. Men are distant from women's problems, or they don't see them, or they don't want to see them. Something has to be done, of course. There always were and always will be problems, but there certainly should be fewer. Everything ends up on the woman's shoulders—the home, the family, work.

Women have to fix everything and find everything. We have so many problems in our lives. In general in this country we have so many problems! Men don't want to face them, and they can't resolve them, and the women take everything upon themselves.

We need as many women as possible in government. I don't know why men think women are stupid. I think that's completely false, just the opposite. Perhaps men think that we are the weaker sex and aren't capable of doing anything, but I think it would be truer to say that men aren't capable of doing anything. A woman can handle everything, even without a man. In our century, in our time, a woman means more than a man.

SEX AND FAMILY

With both my girlfriends and my male friends we talk about how undeveloped sex is here, that adults view it all as some kind of animal relations. But people I know tell me that they think it is a kind of art. Here it is just not acceptable to talk about it. So what happens? Children who are fourteen or fifteen don't know everything, and if they do, they know it from the street. But if they could read it somewhere or if their parents talked to them, perhaps they wouldn't make the mistakes in life that they do. I think that in other countries they talk about this calmly, and here they just keep quiet, we don't even have any literature about it. We only know what people tell us, adults, our friends, girls who have gotten married. So really we don't know anything, only superficially. There's nothing to read. I think they should address this issue, write more books, magazines, so young people would know. I liked the film *Little Vera*.* It's a vital film. But a lot of people think that girl (Vera) is a little prostitute, and I don't think that's the case. We have a lot of families like that. The director showed life as it is in that film, and I think that's absolutely fine.

One young man told me that sex is an art. He told me that when he was eighteen years old he wasn't interested in women. There was a married man where he worked who asked him why he wasn't involved with young women. "Come on, I'll give you a book to read about sexual relations." He read it, and then he told me that he didn't even know something like that could exist. It's an art, like singing, or dancing.

My mother doesn't talk about this subject. She says she has confi-

---

*This film, about a troubled working-class family in a depressed provincial industrial city, created a furor when it was released. Not only did it offer a bleak portrayal of working-class life and the dead-end road of its protagonist, a young woman named Vera, it was also the first Soviet film to contain an explicit sex scene.

dence in me, to be cautious. She is counting on my good sense and consciousness. When I was young and I asked her where she got me from, she said that she went to the store, and a pretty little girl was standing there, and she bought me. Until first grade I thought they had bought me. Then, outside in the yard, the kids started to talk, and somebody told me that children are *born,* and I didn't believe it and said no, people buy them. They all pounced on me, told me that my mother had fooled me. I ran home and burst out crying, and I said to my mother, "Mama, why did you fool me and tell me that people buy children?" She said, "Don't believe them, people do buy children." I ran back out into the yard and told them that people buy children. And they insisted on their own version. I burst into tears again, ran home again. My mother tried to comfort me, and she didn't let me out into the yard again. And later I found out that it was true that people give birth. Then I began to read the magazine *Zdorovye* (Health) and found out about pregnancy.

When I was in primary school I read something in a magazine. And when I was in second grade my little brother was born. And I found out that women give birth to children when I saw my father and mother coming home from the hospital with my little brother. I was nine years old.

I had asked my mother why her stomach was so big, and she told me that she had drunk a lot of water; she didn't explain anything to me. Later somebody said to me, "What's going on, is your mother pregnant?" And I said, "I don't know." Then they told me I was going to have a little brother or sister. I didn't believe we were going to have another person in our family and I thought my mother would love him more than me. I asked my mother, "Is there going to be anyone else in our family?" She said there wouldn't. At first she didn't want to have him because she was already around forty, but she went ahead and had him. Of course now she really loves him, she does everything for Alyosha.

She doesn't talk to me about sex. I don't know why, but very few parents here talk with their children about this. I think children should at least be told that children are *born.* But parents are ashamed. There has to be a different way of looking at sex. Parents think that the children will grow up and they'll understand everything. But in the meantime, before they're grown, a lot of time goes by, and they shouldn't be allowed to make irreparable mistakes.

Some of my friends have sexual relations, but not all. Sometimes they'll talk to me about it, if it's a close girlfriend. If she's in love with him, I think it's fine. But if it's for one day, one minute, I don't know. . . . But I don't think my girlfriends take this lightly. I can vouch for them.

In our class at school three girls got pregnant. They didn't protect themselves at all. One is going to give birth in May, but she already got married. He's eighteen and she's eighteen. They took him into the navy for three years, and she's giving birth in May, and I can't imagine what she's going to do with the child. She graduated with us, she has no money, isn't working, and it's not clear what she is going to live on. Her parents didn't really want her to get married.

Two other girls got pregnant, but they had abortions. They didn't protect themselves. They're both not quite eighteen. They've gotten more serious about this now. They told me that the abortion was horribly painful,* and they've become afraid. A woman is a future mother, and they're worried it might affect their bodies, maybe they won't be able to have children. That's the most awful thing, not having children. Some of my girlfriends think I'm right when I say that before having relations with a young man, you have to think about what the consequences might be, and whether he will marry you if that happens. But life is life, and it doesn't always turn out the way we want it to. To each his own, as they say. Some begin their sexual life at age fourteen, fifteen, some at eighteen, some at twenty or twenty-five. I don't have girlfriends who began at fourteen. But one girl who lives in my building gave birth at age fifteen. I think it's bad, when the girl is still a child herself, but having an abortion is bad for a young girl's body. It's good to have the first child between twenty and thirty. Not before. It's all right to get married at twenty and have a baby at twenty-two, to have two years to live by yourselves and see what the relationship with the husband is going to be like. Who knows? If you get married and have a baby immediately, what are you going to do with the child? Nothing! It's a lot easier without a child.

A woman has the added responsibility of the child, and some men just don't have anything to do with them. Sometimes a woman has children in order to hang onto her man, because if she has a baby he won't leave her. And there are families where they live their whole life without children, just for each other. Different families, different fates.

A child changes a woman's life more than a man's. It is your living being, you gave birth to him, he's your blood. With a man it can be different. They say that a man should be present at birth, to see the torment his wife goes through. I read recently in a magazine that a

---

*Abortions are routinely performed without anesthesia, unless a woman specifically orders it, which is costly.

woman burst into tears at the maternity hospital. Her husband had said to her that if she gave birth to a girl he would leave her and not recognize the child. The next day the husband went to the head doctor. She gave the husband a robe; the wife went into labor. The husband asked the doctor to let him go, saying he was late for work. The doctor promised she would write him out a sick leave, and he heard the cries of his wife in labor. The doctor said to him, "You don't want a girl, but do you know what it is to give birth to a child? What torture it is? Look at your wife giving birth!" He watched, trembling with fear. And when he held the child he said that it wasn't important if he had a boy or a girl, what mattered was that he had a child, he was a father. That really affected their relationship. That's great! In other countries the husband is present during the birth, so that he knows how the poor thing suffers. Maybe a husband will become closer to his wife when he sees. Here they just send out a notice, boy, girl. What difference does it make which sex you bring up? The most important thing is to bring the child up to be a good, worthy person!

I'll get married and we'll see. I would like to have two or three children. For some reason I would like a son. I would like them to be kind and polite; I would like them to be raised well, to give them the best of everything that I have, that my husband has, the best of my parents, so that they feel good about us, about me, about their father. I would like them to respect us and to value us. It hurts when you raise a child and then, later on, he turns away from you. Sometimes here people send their parents off to an old age home. I don't understand how they can. A mother is the closest person you have, the person who gave birth to you, gave you life, raised you, and it's unthinkable to do something like that to her. My children will see how I treat my own parents. If I am boorish toward my own mother, my children will wonder why they shouldn't behave in the same way toward me. It would be insulting if, when I'm old, they send me off somewhere. That would hurt.

I would like to treat my children with kindness. If parents quarrel, children shouldn't hear or know about it. They should see only the good things in a family. There shouldn't be big fights. If he wants to say something to me he should do it when the children are outside or at their grandparents', or we should go someplace and sit and talk, to a cafe, or we should talk when the children are asleep. Children shouldn't see or hear fights. That damages them psychologically and they take things hard. I know from my own experience that when my parents fought it was very hard for me. I thought worse of my father because I saw him insulting my mother, and now I don't respect him at all. I think that children should only see good things in a family; they should see kindness. Children are the flowers of our lives, our angels. And they should be allowed to remain flowers.

BECOMING AN ADULT: "IF I COULD TURN BACK TIME"

During my third year I began working in the department of our factory where they print passes for public transportation. I liked it; the machine we worked on was little and we learned quickly. We were taught by a woman, Auntie Galya. She's on pension but she keeps working. She's been working there since she was seventeen years old. A good woman. She was like a mother to us; she gave us advice, and we loved her a lot. But then they switched us to another department, where they print money. The machinery was different, and there were difficulties. We learned very slowly. Those machines are bigger and more people work on them. We didn't like it. But I can't say very much about my work because it's a closed factory. We get thirty rubles a month, and half of it goes to the vocational school. We work three days a week, for six hours. That was during our practice. Soon we start working, and I don't know how much we're going to get. When we finish and get our diplomas we will become workers, and they'll talk to us differently. We'll work eight hours a day, not six.

I don't want to continue working there because it's very hard. It's not women's work. I don't know where I want to work. In any case, I have to work there; I can't go anyplace else now. We finish vocational school and then we have to work at the school's factory for two years to pay back our education. Until we've done that they won't let us work anywhere else. All vocational school students have to do this. I'll work at the same place I am now, printing money, like it or not.

I don't think it's fair. We understand that the government spent money on us, but if a person can't or doesn't like the work, why should he have to? It's unhealthy. There's zinc there, and it affects your health. And not everybody can get used to waking up at five o'clock and working three different shifts, sometimes at night. It's hard. There's no time left for your personal life. If I work the second shift I start at three and finish at eleven, I'm home at eleven thirty, I eat something, and I don't do anything, I'm tired. You wake up at nine or ten, to get enough rest. In two or three hours I have to go back to work. Or you get up at five, at six forty-five you're already at work, and they let you out at three fifteen. They give you your schedule; you work one shift one week and another the next. Women with small children can start an hour or two later, and they only work first shift.

Our practice is ending. On June 1 we start working. We'll already be the working class. Adults. Big changes are ahead. I think it's going to be really hard—getting up early, not having any time. When you're studying, you have more free time. When you're working, you have more responsibility, you have to answer for your work, you grow up.

Your childhood ends. When children are little they want to become grown-ups, but grown-ups would all like to be young! I also used to dream about getting my passport, I couldn't wait to be eighteen, and now I think, Good God! When you're young you don't have any problems. Mama feeds you, looks after you, washes your clothes, does everything. And you grow up and have to do everything for yourself, and you have constant worries and problems. It's easier to go to kindergarten than to work! If I had finished a general school I could go to an institute of higher education, or a technical college, or wherever I wanted to work. One of my girlfriends works in the same store as her mother, and another is working as a nurse in a kindergarten, and she's going to go to an institute to study this year. Another one is also going to go to an institute to study. One of my friends finished tenth grade [at an academic high school] and she can't find any work at all. That's also hard. Those who haven't been accepted anywhere are just hanging around.

I think a person should continue studying. I will, in two years. I could start studying now, at the same time I'm working, but I wouldn't be able to take it, and I would end up giving up one or the other. And they won't let me stop working.

If I could turn back time, I would decide to go through tenth grade and get my diploma. But there's no going back now. On the other hand it's good that I ended up in the PTU, because it's a different kind of experience, and I've seen what tenth-graders haven't seen. The relationships are more complicated. In an academic high school you know everybody. You come to the vocational school and you have a new collective, new people, a different environment. They say that the kids who study in a vocational school are thick-headed and stupid, but I think that even if a person wants to be an engineer, he should at least spend a little time in a vocational school, so he knows just what the working class is.

It's a difficult moment in my life, but what am I going to do? We pay for our own mistakes. But I don't really think it was a mistake—I learned a lot about life in the PTU; we became more serious about life than tenth-graders, we grew up in the PTU.

Perhaps it's the atmosphere: from the first year we start working, we have a profession. They told us from the first year that we are the working class, that we have a trade, that we have work responsibilities, unlike tenth-graders, and we are more mature than they are. We were already working in our third year, and they told us that we are better prepared than school kids are; they don't have a profession, and they still have the institute ahead of them. But going straight to work means giving up a part of your freedom. Everybody says it's easier to study than to work. I'm not a free person—work binds you, and if you work, you're not a free person. If you work, you're always busy. Outside of work, I'm free.

My mother works a lot—she has two jobs. Because of that she's not free. She would go to the movies, she loves to go to the park, to the circus with Alyosha. But with her work schedule, she can't. We spend half our lives at work—our second home. We spend eight hours a day there.

Still, my mother likes her work. She is conscientious, and I think she is a good worker. She has gotten awards. Whenever anybody gets ill, they ask her to substitute. She's the kind of person who hardly ever says no, even though she has two jobs.

My mother says, "If you don't want to work, go ahead and study!" She would like me to get into Moscow State University, but that's not realistic. Perhaps if I studied with private tutors. But she doesn't tell me which department. She says, "Choose yourself!" so that later I won't regret it and blame her. For some reason she's afraid that later on I'm going to blame her for everything. She thinks that because she's the person I'm closest to, I listen to what she says, and later on I'll feel hurt because I did what she wanted. She wants me to decide for myself. I think that's correct—giving one's child freedom. To go where he wants, not just where the parents want him to go. A person should decide for himself.

I don't think my mother is to blame for my going to the vocational school. She told me from the beginning that I should go on to ninth grade and later to a technical college. But as it turned out, I went to vocational school, I graduated, and I'm going to go to work. Maybe that's good. We'll see what happens.

For now I'm making my own decisions. But until I get married, I'll get advice from my mother. She's a good ally to have. I really respect her a lot. If I get married, I'll consult with my husband, and when my children get older, with them.

A COUNTRY OF PARADOX

LENA

Fifteen years old, ninth-grade student

Lena is small, skinny, and gives the impression of perpetual energy. She keeps her hair short, in an almost boyish cut, wears no makeup, and doesn't care about stylish clothing. She loves sports and in the winter goes for long ski trips through the woods. She tells me that the careers she thinks of pursuing are considered male professions—journalism and cinematography.

I visit her school frequently, and whenever I see her she has something new she wants to tell me about—an article she's read, a television program that revealed some recent scandal. A young man in her class has told me, with an air of amusement, that Lena and her close circle of friends are all "information maniacs." They argue with their teachers and won't stop talking about politics in class.

When I visit Lena at home, she proudly shows me her room. I'm surprised by its absolute order and feminine touch. There is a small hand loom on her desk. She loves to knit.

My mom doesn't work at all. She can't find a job. She's a movie director by profession. When she was young she worked in films and television, but now there's a rule that relatives can't work in television, and my dad works in television, so for the time being Mom can't get a job there, and that's it, no place else will take her. So she stays at home and babysits her grandchild—my brother has a son who's three—and does the housework. She has an awfully hard time because she has two degrees and almost had a third. She went to the foreign language institute—she dropped out in her fourth year—and she graduated from two other institutes. She's an energetic person and not having work is very hard for her. She hasn't had a job in three years.

She's a very active person. She loves to work and she loves variety in her work. She traveled a lot when she was young and made films, too, so that's why she finds it so hard to sit around with nothing to do. She

LENA

wanted to get a job, oh I don't know, as a cleaning lady somewhere, but she says that no one will take her because she's got two degrees. She wanted to get a job as a supervisor somewhere, but she was told that they couldn't take her with her two degrees. She was too smart to be a supervisor.

My dad works in the children's programming division on Shabolovka* on a show called *Expedition to the Twenty-First Century*. For the first shows he shot our school and the kids there.

He's very kind, very cheerful, and, well, he used to do most of the housework. He washed, ironed, did all the cooking, cleaned, dusted. My mom doesn't like doing that stuff. Before, when Mom and Dad both worked, Mom just worked while Dad worked and did all the housework, absolutely everything. Now since Mom's at home she has to do it because, you know, directing—my dad's not just a director; he's a script-writer and the author of the shows and the host and the editor, so he's at work most of the time, on a changing schedule. So he may not work one week and then work only nights the next, for example. During certain times he isn't home at night, he's working, and then he sleeps during the day.

The day after tomorrow he'll be fifty-three. Mom turned fifty this year. My brother is in college. He does a lot of traveling with the other students, hiking. Dad and Mom did a lot of traveling when they were young. Dad went to the Virgin Lands. Then when he was at the Energy Engineering Institute they used to go to the Soviet Far East and give concerts. He went down the Lena River another time with a group. He went to Vladivostok. He's been practically everywhere. Later on he worked on the *Agriculture Hour* show and traveled mainly in the Far East again. Now he's just in Moscow. He'd like to travel, but TV's having an awful lot of problems now with equipment. All of it's pretty old. Say he goes to work planning to put together ten minutes of a piece, but he can't get it done because the machines are constantly breaking down, or the film. . . . Not long ago he shot eleven hours of footage, five reels, for a show. The reels just crumbled in their hands, the stock was so old and there wasn't any other.

On the whole things are going well for my parents. They have everything they need, children, grandchildren, jobs—well, Mom doesn't. My mom is dissatisfied, especially with her situation now, because she's already getting close to retirement age, and our country can't pay a pension to anyone who hasn't worked at least two years before retirement. But she can't get a job. She meets the work requirement. You

---

*Headquarters of the Moscow television station.

have to have worked twenty-five years, I think it is, to get a pension in this country. My mom's worked thirty-two years, and without interruption, too, and now she won't be eligible for a pension. At least not for the kind she would have gotten.

They say that people with similar personalities have a really hard time getting along, and my personality's very similar to Mom's. My dad is very nice and easygoing. Mom wants to understand me and I want to understand her, but somehow it doesn't work out. It's not so much disagreements as, I don't know, something inside.

I have the kind of personality that makes it so I can't sit around the house long. I've always got to be on my way somewhere. Mom's the same. She's a director by profession. That also involves travel. But now she's out of work and she's taking it hard. It's hard for her to sit around the house with nothing to do. Real hard.

I think there should be complete trust between parents and kids. Parents should trust their kids from the time they're born. If parents don't really think of their kids as people, well, let's just wait and see what happens when they grow up. . . . They have to be thought of as rational human beings from the time they're babies. For example, I have a nephew who's three years old. He thinks just like a grown-up. He's got his own ideas. Of course, he expresses them like a child, but sometimes it's amazing what intelligent and interesting thoughts he has. The things that concern him aren't in the least childish, even though he's only three.

He's the son of my older brother, who's an actor. It must be in the genes, because my grandfather was a member of the Maly Theater company and appeared in films. So we've got this dynasty of actors. Yurka, my nephew, has been an actor since he was a baby. And that's instilled in you when you're a baby. If your parents overlook something when you're small, there'll be no changing you when you're my age. And I think that my mom overlooked something like that, I can tell. Even when I really want to talk over something with her I sense that she doesn't really understand me or trust me. Mostly my dad's taken care of me. From the start. As soon as I was born I started to scream. I screamed so loud the walls shook. Maybe that irritated Mom when I was a baby, I don't know, but she had very little to do with raising me and I was almost always crying when I was a baby. But Dad rocked me and made up songs. I would wake him up at four in the morning and my poor Dad would get up and do something to put me back to sleep, tell me stories. So until I was thirteen Dad was literally the only one who took care of me. Mom had practically nothing to do with raising me, she never took any interest in how I was doing, and now I find it really hard. . . . I'm used to it, that when I get home she gives me my dinner and goes off to read the paper or some such thing, and I eat and do my homework by myself. I'm used to not saying anything, I keep to myself. But now my mom's started taking some interest in how things are. But I . . . oh, I don't know, I'd like to tell her, but I can't anymore. I realize that. As soon as I see Dad I start to tell him everything. We discuss things, he sympathizes with me, I sympathize with him. But Mom comes in and I can't even tell her what I tell Dad. What I mean to say is that it's impossible now. I'd like to tell her and ask her things . . . but I just can't. It doesn't work. So those kinds of differences.

And about trust. I have this feeling, not that I'm not trusted—Dad trusts me completely—but Mom . . . I lied a lot when I was a kid. I was a terrible liar. My brothers were the same way. We're actors, so we were awful liars! That's when we were kids. I was really scared of Mom then. If I'd done something wrong I was petrified of telling her. And then once Andrei, I think it was, my middle brother, said something, and Dad said the same thing all the time, that everything wrong you do comes out in the end no matter what you do to hide it. You're still found out. Somehow. At first I didn't believe it, but then something happened, I don't remember what it was exactly, that convinced me. And since then I haven't lied once. But I can sense that to this day Mom still doesn't really believe me. No matter where I go, she asks me, "Who were you with, where did you go, did someone see you home?" She's always got to know. I know that she may not believe me, but I can't tell her a lie anymore.

GLASNOST AND PERESTROIKA: "ALREADY A REVOLUTION"

When Gorbachev first came to power, my whole family gladly welcomed his politics. In the first year things really moved. But now it's already more than three years, and it seems to me that Gorbachev talks more than he actually does. We weren't used to our leaders traveling and giving so many speeches. Andropov and Chernenko were replaced one year apart. They didn't travel anywhere, they were sick all the time, hardly anybody saw them give a speech, but Mikhail Sergeyevich [Gorbachev] is fairly young, fifty-four years old, and at first that all seemed like new thinking; he spoke simply, openly, he talked about perestroika, and his speeches were original. But now it's not the same. Somehow we're tired of it already. It's as if we've already said what has to be said, and yet every day we keep saying the same thing, and very little if anything has actually budged. We need to talk less and do more. He himself says this, but still he keeps giving speeches in great quantities!

Of course Gorbachev is correct, and I'm not criticizing him—quite the contrary, I support his policies—but still he is following the same paths taken by his comrades before him. We talk about—Gorbachev talks about—equality. All these years they've been talking about equality, but there is very little faith anymore that there can be equality here, because talk is cheap. When we turn on the television we see all these wonderfully dressed members of the Politburo, and next to them workers who have practically paid with their entire factory to buy their deputy his suit so that he'll look good. The apparatus continues to function. The superiority of the bosses. The members of the Politburo live in much better conditions than ordinary workers do. I won't argue with the fact that the fate and business of the government are in their hands, but our problems have to be solved as soon as possible. I don't approve when members of the Politburo buy things in special stores, have things sewn in special tailor shops, have things done specially for them. Why? I don't understand it, nor do I welcome it.

And as far as communism is concerned, in general I view it cautiously. I don't think it will ever be accomplished. Somebody once said that it's impossible to live well for a long period of time, because if you live well, some kind of dissatisfaction will always arise. There are people who love each other and are very close to each other, a man and wife for example, and it's the same thing; they won't live happily together for a long time, because no matter what, some kinds of issues will come up, for some reason they will fight, and even if they make up later, the conflict occurred. And the same thing in society, which is after all made up of those same people. It will never be possible for people to live well under communism, the way it's promised. Never.

It seems to me that in Japan, judging from economic and political measures, they have reached one of the highest stages that humanity can. I think that they have a socialist order there, if such a thing does exist. And I don't think we could get much higher than that.

But in general I am against that kind of formulation—building communism, building socialism, the decline of capitalism. . . . My brother has read most of the works of Marx, Engels, and Lenin. Just recently he was telling me his thoughts about them. He thinks that all of these systems—communism, socialism, capitalism—don't exist per se, and as a philosopher named Morgan pointed out, society is divided into stages that are dependent upon technological progress. Man learned how to control fire. That was the first stage, and then, for example, he learned how to obtain iron—the second step, higher. Then he invented something—yet another step higher. So all of those revolutions—bourgeois, socialist—occur depending upon technological progress. For example,

at the end of the nineteenth century and the beginning of the twentieth, technological progress was rapid. The invention of the steamship,
man's desire to fly, all the plans and ideas. And this rapid growth of
inventions that helped advance humanity brought about further political change. Technology and politics are interdependent. A revolution
cannot take place without both of them. Revolutions are always accompanied by a technological revolution; you can see that in any history
textbook. And so I think that socialism is impossible to build without
adequate technological development of society and the developed consciousness of people. It seems to me that in Japan they have all of this.
They have a highly developed culture and consciousness, and they still
have respect for their past, respect for their national traditions, respect
for their elders: children respect old people, wives respect their husbands, and all of their traditions remain despite their modernity and
progress. And according to technological and economic indicators
they've pulled ahead: seven or eight years ago they were producing
recorders and computers that we're only beginning to think about now.
I suppose with that kind of combination of the two factors, it would be
possible to live under socialism.

Look at the conditions over 90 percent of our workers work in, and you
won't be able to say even one word about socialism! I don't know what to
call it! We have technology that goes back to 1905, almost one hundred
years old, and that's what we work with! It's incomprehensible! How can
two such things go together—the end of the twentieth century, on the one
hand, technological progress, flights into space, and on the other, that kind
of old technology. That is the paradox of our country.

And speaking of paradoxes, on *Before and After Midnight** I saw a
woman journalist say that the paradox of our country is that women are
more educated than in any other place, yet we do not have even one
female minister, and in India, for example, they have seven illiterate
women serving as ministers! Here the level of education for women is
much higher than it is for men, and yet at our highest level of leadership we don't have one single woman, and women end up working at
all the jobs men don't want to take. According to our laws a woman is
only supposed to lift weights up to seven kilos, and she ends up lifting
thirty to forty. She has to carry heavy sacks in the stores. We certainly
are a country of paradoxes. We have this great Russian expression here,
"If your wife gets off the wagon, it'll lighten the load."

It's all the same. Yeltsin or Gorbachev. A man or a woman. They're
all the same. We just have to search for talented women, if they're

---

*A popular evening television talk show.

willing to sacrifice their families, because politics certainly takes away a lot of time, all those endless meetings of the Party Bureau. At least here in our country it takes up a lot of time. My friend Ira's parents are in the Party, and her father is always getting held up until late at night at those Party meetings. But even though the amount of time spent on them is enormous, nothing seems to be moving.

Once again, we're faced by that paradox. These constant meetings, all this accounting and reaccounting, somebody gets criticized, somebody else gets re-elected, they clean house—and even so we aren't getting anywhere. And again we see that accountability isn't part of our consciousness. We used to have that, in the first years of Soviet power—Communists, Komsomol members—people respected them. But now the prestige of the Party has fallen, as has the prestige of all of those organizations, because they have become nothing more than a formality.

They confused everything here. In 1917 they confused capitalism and socialism; they mixed everything up. And of course the personality cult played its role. In 1937, when millions of people suffered repression, were sent to camps and prisons, they were making films with titles like *Volga, Volga, Cheerful Young Fellows,* and *The Bright Path.* People were full of enthusiasm, the country was moving forward, inventions were made, and at the same time there was all that repression. It's not possible! And what was going on in people's minds? When he was being executed, Tukhachevsky's final words were, "For the Motherland, for Stalin!" But it was on Stalin's orders that he was being shot! People went into battle for Stalin, and he was drenched in their blood!

This is really a country of paradox. You can't judge our country looking at only one side of it. There is so much criticism of the current period, there is nothing in the stores, people are ill natured and angry, nobody wants to do anything, and yet look at what kind of people also exist! The kinds of discoveries being made, how many ideas! Not long ago somebody invented a wheelchair for invalids that climbs up stairways by itself—and at the same time the bureaucratic system won't let it be produced.

Now we have the cooperatives. In the shape they're in now, I don't think very highly of them. What they do now used to be called fraud, unearned income, anybody doing anything he could get his hands into! That used to be prohibited; it was called criminal activity. Now they're letting anybody make anything they want and it might not have any quality to it at all, it might be nothing more than a dyed-over undershirt with some snaps stuck on it! They sell it for an outrageous sum and you wash it once and the thing has lost its color and shape!

We had cooperatives in the 1930s, but we ended up condemning them, stigmatizing them, and then they closed them down. Now we've found out that we need them again because they will lead to a strong and developed industry and economy. When the government is able to compete with the cooperatives and can provide people with enough food and clothing, the cooperatives themselves will become unnecessary elements and will disappear.

For now the cooperatives can charge whatever they want, they don't really care about the quality, and the government doesn't give them any competition. If even the government doesn't care, what can you expect from the cooperatives? They've been around for two years already here, and they aren't changing at all, the prices keep going up; the government is producing fewer goods than before.

There are two ways to go here. If the government takes it upon itself—and I think it will—if the government gets itself together, then I think everything will be fine. We have a lot of good people here, enterprising people, like Zaitsev, our fashion designer, Fyodorov and other doctors, artists, and all of them are in state-run enterprises, even though they work independently of each other and haven't unified themselves. If there are people like that all over the country, the need for cooperatives will disappear.

But I think that if nothing changes in the next three years, if the government remains the way it is, then there will be nothing, no changes in the economy, and prices will go up to who knows how high! And people will still keep buying! And then there will be shooting and riots! But Russians in general are a tolerant people.

Still, we have the kind of situation that Lenin wrote about here. The characteristic of a revolutionary situation, in any revolution, in any country, is the impoverishment of the masses at a level higher than usual. And in our country there is work sabotage, nothing's available, nobody wants to do anything, and so it seems that the first point is fulfilled. Next, the impoverished masses can no longer live in the old way, and the upper classes cannot either. Of course here we are supposed to think that we don't have higher and lower classes; everybody is equal here. Basically ordinary workers here don't want to keep living in the old way, and, in any case, they can't. And those on top—that is, our leadership—also cannot live in the old way.

Glasnost, perestroika. Forces capable of carrying out a revolution are taking shape here, and basically all sectors of our society are concerned about perestroika. On some level that is already a revolution. That is, not with weapons in hand, but nobody ever said that rivers of blood have to flow for a revolution to take place, so what's going on here is really a different kind of revolution.

Look at what's going on in the Baltic and in Central Asia. And we've gotten to the point that there was martial law in Baku; in other words, there were tanks and troops on the streets of a socialist state. We haven't had anything like that even once during the last seventy years! And the Baltic area has said very simply that it is going to secede from the Soviet Union!

I went with some kids from school to Tashkent (in Uzbekistan) and we talked to some young people there, and they told us that the same month we were there they were experiencing a lot of tension with Russians. There have been instances when people stopped trams and buses and demanded that the Russians get off. It's reached that level. This is such an interesting situation, very similar to a revolutionary one. Things are not the way they normally are.

Things have to change. People have to change. Look, in our country, Russian people have been known for their love of work since ancient times. Look at the cathedrals we built, the kinds of beautiful jewelry we have! We've had everything. Look at all of those power stations along the Dnieper built in the 1930s, all of those Komsomol construction projects, the Baikal–Amur Railway! They were built on nothing more than enthusiasm by young people filled with energy and the desire to work. They built and they built well. Those old buildings that were made under Stalin and Khrushchev were the ones to survive the earthquake in Armenia. So we do know how to do everything here. It's only been in these last years that silence was encouraged, poor workmanship was encouraged, bribery was encouraged—and even if it wasn't encouraged, people just looked the other way. A construction worker would mix a little extra sand or water in the cement, nobody paid attention, so he'd turn in his work with its imperfections, and the next time why should he even bother trying? He'll do an even worse job. That's what things have come to around here; people are used to it. It seems to me that we have to get rid of that habit of carelessness and unconcern, that way of thinking that just anything will do.

And from the period of stagnation, we can't seem to get out of the habit of being used to voting "in favor" all the time. And it might even be that the true points of view are silenced here, by the vote of the majority. And I think that began after the time of the Revolution. Before the Revolution, under the tsar, the majority had to submit to the minority, they listened to and obeyed his orders. But with the coming to power of the proletariat, everything got turned on its head. In the 1930s the ideas of leading scientists like Vavilov often simply were drowned in the masses. Look, for example, at Lysenko and Vavilov—the majority was for Lysenko. And all because of some totally useless discoveries that nobody needed, certainly not science, and they simply destroyed Vavilov's talent. We don't even know how much was destroyed. A single person is not in a position to oppose everybody else in our system, because people here basically don't understand what it is they are voting for, and if all of a sudden someone is against the majority, people won't trust him. He might end up in trouble at work, and because of this everybody always votes "in favor," just in case. That's the way things are around here.

And then we have the habit of giving every moment some kind of concrete definition: this was the personality cult, that was the period of stagnation, this is perestroika. I don't like those precise definitions, those borderlines between time periods, when the stagnation began, when it ended. Now, stagnation has supposedly ended, but stagnation still exists. Now we have perestroika, but nonetheless our bureaucracy hasn't been done away with; in so many institutions they are still demanding those folders full of papers and documents; they still attach more meaning to papers than to a person. I don't think you can distinguish things so sharply. For me, for example, the period of stagnation is completely connected to my parents; they were born before the war and their conscious life took place during the period of stagnation. I don't know how that affected them, but I really don't see any stagnation in them.

REVOLUTION AND DICTATORSHIP

We've all started talking about the personality cult now, but what about looking at how the Revolution took place, under what banners? The idea was that workers and peasants were supposed to come to power and create the dictatorship of the proletariat. But a dictatorship, no matter what shape it takes—proletarian, not proletarian—is still a dictatorship, which means blood and terror, and anybody's blood, war, enmity gives birth to evil. It's no small thing that those who didn't support the Revolution were forced to emigrate in 1917, and those who didn't leave were simply killed, and add to that the Civil War, and we end up with an embittered people, all of those Pavlik Morozovs,* people who were considered heroes for seventy years who raised their hand against

---

*A boy who was glorified for many years by Pioneer leaders and educators as an example of heroism. According to the traditional version, Pavlik denounced his father, head of a local governing council, for cooperating with the *kulaks* (wealthy peasants) and lying to Soviet troops sent in to collect grain. The boy was then murdered. Thereafter he was celebrated as a martyr who had put loyalty to the Revolution above personal loyalty to his father. However, in 1988, articles in the Soviet press began to question Pavlik's status as a hero. Intense discussion in a series of articles raised doubts about both the story and the morality of Pavlik's action. Now many people consider Pavlik an example of treachery and simple-minded dogmatism rather than of heroism and bravery.

their own brothers, their own fathers! For seventy years we've been teaching our children since the first grade that Pavlik Morozov was a hero; he did his own father in and *that* was encouraged! But I don't know how to judge that—a child raises his hand against his own father, and *that* is encouraged?

And look at the people who came to power. Perhaps they were not bad people, peasants, workers, but the entire intelligentsia left Russia; we wiped out all of our culture and now we are clutching at our own throats. Look at Comrade Bogdanov, Lenin's closest friend. He had some disagreements with Lenin about philosophical questions, so we don't know anything about Bogdanov, about his life, only what we know from Lenin's work, which they study here at the university. Lenin really gives Bogdanov a tongue-lashing, but as it turns out he was a great philosopher, a talented man, a great intellectual, and in some matters his work probably was superior to Lenin's.

So we see that even when Vladimir Ilich was in power, both culture and strong personalities were destroyed. And so basically during all those years of the Revolution the best of our culture, science, and art emigrated. Probably because a revolution is such a spontaneous thing that once it starts you can't stop it. And it didn't depend upon one person alone. Almost as if by inertia the Revolution began and it was impossible, after 1917, to stop that flow of emigration, which arose spontaneously, as did the Civil War. That had to happen. There were two groups in opposition to each other—the Bolsheviks and their allies, and the other groups; the Reds and the Whites—and their differences couldn't be resolved by peaceful means.

It's turned out that the archives and all the other sources of information from which we study history are false; they have been changed and rewritten several times. So it's very hard to make judgments about certain people and parties. In 1917 they erased the meaning of all those other groups that were part of the RSDLP.* All of the Mensheviks, the Cadets, the Socialist Revolutionaries—there were a lot of them but here we just have two big groupings: Whites on one side, Reds on the other. And perhaps some of those other parties were right, but we don't even know about them. The Bolshevik Party blackened the reputation of all the other parties. In our history textbooks we read about some disagree-

---

*The Russian Social-Democratic Labor Party, affiliated with the Second International. It was founded in 1898. At its second congress, in 1903, a split occurred between the Bolshevik and Menshevik factions. The Bolsheviks, led by Lenin, advocated independent action by a united front of workers and peasants. The Mensheviks believed that cooperation with liberal forces would be necessary to lead Russia through a stage of capitalist development before socialism could be achieved.

ment at this congress or another, on this question or that, and then
they tell us Lenin's point of view and the Bolsheviks' point of view, but
there are no documents or sources of information, no speeches of another party, documents from which we could judge the position of
another party, another point of view, so that we could form our own
opinion and point of view.

We don't have enough facts about the Civil War and we really don't
know how to analyze it. Look, we're in ninth grade already and what
can we say about the Civil War? What do we know about it? We know
that there were Whites and Reds, but for what reason—ask us what
started the Civil War, what the disagreements were—we don't know
anything about it, and probably even our parents don't know. They
know even less than we do. They know the things they were taught, and
as it turns out, the way they were taught was not the way they should
have been at all.

And about Stalin. Stalin was an extremely strong personality. He was
a person who was able to bring the entire nation under his control, get
rid of anybody who wasn't his friend—that is, anybody who didn't approve of his politics. I suppose one could consider him a kind of genius,
in the sense that he was able to set himself in opposition to this entire
huge nation and nobody was able to thwart or oppose him. But on the
other hand, there were all of these millions of people killed, thirty
thousand in Belorussia alone were killed, which is the same total as the
number of Communists killed by Hitler—and Stalin killed that many in
one camp alone! It's hard for our Soviet comrades to really judge this
until there's more discussion.

It seems to me that the Russian people always have to have someone to
worship, and now that they have given us freedom, we don't know what to
do with it. From what angle to approach it. So far all we are doing is
shouting. And Stalin was able to create some discipline in the nation; of
course, I do not worship him, but at least he did create some discipline,
and under his leadership people couldn't get away with sloppy work. But
of course if he didn't like something, then there were all of those prisons,
those camps. That wasn't discipline, that was panic-driven fear not to do
this or not even to say that, against the Party, against the line we were taking.
That wasn't discipline, when one wrong word to someone could mean
death, and not just for that person alone but for his loved ones as well. Still,
at least there was some quality to the things we produced, all those books.
We look at the books our grandmothers and great-grandmothers had, the
kinds of goods they had, the food products, and we see that things were
not so bad. The economy was in good shape then. In general it seems that
the Russian people cannot be left to their own devices. But it's also wrong

to use the kinds of methods Stalin used. That was a military dictatorship, something of that sort. So of course the economy was developed then, but I think that he is the reason that a part of our people is, well, not weak-willed, but obedient and resigned. Whatever direction the current runs in, the people run with it. So now we have glasnost and everybody shouts, "That's great!"

And I have something else to say about dictatorship. It seems to me—and I've been convinced of this by reading our newspapers—that any kind of violence, no matter what splendid goals it's committed for, no matter what ideals—the building of socialism—that any act of violence, any blood spilled makes any society unworthy. Lenin, in establishing the dictatorship of the proletariat, was using the experience of the Paris Commune, which also established a dictatorship, the Jacobin dictatorship. We consider the Jacobin dictatorship something wonderful, but of course we have to look at it that way because we did the same thing here! But it seems to me that not all countries consider a dictatorship to be the right way, in other words, we condemn Pinochet's dictatorship in Chile, but basically we did the same thing here. We court-martialed people, and without a real trial and investigation we shot innocent people.

Lenin based himself on the experience of the Jacobin dictatorship, but in the Jacobin dictatorship those Parisians who applauded the execution of the king—those Parisians didn't go anywhere; they stayed in their Paris to live after the execution of their beloved king, and with that same great applause they greeted the execution of their Robespierre, who had, before that, been the one to order the execution of the king! In other words, Robespierre, in establishing that Jacobin dictatorship, paid a heavy price because the dictatorship, even though it is considered the peak of the French Revolution, was really quite a bloodbath. A tremendous number of people were destroyed, the same as happened here after the Revolution. Anybody who disagreed was shot, or persecuted. Writers who didn't agree were not allowed to write, or rather, to be published, and they starved to death. Artists couldn't show their paintings, nobody bought their work, and the same thing happened in all areas of culture.

We haven't yet gotten to the point of discussing dictatorship here, but I think we will, because I already have heard people who share my point of view. I think that people are silent now simply because there aren't any documents available yet, and so people aren't able to form their own opinion. But it's hard to really judge all of that until all the documents are released and all historical archives are opened, so the people will know what's happened in our history. . . .

If we'd gone on the way we had all those years, who knows how it would all have ended? Stopping in time—that's what's most important. We said one thing and did another. In other words, nobody trusted anybody else. Supposedly there were equal rights but actually our leaders lived better than ordinary people, to put it mildly. I don't even know how perestroika will go. It's very hard to change the people of this country. They're very set in their ways. It's really hard to change your habits if you've lived one way for a long, long time and then suddenly everything changes. Really hard. It takes years and years. Even now supporters of Stalin are turning up in the press and on TV. With all kinds of ultimatums and suits in Stalin's defense. I think there's a lot of stuff in defense of Brezhnev now, too. But now the people who knew Brezhnev and were on good terms with him—all those bodyguards and friends—now that perestroika's come along they're tearing him apart. A year ago they'd have sung his praises. I don't really like it very much: nowadays you can't open a paper without . . . Like, for example, not long ago I read this article in which this bodyguard of Brezhnev's, I think it was, gloated over how he and Brezhnev had gone out drinking and so forth. Of course, we should know the truth, but he was our general secretary for nearly twenty years, eighteen years. No matter what kind of person he was, he was our leader, he was considered our leader then, and now the way they run him down . . . I don't know, I don't like it, the way they're treated. Yesterday we praised them, and now we drag them through the mud.

Gorbachev's policies are fine and good, but things are still very difficult here, because it's very hard to go straight from stagnation to perestroika. And if we don't do anything then he won't be able to. But I don't think it can go on long because he might give out soon. He's under pressure. It's hard to reform people who take bribes and steal from work. It's a big job.

PROBLEMS OF SOVIET YOUTH:
THE ARMY AND THE KOMSOMOL

One of my brothers, Andrei, was sent on some kind of secret assignment in the military. He served not far from Murmansk, in the North, on a totally uninhabited island, with only a military base and missiles, and the only connection with the outside world was a boat that left the island once a week for the mainland, and there were no civilians there at all, only officers' wives. And he had to serve three years there, as they always do in the navy, and the climatic conditions were very difficult, and cold, and all of that takes a toll on the psyche. He went there with five other young men from our neighborhood, and he ended up burying those five with his own hands. One of them was run over by a tank during maneuvers, and another one went to take some document somewhere and was caught in a blizzard and they didn't find his body until springtime. And then Andrei's finger started to fester and he ended up in the hospital, and so instead of his three years he was in the hospital for half a year and then they released him, and he didn't serve any more time in the military. Nobody in my family has had a normal time in the military.

Young men change a lot in the military. Sometimes you simply don't recognize a person after he comes back. He might have gone off to the army warm and gentle and return full of hatred toward the whole world.

And a lot of our young men aren't ready for the army, and they can't get used to the burden immediately. They need to be prepared, morally as well as physically. I think this preparation needs to take place starting in school. The lessons we have in military training are not sufficient for young men to prepare for their future service in the army. Really we don't get anything; we have target practice using weapons from before the Flood, we learn how to use gas masks that went out of use thirty years ago. In other words, those lessons make no sense and they do nothing to train us morally.

Girls train, too. But traditionally here people consider that a woman has no business in the army. I think that's the way it should be. A man should occupy himself with men's business, doing battle. Of course I am categorically against war, but if they are forced to . . . A woman's destiny is to wait for her man her whole life, first to wait for him to come back from the army, and later to come back from work, from trips.

And that's a big difference between us. We girls know that we are going to finish school, go on further to the university or an institute, but the boys know that they still have those two years ahead of them when they will be cut off from the world. Thank goodness I won't have to serve.

I remember when I was at summer camp and Dad wrote me that this young guy from West Germany had landed a plane on Red Square. I'm grateful to him, because there was so much talk here about how our borders were so well guarded and they still couldn't do anything. There were planes in the air, but the radar couldn't find him, nobody could find him. He flew right through to Moscow. It was brilliant! He showed our air force and the military that things aren't as wonderful as they say. It was a brave thing to do. I think it was great. Nobody had done it before anyway. I mean, we don't have a border with the Federal Republic of Germany, so he must have flown through Poland, I guess. . . . He crossed several borders without being stopped. He deserves credit just for that. A lot of kids are on his side. Just about everybody, in fact. I haven't heard any of the kids criticize him.

We have these jokes that our soldiers spend their time painting the leaves and the grass green and things like that. Well, my friend Sveta was joking around with some friends of hers who're in the army and said, "So do you paint the leaves green?" They got upset. "What are you laughing at?" Not long before this a lieutenant had brought them a bucket of whitewash and ordered them to paint over the dark patches on the snowdrifts. I mean this is no joke, they really did paint the dark patches on snowdrifts. What can you say?!

Right now soldiers aren't very popular. They've lost some of their popularity. I don't know why. They're considered a little retarded. It's really rare to see a soldier, an officer, who stands out. The lieutenants who've just graduated from military academy aren't too bad—they're in good physical shape and they know how to do a thing or two, but later on, the higher they go up the ladder, well they don't really do anything. I mean. . . Not long ago Artem Borovik, the journalist, published a three-part series of articles in *Ogonyok** on the American army, and it appeared on *Vzglyad*.† He said that if your officers don't make the grade because they're either overweight or out of shape they're just thrown out of the army. That doesn't happen here. Our officers weigh tons. They can't move. Their uniforms look like they've been stretched over a barrel.

In general we have just two kinds of teenagers. There are some fantastic people, enthusiastic, artistic, interested in everything. They want to change things, get involved. And then there's the majority that seems like this . . . this homogeneous mass. No matter how close I come in contact with them I can't figure out what they think about, what they

---

*One of the most popular weekly magazines, known for its investigative reporting and its highly critical perspective.

†*Vzglyad* (View) was a popular late evening television show that combined news and entertainment, aimed at a young audience. Its features were always unusual and often controversial, such as an interview with neo-Nazis and anti-Semitic members of the group Pamyat. Many people were outraged that they were allowed to speak on a popular television show, but the journalists defended their choice by pointing out that their aim was to create public awareness of a real threat. Created by young journalists, *Vzglyad* was an example of the remarkable impact of glasnost on television programming. In the university dormitory where I lived, watching *Vzglyad* was a Friday night event, and the communal television rooms barely contained even standing room while the show was being aired. In January 1991 *Vzglyad* was removed from the air and its broadcast prohibited.

talk about. If you read, though, or watch TV, the impression you get of them isn't very nice. Not pessimism but a total lack of desire to do anything. Hanging out in courtyards and passageways.

And the Komsomol today isn't what it should be. All the people who work for the Komsomol have turned into the same kind of bureaucrats the Party has. The Komsomol isn't doing any real work. All the Komsomol construction projects, like BAM* for example, the last big construction effort that everybody thought was so successful. . . . It turns out now that they did such shoddy work that it's losing millions. Our Komsomol did one heck of a job!

The way the Komsomol is now it's worthless. When it was new in the 1920s and 1930s it really had a role to play. The enthusiasm we talked about was there. Kids were excited, they believed, they wanted to do something, they were building communism. But now we don't even have a goal. I mean, what goal do we have now? All these years we were building communism and now we're coming to the conclusion that we didn't even build socialism. No one can say what system we've got now, or what we really want. And all desire to do anything's gone. Nobody knows what to do.

In other words, a kid's born, grows, finishes preschool, starts school, the first grade. Now what. . . . It's senseless to even talk about his having political views; he's just out of preschool. Right away he's given a pin—he's an Oktobrist. They all recite in unison, Oktobrists are friendly kids, future Pioneers, the seven rules of an Oktobrist. . . . He's already part of some organization. Three years go by and now he knows, even though he's little—even at that age kids worry about whether or not they'll make it into the Pioneers—he knows that he has to be accepted into the Pioneer organization. It's supposed to be voluntary. That's the idea. But if you aren't in the Pioneers you can't become a member of the Komsomol, and if you don't become a member of the Komsomol you can't join the Party and you won't get into college. So when you come to the end of Pioneers, you're fourteen and technically you're not a Pioneer anymore, and you're not a member of the Komsomol, and it's all become so insincere. . . .

I'm applying to enter the Komsomol now. On the form you have to write why you want to be in the Komsomol. Basically everybody's got the same reason—they want to get into college. I, for one, think it's a completely unnecessary organization and I don't want to join it, but in our society I don't have any other choice. And if you take a look at the

---

*One of the biggest recent Komsomol construction projects, the Baikal–Amur Railway, a major rail link between Siberia and the Soviet Far East.

crime statistics—I'm talking about crimes committed by juveniles now, not adults—those kids were Oktobrists once, they read the same books, recited the same rules about studying hard. Even so, 90 percent of our kids are flunking and don't do anything at all. You don't have to belong to some organization to do well. For example, neither of my parents belongs to the Party. I don't think they've ever wanted to. Thank goodness! God knows how that would have ended. And now it would be impossible to raise the prestige of the Komsomol and the Party, because they've reduced people to thinking so conventionally.

In 1917 or 1918, after the Soviet government was established, one of the mistakes that was made was the separation of church and state. The church had always preached charity and caring for others and love your neighbor as yourself and commandments like that. There was a long tradition of those philanthropic societies. But the Soviet government got rid of that stuff all at once and issued laws like "No spitting," and "Don't litter." But laws don't solve everything. If a person doesn't realize that something's wrong, the biggest poster in the world won't make a difference. He'll still spit or litter. It doesn't make any difference whether he's in the Komsomol or not, a Pioneer or not. Now we're going back to religion. Monasteries and convents are reopening. But something in people has been broken, and it'll be very hard to fix it, probably impossible even. Maybe you can do something, but . . . It's really hard to foster love and kindness in a society as angry as ours. Even if a family brings a child up to be kind, he'll just be kind inside, because in our society it's very hard to be kind all the time, not to litter or spit or whatever. To treat others decently. That's what I think.

SOCIALISM AND CAPITALISM:
THE SOVIET UNION AND THE UNITED STATES

Look, I don't even know what socialism is. It's very hard to judge what true socialism is. If you call what we've had around here for the last seventy years socialism, then I am against that kind of socialism. And if you judge socialism by what's going on here now, then you still won't understand it. In other words, the formulations of socialism that we are accustomed to don't fit what's going on here now. The things we have now—the cooperatives, self-financing, the decrees allowing families to start their own enterprises and allowing money from cooperatives not to go totally to the government—to me these seem to be capitalist elements on some level. Elements of a capitalist structure. And yet this is what we're calling perestroika.

I think that socialism is a way of life that is very difficult to build. Our people have already become accustomed—even if they seem like little things—to getting to work late, taking time off from work, not feeling much responsibility toward their work, and yet these are the most important things. This is what the quality of work depends upon. And the quality of work depends upon the conditions of work, and it seems to me that while in socialism that does not necessarily mean full robotization or automatization, still, work conditions have to be much better than they are now and there has to be less bureaucracy.

There should also be enough in the stores and goods should be of a high quality because a person should not have to spend much time thinking about little things like service. If a person goes to a store he should be greeted nicely, have things offered to him, and spend less time thinking about what he has to buy. Right now people's heads are full to the brim thinking about where to buy something to eat, where to get clothing and shoes. And even though they say that these are not the most important things, if all of this were done the right way people would be more interested in other things. People don't have time to go to exhibits, to the theater, to the movies.

The structure people live in is dependent upon their consciousness. You can call it what you want—socialism, capitalism, communism. They say that in communism there will be no money, but in my opinion if there isn't money anymore it will be because people will have a highly developed consciousness—but consciousness, no matter how much we've tried to build it, can never be built; it has to be cultivated. And I think that that is what socialism is—consciousness.

Education cultivates consciousness. It struck me that there was always a custom in Russia, especially under Peter the Great, of bringing in all kinds of teachers, craftsmen, singers from abroad, from Germany and Sweden. We need to do the same thing now. What a culture Russia would have! And I think we're moving in that direction now. Of course, now we have companies instead of teachers. In other words, we make contracts—come and teach us the right way to live and work.

Peter really did make our culture what it is. We had wonderful craftsmen, too, but I'm talking about the foreign teachers he hired. Well, take the movie *Young Russia*, a fantastic movie that's at least the second good movie about Peter. It shows the period of Russia's development starting in 1700, the war with Sweden, how Peter built the navy. It gives a really interesting picture of Russian attitudes, and how they learned from foreigners. I think it's like, not that our culture was ruined because we were overrun by those craftsmen, it's just that Russians . . . well, those peasants, what did they know? I mean, what kind of skills and all did they have, building skills?

There's a scene in the movie where the peasants have built their first big ship and they start to celebrate. Peter arrives and his associates tell him to take a look at what they've built, that first Russian ship of theirs. They'd kind of slapped it together and plugged up the holes, and ships were wooden in those days, you know. So while they were celebrating, Peter inspected the ship. When he saw all the shoddy workmanship, he disembarked, ordered the moorings cut, and set the ship adrift. It sank in the river with the workmen who were celebrating on board. He showed them what kind of ship they'd built. So in that way foreigners, especially Germans, have taught us things, and Germans have always been known for being meticulous and punctual.

There's a lot in the papers now about how amazed Russians are when they go abroad and see the work of foreign builders. For example, the Japanese buy timber from us. They have these no-waste technologies, and all the twigs and needles, they have this special equipment that collects the needles, and eventually they're used in all kinds of shampoos and concentrates that the Japanese sell to use. But we burn all that stuff!! Well, I think we need to learn the right way to run our economy and build things, because basically we don't know how to do anything. I mean, we do build things and you can live in them but if you take a look, everything's slapped together. It's our generation that's going to have to learn all this stuff.

I think that America is a fantastic country. Enormous. My impressions are kind of disjointed because I mostly associate America with cowboys and prairies. In the sixth grade we were really into Mann Reid's *The Headless Horseman* and *Oceola: Seminole Chief* about all of those Americans. Last year I read a very interesting book by Margaret Mitchell called *Gone with the Wind.* I really liked it too. My impressions . . . I really like America. The Riga Film Studio produced a movie called *Rich Man, Poor Man* about America.* It's the story of an ordinary family: a mother, father, and two boys. The boys grow up. One of them becomes rich, and the other becomes an athlete, and goes to prison. . . . The movie shows rich Americans and poor Americans. It was tastefully done. And recently a lot of positive reports on your country have started appearing in our press.

Basically we don't know anything about ordinary life. I mean, before we were told that America is a country where there's unemployment and the capitalists oppress the workers, all about the different demonstrations you have. And they always criticized your movies, said that they were immoral, pornographic, decadent, violent. Now we enjoy watching them!!

---

*Lena is probably referring to the American television miniseries of the same name, which was aired on Soviet television.

There are a lot of children's satellite link-ups now, and then I really like all the link-ups Pozner hosts with Boston and New York and Washington. Compared to us of course, American kids don't get uptight about talking to other people. I don't think they worry at all about what they're going to say or how they're going to say it or what people from other countries will think of them. They discuss all kinds of things, political issues that not all our people would discuss that freely. And then they don't have the problem of what to wear. What I mean is, with some of the participants from our side you get the feeling they went around to all their neighbors just to put together an outfit that would measure up. . . . But your people don't give it much thought. They look the way they look. No inferiority complexes. People here think about what they're going to wear to work the next day. If I wore this blouse to work today how am I going to wash it out so that it'll be dry by tomorrow, and what am I going to wear when I go out tonight? Everybody's thoughts here are focused on the same thing: how to get a hold of clothes, groceries, and so on. I think Americans have more pleasant thoughts.

TRUTH AND GLASNOST

The government tells the truth now. But when it comes to doing something though, no results.

Just take our history exams. Really, you have to give them credit for coming up with the idea of going back and writing a new textbook, a good one that tells the truth, but basically nothing's been changed.* They get off to a good start and then they just can't seem to finish the job.

There's a debate now over what to do with the history teachers who taught kids before perestroika and are still teaching. In other words, if they taught history wrong before perestroika, then they were lying to their students, but if they told the truth, then they're lying now. See? It's a vicious circle. History teachers are being called victims of the times. In other words, they're totally at the mercy of what's happening around them. They'd be happy to tell the truth, but then they aren't always given the greatest information. Our history teacher's told us that when she wrote her senior thesis she was forbidden to include the stuff

---

*At the end of the 1988 school year, final history exams were suspended for graduating tenth-graders. New, radically different perspectives on Soviet history, particularly the Stalinist era, made it impossible to conduct exams based upon the old history curriculum. The old textbooks were criticized and declared worthless. Most teachers stopped using them, even though there were no new materials to take their place.

she'd found in the archives about the Revolution and what actually happened. About Stalin.

Things are being printed that couldn't have been published before— well, like about 1917 even. I think it's interesting, for instance, to observe this stage, to leaf through the papers from the past four years and see how slowly, gradually, the truth is revealed, first by dropping hints, then saying more, and now they've started printing actual documents. In the last issue of *Ogonyok* there was a big article by this American professor who wrote a book on Bukharin not long ago, and now they've printed excerpts from his book.* It gives some interesting facts about Stalin and Lenin. It turns out that what we thought was true isn't. The usual story was that there was an armed uprising, the Provisional Government was captured, and there were injuries and damage when the Winter Palace was taken, shots. Turns out that wasn't so.

Television is changing too. There's a new show, *Good Evening, Moscow*. It gives all kinds of news and reports on our city. There's this one segment, "Express Camera." When Yeltsin was still in office† it was a hard-hitting feature. First of all, it was produced by young journalists and they pretty much did what they wanted. They said things that weren't usually said out loud. They showed what you could hardly call the best side of life here, and they weren't afraid to show it openly. Not really big problems, but Moscow problems, city problems. The renovation of a library that's damp, for example. Problems like that. Now, first of all, they've cut "Express Camera" down to a few minutes. The reporters don't have time to say anything, and the segments aren't as hard-hitting. Before, as soon as "Express Camera" paid a visit to a commission or agency, changes were made. Now nobody's the least bit scared of them.

MEN AND WOMEN

I think both parents should do the housework, and they should teach their children to do it. It shouldn't just be the mother who's responsible for the housework, for cleaning up the apartment. I'm just basing this on my own experience. In my family it's Dad who does most of the housework. Mom doesn't like to cook or clean or do the laundry. Before Mom just worked. Dad made dinner and fed us supper and cleaned up. That's basically the way it is now, too. What I'm really grateful to him for is raising us that way.

---

*Stephen F. Cohen, *Bukharin and the Bolshevik Revolution* (Oxford University Press, 1980).

†This refers to Boris Nikolayevich Yeltsin's tenure as head of the local Communist Party organization in Moscow. He was removed from this post in 1987.

Of course, it gets annoying sometimes, when he's at our heels—you didn't clean your shoes, close the door, turn off the light, turn off the faucet, put everything back where it belongs. We've gotten used to it I guess, and those habits will stay with us. And I think that a husband and wife should split the housework, because nowadays men and women work the same hours. Why should a woman stand at the stove every evening making her husband's dinner or supper? I think married couples should do everything together. Say there's some family celebration—make supper together and then talk over tea, all together.

I'd be for reducing the hours a woman works, even by just half an hour. So that she could get home earlier, fix something, pick up around the house, and relax at least. The way it is now, the woman sometimes gets home later than her husband. If he starts work earlier. The husband's unhappy and the woman's tired. That leads to irritations and arguments over silly things.

If it's customary for the woman to do the housework, and if she has to do the housework, then give her time to do it. But in the meantime it should be divided up evenly.

There are a lot of angry women around here. The ones who're angry are mostly the ones with big families, or a family to feed. They have to fix the meals and do the shopping. Right now—of course, I hope this will change—it's really hard to just pick up something at the store. You have to stand in those endless lines, pushing and shoving. Maybe the woman doesn't want this to happen, but the slightest irritation, aggravations of any sort, they build up and finally come spilling out. Somebody steps on your foot in the morning crush on the bus and that right there puts you in a bad mood. Push somebody in the bus by accident and you'll get such a telling off you'll want to die. It all builds up and by the evening people get home from work tired and still kind of angry from the morning and not having enough sleep. Somebody's in a bad mood and there's kind of a chain reaction. An argument breaks out, or she takes it out on her family, her exhaustion—it's more that than anger. The women themselves don't want it to happen. A lot of women can't keep their temper in check.

Some men are like that, too, but men probably don't go to the store as much. My dad's probably the only man in the Soviet Union who does the shopping. Mom just goes to stores that sell clothes, department stores. Dad, Andrei, and I are the only ones who go to the grocery store. Mom goes shopping very rarely, and men very rarely come in contact with that world. Service here isn't particularly good. What I mean is, our salespeople have sharp tongues, too, and after a run-in with them you won't want to set foot in a store. You can understand them, but still . . . Men, on the other hand . . . they go to work in the morning. Most men have cars, so they go there in their car, so they don't have to deal with any of those public transit hassles, the crush. Or they get out their paper and they're in another world. They aren't part of that close contact. Men socialize less. They're less social by nature. Of course, there are some talkative men, but mostly they're reserved and serious, the way men are supposed to be. And they just don't pay any attention to those squabbles and fights. I think they're less easily irritated. Like for example, if you get on public transit in the morning you'll see that most of the people sitting down in the crush are men. They sit there calmly while old ladies stand right next to them. They have no intention of giving up their seats. Well, when a woman sees such total disrespect, how can she keep her cool? Every little thing makes her lose her temper. So men have a lot of influence, too, over the way women are.

With us the woman is traditionally the homemaker. She raises the kids and devotes her whole life and energy to finding food and clothing, and so the short time she has slips away. It was put well in that piece: friendship and love demand time, but when that time comes it's sometimes spent hunting for all kinds of makeup and food and heaven knows what.

I guess it all changes after college. Because in college, too ... It's a paradox. On the one hand there are those informal organizations and those slouching punks and heavy metal freaks, but on the other hand if you look at the Witty and Clever Club there are all these funny, young, energetic guys and girls you've got to admire, but then after college all those girls get married. . . .

If you want to make dinner here you have to hunt for the ingredients. . . . Let's say I want to make soup. I need beets, carrots, potatoes, meat. . . . Leg of lamb, say. Well, to find those ingredients I'd have to comb half of Moscow. One place doesn't have meat, the next place doesn't have something else. That's probably why.

I think from our conversations with you we've found out that American women never do any sewing or cooking. When we go out we can't be sure that, say, we'll be able to get a decent meal at a cafeteria. The one at my school is good, actually, but my brother never knows whether he'll be able to get something to eat at his cafeteria. Usually there's nothing there or it's crowded, so everybody's hungry and grouchy. The same thing with clothes. I'd rather spend sixty rubles on cloth and sew myself something than spend just as much time hunting for some piece of clothing.

THE FUTURE

The way I see my future I'll finish school and enter college, I haven't decided which yet. Probably the All-Union State Film Institute. To become a cinematographer. I'm going to pick a career that involves travel. Then I'll get a job after college, get married, have a lot of kids—four. And then get my kids settled. What else could I want?

I have some idea of the kind of man I want to marry. He should be kind and intelligent and love children, and me. And, as the newspapers say, he should be unpretentious. In other words, a regular guy. Kinder. And I think he should definitely be handsome. He should earn enough to live comfortably. Preferably his job should involve travel, too. If I have the kind of job where I'm gone for long stretches, why should he have to sit at home alone? With the kids. And we'll raise our kids to be healthy, strong, and athletic. Get them involved in sports at an early age, take them skiing in the winter and biking in the summer. Of course, there aren't any husbands like that nowadays. Where can you find them?!

Because nowadays most men look for wives who don't like kids either, who don't want kids. Most men want to have an apartment, an important position and a car, a house in the country, money. So they marry the kind of women who dream of their husbands having an important position, a car and a house in the country, so that they can brag about how rich they are to their friends. I don't need that. I don't think that's what's most important in life.

I probably want to have lots of kids because the more you have, the closer the family is. Though that's not always true. There are three kids in my family. It's great when you all go on a trip together. It's always noisy. I don't like it when it's quiet.

I don't know yet how everything will work out. Whether I'll get into the institute. The competition's really stiff, and they don't like to take girls in cinematography. It's a hard job what with the cameras and all. The competition's stiff, but I'm going to give it a shot. Women are considered fragile, and next to those big cameras . . .

FREEDOM: "STILL TOO EARLY"

I think that freedom is when, let's say I want to go somewhere—here you've got to have a pass to get into most places. I want to see a movie—I go see it. I want to tour the country—I do it. I buy a ticket without any kind of background checks. Why is it that in my own country they check up on me and make me prove my identity? I should be free in my own country. I'm Russian. I was born here. I have every right, theoretically, to go to Vorkuta or the [Soviet] Far East or the mountains if I want, to buy a camera to take pictures there if I want. Say I'm studying ancient history: I buy a ticket to Greece and see Athens, the

Acropolis, Rome. If we're studying the Renaissance—I go to Italy. If I want to see how the West Germans live—I go to West Germany. If I want to visit America—I go to America, and not just for business or in a delegation, when I can only change thirty rubles and have to feel ashamed. . . . There have been these bitter articles by people who've been abroad, especially to West Germany, which we did defeat in the war, after all, and there's our tourist with that handful of marks he's been given, wondering how he'll survive till it's time to leave, but he wants to go here and there, he wants to buy something at an international auction, fly to New York. If I want to change a hundred, I change a hundred, if I have a thousand to change . . .

I was part of a youth delegation when I was in the seventh grade, and the questions we were asked—What is the purpose of your trip abroad? Do you have in your possession any ammunition, drugs, hard currency, weapons? How much and why? And the same questions coming back.

Say I want to go to the country. I can go there, live there a few years, and come back. I know that I have an apartment in Moscow.* When we can do that we'll be free. When a person feels free and isn't at the mercy of anybody else. When, if I go to America, say, I'll know that no matter what I say to any Americans I meet, it's not going to affect me or my kids somewhere on down the line. When it won't matter what my last name is. A lot depends on what your last name is. In the 1950s and 1960s people were turned down for jobs because of their names. Even my friend Ira. Her last name is Feltsman. Her mom was turned down by an institute. She works at a factory and starts at seven, which means she's got to get up by five or five thirty. She wanted to get a job closer to home, that would be nearby. They kept her waiting for a whole year and then they turned her down, and at her old job she'd lost her seniority. It's the same old stupidity. She'd worked twenty years, quit, and then she had to start over from scratch. And to get that much seniority again she's going to have to work another twenty years. What kind of freedom is that? If I want to go work somewhere, say, I can sign a contract and when it's up I can leave, and I know that I'll be able to get work someplace else.

Say I go someplace to apply for a job. They just won't take me. They'll say I have to have an internal passport or a birth certificate, another interesting document. We ran into this in Vladimir. I mean I had to produce my birth certificate to check into a hotel. Say I come to

---

*This refers to the complications of registering one's place of residence (the *propiska*). Moving from Moscow to another place involves the risk of losing the highly coveted Moscow *propiska* and the legal right to a Moscow apartment.

some town and I need a hotel room, but they can't give me one. Why? What difference does it make whether or not I'm an enemy of the people, whether or not I'm a spy? I need a room and I get one. Say I want three still cameras and ten movie cameras, it's a quirk of mine, I want them. But here you can't bring more than three into the country, and they can't be valued at more than what you changed.*

Of course my parents aren't free either. What kind of freedom do we have here? My own mother hasn't been able to get a job for four years. Why not? She wants to work. She has ideas. She always has ideas. I think she's a very talented person in her own way. She made some good documentaries once. When she worked for the studio. What I mean is, she wants to work and she has some ideas but they won't take her. She can't get a job. And then all her life she's dreamed of going abroad, taking a trip to Bulgaria. I don't know why. But she hasn't been able to, either because she doesn't have enough money or there are some kind of papers she has to get. The same goes for Dad, too, pretty much. There are always bad feelings in the unit, disagreements between editors. They yell and scream. For example, they both work in TV a lot, making original programs, and most of the ones Dad's done lately haven't been shown. Mom's too. When she worked for television she did this show about physicists. There's this secret town outside Moscow called Dubna. It's classified. And her show was about how they spend their free time. It couldn't be shown just because it was a town of physicists and how can Soviet physicists joke around? So it wasn't shown. In other words, she was supposed to think about how she could change it, what she could add. And it was a shame because she'd spent all that time. And the physicists also wanted to see it, and it didn't really show anything, what's most interesting. What kind of freedom is that? It's still too early to be talking about freedom.

---

*This refers to the amount of rubles (which is limited by the Soviet government) that can be exchanged for foreign currency.

"WE ARE NOT AFRAID OF ANYTHING"

ILYA

Sixteen years old, tenth-grade student, special English school

I meet Ilya through the fourteen-year-old daughter of a friend of mine. Both of them study at one of Moscow's better special English-language schools. We agree to conduct our first conversation at my friend's home. It's hard to arrange, because Ilya is busy most of the time preparing for entrance exams to Moscow State University, where he would like to study next year.

On the designated day, I arrive first. When Ilya rings the bell, my friend opens the door, greets him with a formal handshake, and says, "Good afternoon, Comrade Professor!" Ilya blushes a little, as if embarrassed. When we are introduced, he shakes my hand and is quite polite.

Ilya is thin and slight and has soft, delicate features. He is not very interested in talking about personal subjects, and reserves his energy and enthusiasm for politics. We sit in the study room, door closed, and begin talking. At some point in the conversation we hear a soft knock on the door. My friend's daughter, who has a noticeable crush on Ilya, enters, wearing an apron, carrying a tray with two milkshakes she has prepared for Ilya and me. She tiptoes in politely, gives a slight nervous curtsy, and backs out the door, as if she has been interrupting an important meeting. I notice that Ilya does not feel the least bit uncomfortable being served by this young woman, and I can't help but think that this moment reveals the groundwork that has already been laid for the future relationships these two young people will form with the opposite sex. It is a gesture of kindness, but there is something disturbing about it.

Ilya's father is a well-known psychiatrist who evaluates patients in a hospital emergency room. He is also known as a poet. His mother is a candidate of economic sciences (Ph.D.) whose field of specialization is comparative international economic analysis.

ILYA

I've lived all of my life in Moscow. I love literature and history, not only Russian but of all cultures in general. I've always been interested in the humanities. And seeing that our society has become so politicized nowadays, like it or not, you get caught up in all the political information we have around here. That's why I became interested in areas like economics.

This is my last year in school, a really difficult year for me and my classmates because we're getting ready to take final exams in school and entrance exams for the university. Everyone is either taking special courses or studying with a private tutor, which costs money, because trying to get into the university is a serious matter and takes a lot of effort. Probably this is why there isn't time for anything else. We have to study a lot.

All these years of school, my favorite subjects were literature and history. Math and physics always made me suffer. In literature I was always pretty successful, and when we held the "Literary Olympics" at school, I always did well, always won a first place. This year our school's team participated in a televised literary competition and we won prizes, so, judging from all this, it seems I have certain abilities in the humanities. However, whether or not I'm going to get into the university—I'm not so sure. It might work out.

My favorite literature is nineteenth-century Russian classics, Tolstoy, Dostoyevsky, Chekhov, Pushkin . . . not just because I'm a patriot but also because it's great literature. If we look at twentieth-century literature, well, we have a lot of journalistic work that they didn't publish before. There's a lot being published here now that wasn't before, some of the best writers, without a doubt, Andrei Platonov, Trifonov . . . some poets who are only starting to be published now, who had only a little bit of their work published—Mandelshtam, Akhmatova, Pasternak, Joseph Brodsky. My greatest interest is in Russian literature, although of course I'm interested in world literature too—without world literature you won't get far.

I've had a chance to read a lot of books published in the West. I've read Western editions and also what's known around here as samizdat, that is, people type things themselves and make carbon copies. During the deepest stagnation my parents had the opportunity to get to know foreigners and dissidents, so we had that kind of literature in our house, including some of Solzhenitsyn's.

My parents are divorced. I live with my mother, and my sister lives with my father. I have an excellent relationship with my father, I talk to him a lot, and it's hard for me to talk about the divorce. They loved each other, and they're educated people, and look . . . when all of this happened it was terrible. And it's a big problem here. There's a high percentage of divorce here, the same way you have.

Sometimes I have conflicts with my parents; I want to do one thing, and they tell you—even though you're already basically a grown person—they begin to give you advice, tell you that things should be done this way and not that way. As far as these things go, it seems to be good in America, because young people try to be independent, and even materially they have the right to their independence. Here you have to get into fights with parents every once in a while. I struggle for my independence, and I think my parents are getting used to it. It's an ongoing process! They keep track of what I do. And sometimes you don't really want that, having somebody keep track of you.

POLITICS IN THE USSR: "A QUESTION OF SURVIVAL"

My mother's running a seminar at her institute right now. There are many famous economists taking part in it, and I got to meet them! Her field is really the comparative economic analysis of different countries, but at the moment she's absorbed by the same enlightenment process as all of our famous journalists, economists, and even historians are.

Shmelev was there, at the seminar . . . he's one of our best-known economists and journalists who became famous for his article "Advances and Debts," which drew a lot of attention in 1987 and was discussed quite a bit on Western radio. He brought all of our problems to the attention of the press in that one article. He offered some of his own solutions; he believes that the only way out of the bad situation we are in now is a market economy. I agree with him. So far, humanity has not thought up a better economic system than the market economy that exists in the West.

The experiment that has been going on around here for the last seventy years has not had any success, and even though Gorbachev says that we now have more socialism, still, call things what you want—socialism, capitalism—there are simply objective laws in economics that are better off not being broken, the way they break them around here. For example, that thing called competition, and everything that goes along with it. Our planned economy so far is in bad shape!

You can really argue whether the revolution that took place here in 1917 was governed by historical laws or not. Probably the things that happen in history are law-governed and that's why Russia is always different from the rest of the world. On the one hand, there's this attraction to the West, and, on the other hand, we're not really a part of Europe, so we've always had these complications in our historical development. Our revolution was made in order to establish general equality, social justice, but they ended up creating what we call a leveling off, a kind of artificial attempt to make all people the same. I don't think there's anything terrible if one person works better than another and earns more. I think that's completely natural. And that is what our history, and world history in general, has shown. I don't think that there is any kind of social equality around here anyhow because there are people here who are more privileged and people who are less privileged.

Then we had Stalinism, the absence of democracy. I don't consider Stalinism something isolated, because looking at all of our history it's clear that dictatorships have always existed. There is a wonderful novel published here, *Life and Fate,* by Vassily Grossman, in which there are direct parallels drawn between Stalinism and fascism. I think that in many ways these two things have the same roots. And even though people are reluctant to talk about that here, they both are very similar to each other, as are all dictatorships that have ever existed. So many people died, which corresponded to the psychology of those times, and its legacy has remained here up till now—Stalinism hasn't died yet, it sits inside of people and, unfortunately, inside the people in power.

People still have that fear, that fear to talk, although, thank God, the time has come when people have started to talk, and for that alone we should erect a monument to Gorbachev. People have started to talk more and worry less about what will happen to them because of what they say. But the reforms going on now remind us of Khrushchev's reforms, and they were unsuccessful, so people are afraid that once again it is not going to succeed. If Gorbachev doesn't succeed in restructuring our economy, there will be total collapse in our country, and there is no going back. So of course our people have become quite active and agitated.

I would like to be an optimist because I do believe in Gorbachev. At the moment there's a lot of opposition to him among bureaucrats, lots of ministers of that same structure that was founded during Stalin's rule, and naturally these forces are trying very hard to counteract the reforms. But the fact that it's truly gotten . . . well, I don't know if we can talk about absolute freedom of speech, but certainly our mass media and press are free and people are talking. To think that four years ago people would have said what they're saying now . . . well, it truly does make you happy.

Russia is a country that always takes such a strange path, really, if you look at history you see that other countries have had a kind of normal development—Europe, America, they keep moving ahead.

They go through certain stages of development and in general it works. But in Russia there is always some kind of abnormal path of development.

It's hard to say concretely what will happen in our country in the near future. But I hope, based on everything I've been reading, that at least in terms of economics and politics we will strive toward what you already have, and I hope that we're able to achieve this: a market economy that will give us a certain amount of material well-being and, in the political arena, democracy and a real choice of leadership.

I know that you are not a society without problems, it would simply be wrong to say that, but all problems are not alike, and the ones we are facing are far more serious than the problems facing you. You have unemployment, but I think you can solve that problem by the end of this century. That's a far less serious and fundamental problem than what we're facing. We are simply in a sorry state! Even though we are considered one of the superpowers, economically we are quite close to Third World countries, and as of yet there's been no real progress. The problems you have are simply not as horrible as ours. Ours are a question of our basic survival.

Our standard of living is really low. Our economy is collapsing and we need some serious reforms, the sooner the better, so that the very survival of our country doesn't come into question. There are now such pessimistic prognoses that by the middle of the 1990s our economy will collapse completely, and then it's possible the military will intervene, and nothing good will come of that.

There are people against the reforms, but they don't say they're against them. During the period of stagnation they received certain privileges they want to keep. This is particularly the case of bureaucratic circles, the administrative apparatus that's taken on such huge proportions here, the ministries. It's a natural development to get rid of them; the only ones who will remain are those who actually do something. But of course they're fighting for their positions. There's a battle going on; there are still people who have a Stalinist psychology who are against glasnost, against the cooperatives, who think we are playing into the hands of the West; in other words, they are throwing around a lot of political slogans. But thank God there are a lot fewer people like that around now.

All of these politics have tired me out! Politics in Russia has always been different from politics in America because with you Americans it's all the same whether you elect Bush or whether you elect Dukakis. In the final analysis, nothing much really changes. That's the way it seems to me, for the average American. His life won't really change much.

And here it's the first time they've really given the people a chance to elect from two or more candidates. On the one hand there is truly a grass-roots aspect to the elections now,* but on the other hand the Moscow Party authorities are trying to exert pressure to vote against Yeltsin,† which has had the opposite effect and has acted like an advertisement for him. I even saw a poster written in markers "Vote for Yeltsin: For Justice, Democracy, Truth." Signed by fifth-grade students of School No. 4. Even little children have gotten caught up in this! That was really interesting to me. And now they've published the list of the new deputies and I am pleased with practically all of them, and I'm happy that they've gotten rid of a lot of Party functionaries.

There's a debate going on about whether or not we need a multi-party system. We have only one party, if you can call it that, because within the Communist Party there are forces that are completely opposed to each other, even within the Politburo itself. Gorbachev and Ligachev are completely different. So there already exists something like a multi-party system, even though it's within the framework of one party.

In our school there was a lot of heated debate during the electoral campaign: "Who are your parents for? Who are you for?" Everybody was very concerned about it. Our teachers talked a lot about who they were going to vote for and why.

In general we are trying to approach what is, in my opinion, the best that humanity has been able to achieve, no matter what it costs, which is your system, in the United States. Of course you have your difficulties, but seeing as humanity hasn't yet thought up anything better, we should strive to achieve in our own way that which exists in the West; that's my own opinion. Restructuring the political sphere and the economic sphere, all of this is in essence perestroika, which, without a doubt, we need here like a fish needs water.

Your political system is fairly democratic and doesn't contradict your

---

*The election of deputies to the Congress of People's Deputies, the Soviet legislative body, in March 1989, in which many Communist Party candidates were defeated and opposition figures such as Andrei Sakharov were elected.

†Boris Nikolayevich Yeltsin, the controversial Communist Party reformer who was removed from his post as head of the Moscow Party in 1987. An outspoken critic of Party privilege, Yeltsin was highly popular among Muscovites, who credit his tenure with various improvements in city life. Yeltsin's political comeback occurred during the March 1989 elections for the Congress of People's Deputies, when he won an overwhelming majority of citywide votes in an electoral race against the Communist Party candidate. Since then he has been elected president of the Russian Republic, the largest and most powerful republic of the Soviet Union, and he remains extremely popular among the general population, offering a serious challenge to Gorbachev's leadership.

economy, which is such a problem in our life here—and who could help
but be enraptured by your economy, which we could use so much around
here? In general things are looking up for you, and in any case you always
have opportunities to achieve something. We would like there to be some
kind of sense of being provided for. . . . Who could be against that?

People here love to say that your democracy is bourgeois democracy
and that the people don't really govern, the affluent class does, that you
have a certain aristocratic uppercrust. But still, from what I understand,
Americans are satisfied with what they have. Of course one always wants
things to be better, but, as far as my contact with Americans has shown
me, they are basically content. They used to say that things were bad
over in America and good here, and of course they weren't—you can
imagine if everything is still so far from being ideal *now*.

Still I, for example, cannot say that I am dissatisfied with the Soviet
Union; I was born here, this is my country, and there is such a thing as
patriotism. But if we speak about specific things and make a compari-
son between what you have and what we have, then without a doubt we
want to achieve what you have already been able to. In the first place—
and I'm talking about the entire population now and not just the intelligentsia—your material well-being. People, after all, have to live with
their earthly needs! And people whose view of things is broader, the
intelligentsia, well they . . . before there were dissidents who said that we
really needed democracy, freedom of speech. And now everybody is
saying what before only the dissidents used to say. At least all of this has
come out from the underground now. It used to be that there was only
one point of view—the point of view of the government, the leaders.
There simply couldn't be any others.

We even feel this at school. We have to take a history exam in school
to get our diploma this year, and it's very difficult because new facts
about our history keep coming out, and if you look at a tenth-grade
textbook you'll see that what is written there is not at all what is being
said now. That old textbook was written on the basis of a short course
on the history of the Party written by Stalin himself and talks about
Bukharin as an opportunist and the worst kind of person. There are
already different points of view than the one that everything was fine
and only a small number of people died. All in all, a lot of false information and lies. And still there's no new textbook. So as far as Soviet
history is concerned, there's no real clarity. They don't know what
material we should study from—maybe from what's being written in the
newspapers. Cohen's book on Bukharin came out, so we might be able
to use that, or maybe we could use something by our historian Roy
Medvedev. The history exam this year is going to be given in the form

of a conversation. Each student will prepare a talk on a particular topic, and the examiners can ask him questions about it.

Before we had glasnost, it was impossible to believe the information we got here, and the only truth I could get was from Western radio. I still believe in Western radio to some extent, especially since my parents spent time with dissidents who confirmed what we heard, and on your radio they spoke about what we didn't speak about here, or what they lied about here. But now a curious thing has happened. Before when a group of intellectuals gathered, they talked about what they heard on Western radio. But now when intellectuals get together, they tell each other about what they've read in *our* newspapers, *our* magazines! And this is why we say that Western radio hasn't gone through perestroika yet. Really, there's much more interesting information in our newspapers now than what we can hear on your radio. It's much more interesting to watch our television and read our newspapers. We have progressive newspapers, reactionary newspapers, and even some that maintain neutrality. I've already gotten tired of being surprised by what they're printing around here! Whenever you run into somebody you immediately ask, "Did you read what they wrote in *Ogonyok? Moscow News?*" These are the things they used to have to print in samizdat around here, or that people had to smuggle in from the West.

It's interesting to hear the views of Western radio about what's going on here, the view from outside, but you really only know what's going on here if you live here, from direct observation. There are Western journalists living here who report on what's going on, but they have their own orientation, and it's different. We live here, and we simply have more interesting information and are following this process as a struggle. Western radio gives its own viewpoint, and although of course it's interesting sometimes, "Your own shirt is closest to your skin," as they say here.

Things are changing. I remember perfectly well how things used to be around here. There still haven't been any changes in our economy, but there have been tremendous changes in foreign policy. But the biggest, most revolutionary changes are taking place—and I say this already for the tenth time—four years ago it would have been unthinkable, any newspaper you grab now, even one considered neutral, and it almost looks like an illegal pamphlet, of the highest revolutionary nature!

VIEWS OF CHANGE: GENERATIONS

My generation has a problem that probably wasn't so evident in preceding ones. Even now, when so many new facts about our history are coming out and the authority of those in power and of the mass media has been undermined, in spite of the fact that what is going on here now is wonderful, a great percentage of people are apathetic because they don't believe in anything, not much interests them, and of course that's really sad. But you can still meet up with people quite often from the generation of the 1960s who are quite active.

I'm interested in politics, and I'm surprised when I meet people who aren't. Look at the elections we just had here! And then you talk with people, with my peers, you find some who have just barely heard about any of this, hardly know anything, and don't care about any of it. My school, given its specific nature,* has a smaller percentage of these types, but outside of school I have often met people my age who are not at all interested. That's so surprising to me.

It seems to me that my parents' generation developed immense faith in the 1960s, during Khrushchev's time, when there was a general rise in social movements. If you compare the 1960s with the previous period of Stalinism, it's like night and day. And at that time the generation of the 1960s was twenty to twenty-five years old, they were young people who were already free from that mad fear cultivated by Stalin, and really, that's when our poets appeared—Yevtushenko, Voznesensky, Rozhdestvenny. Their poetry has a social nature. In the economic sphere a lot of young scholars emerged, and they certainly had faith; many of them joined the Party in those years, and then in the 1970s they became disappointed and disillusioned. But it is precisely those people who are carrying out perestroika now, those who had so much faith in the 1960s. Of course they view all of this with great apprehension, because they already saw those previous reforms destroyed and they can imagine that it might not work now either. But once again they're the ones who have become socially active. There are certain circles of young people who are active, but really that generation of the 1960s is the stronger one now.

Personally I have a mixed kind of relationship to the question of faith. On the one hand, I think it is probably very hard for a human being, because of his psychological makeup, to live without believing in anything. Without a doubt a human being must . . . something has to make his eyes light up, he must be able to respond to something, and it has to be something close to him. And on the other hand, the experience of our history . . . look, I find purely blind faith deeply repugnant, when people . . . well, you can compare it with religious fanaticism. . . .

---

*Ilya's school has long been considered one of Moscow's most progressive and open. The principal is well known and highly respected by reform-minded educators. Ilya comments several times on the elite, intellectual nature of his school, and he refers to himself and his classmates as privileged.

But I have great respect for religion; I haven't been christened and I'm not a believer, in the sense that I observe any rites or go to church, but in my soul I think I identify myself with Christians. I think that Christian principles are something eternal for all of humankind.

Love for your neighbor. In the Gospel the second commandment says, "Love thy neighbor." That's what Christ talked about. I think that's very important, especially in this world of ours with all its contradictions. I think it's very important to preserve humaneness.

Of course I doubt there's any concrete religious framework in my consciousness, although if you asked me what religion I feel the most affinity with, without a doubt it is Christianity. If you asked me to specify Russian Orthodoxy or Protestantism or Catholicism, I'm not sure.

Before, the information we had about religion was virtually all negative—that well-known phrase, "Religion is the opium of the masses." That was the only world view, which I would call "false atheism." Because a person really should at least have some knowledge of what he is struggling against! And here they were atheists out of ignorance. They didn't really know what religion was and still managed to call themselves atheists.

In general I have great respect for religion. Even though for seventy years they have been cultivating a completely barbaric attitude toward religion, starting with their tearing down churches and cathedrals. There was so much propaganda against the Church.

My parents have the same attitude toward faith that I do. You could call this "believing atheism." In other words, they don't follow any religious canon but maintain rather general humanitarian positions, and of course they are sympathetic to Christianity.

If you take my parents' generation and people even older than they are who grew up during Stalin's time and spent their youth when he was in power, some fear still remains. And without a doubt, what distinguishes my generation—perhaps I'm not correct, but it seems to me that in general, we aren't afraid of anything. I'm not saying we're ready to go out there and fight, but basically we haven't become scared. I think I'm right in saying this. As far as my own parents are concerned, in this sense we have very much in common, but there are people who, up to the present, are still afraid. "Look, you talk and talk, and then what happened before is going to begin all over again." Of course they have a reason for these warnings, but I think one has to take an optimistic approach or else how can you go on living?

An example of this fear, well, there's a joke going around. It takes place in a prison camp: 1992. Roll call. "Baklanov!" [editor of a progressive magazine]. "Present!" "Yakovlev!" [editor of *Moscow News*].

"Present!" "Afanasyev!" [progressive historian]. "Present!" "Korotich!"
[editor of *Ogonyok*]. Silence. "Korotich!" Silence. "Korotich!" "Present!"
"Why didn't you respond right away? The time to keep your mouth shut
is over! Now it's time to account for yourself!" That's the kind of joke
we have here. And of course, it's real. People have learned from bitter
experience in the 1960s, when there were progressive reforms and they
simply put a stop to them. Many of the people who could be counted
on became disillusioned. That's reality.

It seems as if that generation became disillusioned, but they have
started to believe again. People around fifty. And among youth, people
of my generation, even though this didn't happen in front of their eyes,
still, they have a general lack of belief in everything. Among my peers
there are apathetic people who don't believe in anything, totally passive
people.

You always find some people who are active, no matter what kind of
generation it is, even those that people have considered lost generations. But it's another matter to ask what the percentage of them is. I
know of ecology movements, composed basically of young people, and
in the events going on now in Estonia, in general, in the whole Baltic
region, there are very active young people there now, although again,
the leadership is mainly people from the generation of the 1960s.

It's hard for me to say if there are possibilities for me to do something concrete because I don't participate in any movement, although I
would join with pleasure; perhaps it's just that I haven't really found the
opportunity yet, or perhaps I simply haven't thought enough about it.
No, actually, if there were an opportunity I would join with pleasure.
For now, I can call myself an active observer and contemplator of what's
going on. I read newspapers and every day I find myself discussing
history, foreign politics, domestic politics, the economy, ecology, all
kinds of topics with my parents and with some of my peers. It always
affects me when people start talking about these things. I think that I
follow what's going on really carefully, and I try to get my information
from many different sources.

This might be somewhat immodest of me, but I consider myself one
of those people who support perestroika actively, and I consider that to
be some kind of contribution. But I don't really have the feeling that
my generation can influence perestroika. I could certainly talk about
how perestroika influences us! Without a doubt we are becoming more
responsible and freer. We have been freed of the fears that the previous
generation had and we are able to talk more openly. But the feeling
that our generation as a whole can affect perestroika—that I don't
have.

You couldn't really call us the children of perestroika. But on the other hand there are differences between us and our parents. They're still afraid of something—sometimes even *my* parents tell me to watch what I say over the telephone. But I don't have any fear inside of me. I'm not afraid. I *want* not to be afraid.

My grandparents are alive. Their generation is more complicated than my parents'. My grandfather was a famous economist who took it upon himself to write a letter to Stalin in 1952, telling him he didn't agree with some of his economic policies. For some strange reason he wasn't put into prison. Maybe they just didn't have the time to do it, because really what he did in those days was considered suicide. My grandmother was also an economist. Their youth began in the years of the Revolution, in the 1920s, and their adulthood was spent during Stalin's time, Khrushchev's, Brezhnev's. And what happened during Stalinism left a great mark on their generation. My grandmother and grandfather always understood who Stalin really was. My mother says that her parents always referred to him as the Boss, they cursed him, thinking that their daughter didn't understand. Those were terrible days, but many people of that generation remain Stalinists even today, even though all the facts speak against it. It's the result of the blind faith that was cultivated then and still exists in many ways in Stalinist views. Sometimes you can see them on television, and I myself have met a few . . . during the elections people gathered on the streets and began to argue about things, and often you could find an old woman or man who would say, "Your perestroika isn't true, during Stalin's times everything was fine, there was order, and Bukharin and Trotsky were enemies of the people." And those who did understand what had happened are a very frightened generation, because in Stalin's time it wasn't possible to speak or think for yourself. People who are still afraid to speak are basically the ones who lived through the war. The Stalinist argument is that Stalin won the war, even though now it's known how many mistakes he actually made, and perhaps there would not have even been a war if Stalin hadn't made those, well, to put it mildly, "mistakes." But still they say, "Stalin won the war." That faith remains. That's a very complicated generation, although there aren't many of them left.

My father is older than my mother and he remembers more. He was at Stalin's funeral. He says there was a frightening crush of people, probably organized by Beria himself. Perhaps my father himself believed in Stalin, when he was a little boy. A lot of people believed that what was going on—the repression and things like that—was the fault of some local powers. He came to his own conclusions about what had gone on even before it was revealed by Khrushchev. In 1953 he finished medical school and went to Norilsk, where there were huge prison camps, millions of people. And it just so happened that he ended up there during the time of "rehabilitation." He tells about it: Three people sitting in an office, one a local Party boss, another from the region, and another from Moscow. They would bring a person in the office, talk with him for a few minutes, and then let him go free. He says that even though there were many real criminals, for the most part the people there were innocent. And that's precisely when people got active—in the 1950s and 1960s. That's when my father got actively involved; in his poems there are a lot of references to the camps.

My grandfather who wrote to Stalin was on my mother's side. On my father's side my grandfather was sent to prison in 1937; he was an engineer who was convicted of having proposed the construction of schools right next to the railway because he intended to harm children, so that they would get run over by the trains. Sabotage. An absolutely absurd accusation! Well, they sent him to prison and half a year later in the camp he ran into the public prosecutor who had conducted the trial against him. My grandfather asked him, "Why did you do that, of course you knew that those were the ravings of a madman!" And he answered, "If I hadn't held that trial against you, they would have sent me to prison immediately. But as it was, they sent me there a half year later." But my grandfather was actually lucky because thanks to my grandmother's intercession—and this was an extremely rare occurrence—they let him out in 1939. He was only imprisoned for two years; he stayed alive.

VIEWS OF CHANGE: WORKERS AND INTELLECTUALS

It would be easier for me to compare people according to social strata rather than age or generation. Without a doubt, perestroika depends upon the intelligentsia, because the intelligentsia is basically who's responsible for carrying it out. I can't really say what the working class supports because I have very little contact with it. But in order to really understand what's going on around here now a person has to have a high cultural level. I've noticed that there is a kind of reaction, basically among workers, that because nothing has happened in the economy those people who aren't very cultured say, "Perestroika, perestroika, all they do is talk, it's all a bunch of hot air, nobody's doing anything, there's nothing in the stores, things have only gotten worse! And now these cooperatives have appeared! They've bought up all the sugar!"

That is such an uninformed way of thinking . . . but it's true that for simple people it's what's the most important, that there be something in the stores. When people really get something, that's when they'll really believe in perestroika. And until that happens, there will be all of these intellectuals' discussions. But you see, I think that in order for something to happen in the economic sphere we have to go through all of this process of conversations, discussions. Up till now we haven't really had specific ideas about what has to be done.

Simple people judge by whether or not it's gotten easier to live, and up till now, materially, life hasn't gotten any easier for them. When things get easier for them, then there will be great support for Gorbachev. But in the meantime, not only has it not gotten easier for them to live, it's actually even gotten worse. But you can't blame perestroika for that. The economy is in a bad state and it's getting worse, but this process began way before perestroika.

The thing that undermined Gorbachev's authority with part of the population—although they basically still do love him quite a bit—was the anti-alcohol campaign. It was done in a really inept way, through administrative methods.

I know that scientists here are saying that if nothing happens soon in the economic sphere then the opposition is going to have a lot to say about what goes on here. Things will be difficult for him and his authority will decline. The truth is that we don't know what's going to happen with the economy here. Our aim now is to develop a market economy, but that idea is facing so much opposition!

The cooperatives are part of this. Basically I think they're a progressive development. It's natural that the work of the cooperatives is connected to the biggest difficulties we face in our daily life. The cooperatives are trying to fill in the gaps in the service sector, consumer goods, even medicine. It hasn't always turned out well, but you can hardly blame the cooperatives for that, because there are objective reasons. After all, your market economy that I love so much is in the good condition it is in now, and yet it too had its own period of the so-called Wild West, with its cowboys and all that terrible muddle. We have to live through that kind of period here now! The most serious problem isn't that, rather it's that the cooperative movement has all kinds of limitations placed on it by the ministries, which are also fighting for their survival. So at times it becomes impossible for the cooperatives to obey the law. People are finding goods there, but at very high prices.

On my way to school there is a cooperative that sells *chebureki*.* Hungry people walk by, and even though the prices are pretty high, they buy. You'll always find people there, and every time you stand in line—because there is always a big demand—you find someone who criticizes the vendor for his high prices and says, "Look, you're a young man after

---

*Meat wrapped in dough and deep-fried.

all, why don't you go out and work? What you're doing now is speculation!" The vendor usually doesn't say anything, or if he answers he'll
say, "If you don't want one, don't buy it."

Now, you hardly ever find *chebureki* in a government-run stand, and if
you do there is usually such a huge line that you're better off spending
a lot of money than humiliating yourself in those completely absurd
lines. As far as I know, the people in cooperatives are not making
excessive profits, because what's happened is that in order to get the
raw materials to make anything they have to pay several times more
than state-run enterprises have to.

Even if people in cooperatives were making excessive profits, I don't
think there would be anything terrible about that. It just produces
envy in people, and that's related to the psychology that developed
here over many years, when everybody was leveled off, and any kind of
inequality created resentment. Ordinary citizens who receive miserable
wages for the hardest work have a negative reaction to the people in
cooperatives, who probably earn more than anyone else. But personally I feel fine about cooperatives and think that they are part of a
normal process. People who earn more than others have the right to
live better than others. The cooperatives' survival is part of all the
changes taking place in our economy, and they are one of the successes of Gorbachev's reforms. Cooperatives are filling in the gaps that
exist in our economy. It's true, unfortunately, that their prices are
high, but you simply have to think a little and realize that it's a temporary phenomenon, and it's wrong to blame the cooperatives themselves for it. After all, we are paying for the bad economy we've got.
People accuse them of being speculators, but I say, if they're involved
in anything illegal, go ahead and punish them! The ministries are
boycotting their activities and are passing laws that just don't give them
any room to move. But I say, if they're breaking a law, send them to
court, convict them. If not, then why curse at them, they're getting
down to business!

The attitudes against cooperatives are very much connected with the
psychological barriers that still face us. One of the characteristics of
socialism is state ownership of the means of production, land, and
natural resources. We have to get away from this. We have to get away
from dogmatic convictions, because the economy should work the way
an economy should, and not because they want to follow some kind of
theory. The cooperatives will be part of Gorbachev's success or lack of
success. There's nothing new to discover here; the market economy
already exists, and in various forms! Sweden has a high level of national-
ization, but it has a market economy.

THE IDEAL OF SOCIAL JUSTICE

Social justice was one of the first questions to be raised here, but it didn't happen. In spite of everything there are the more privileged and the less privileged.

A revolution that tries to level everybody off by taking away from everyone and dividing it up into halves has never led to anything good. I think that if you want to become rich, you simply need to work better. And the chance to do that exists in your society. Of course you do have your aristocratic circles, in politics, and rich people, but personally, from the point of view of my own psychology, I don't care if the person across the street lives in a luxurious villa and has ten cars. . . . I don't even care how he got that wealth, through inheritance or if he earned it himself, the most important thing is that he didn't break any laws to do it. I want to earn as much as I have the opportunity to, and I really don't care if somebody across the way has more opportunity than I do.

In your country a person who has a goal will be able to achieve it if he really wants to, if he has the right capabilities. As far as I know, even the children of the rich aspire to start from nothing and earn money for themselves, and things like that. I know this from my own personal contact with Americans and from what's written about it in newspapers. It's well known that children strive to be independent and they even move to other cities and begin to earn their own money. They start to earn money early, even if it's only a small amount. Of course a person isn't to blame for being born into a wealthy or a poor family. But if a person wants to accomplish something, he'll have to work. I think that it's only in utopian systems such as socialism and communism that they have all these conversations about general equality.

I'm against characterizing a nationality, but it does seem to me that Americans are a very hardworking people, and in fact, when they speak about our having the same kind of economy as you have, I don't believe that we could have the same kind of success as you quickly because . . . well, I'm not saying that Russians are lazy, but there are some traditional things, views, and you Americans . . . Look, there were a lot of people here who knew how to work, but during collectivization the people who worked the best of all were called kulaks and they had everything taken from them.*

---

*Kulaks, or wealthy peasants, were able to produce in large quantities for the market. They rented land from owners and hired agricultural laborers to help work it. A campaign of "dekulakization" began in 1929. By 1930 their land and property had been expropriated and most kulaks, as well as many of their families, were sent into exile, arrested and sent to camps, or were killed. As new perspectives on collectivization emerge, some historians have condemned the campaign against the kulaks and their families as an unjust and tragic repression.

In your country you simply would have called them farmers! They were really the best people we had, they worked the best, and without a doubt everybody should have depended on them. But they suffered for that! That's one objective reason why things won't get better here right away.

And then I don't think it makes sense to place too much emphasis on the question of social justice, but of course this might just be the position of a Soviet person, because we've had to put up with far too much on account of these yearnings for social justice.

Of course in your country the problem of racism and discrimination still exists even though by law everybody is supposed to be equal, but at least people are talking about it. There are organizations that struggle with that issue, and, as far as I know, there's been some progress in this area. At least you can talk about the problem, which I think has objective reasons, because of the history of black people, after all, they were slaves, and of course that kind of deliberate injustice takes a long time to smooth itself out.

I myself am a Jew, and I've encountered anti-Semitism and some chauvinism. But the nationality question is more complicated to resolve than anything else. Look what's going on around here—in Karabakh, and the Pamyat society. It's always the most complex question because it means a complete change in people's awareness, and that comes about over a long time. I'm not saying there isn't a problem of black people in the United States, but I think you are at least trying to find some solution to it. But a black person born today as opposed to a black person born thirty years ago, when a black person might not have been given a job, or there were separate restaurants for whites and for blacks . . . now, there are antiracist laws thanks to what Martin Luther King did.

I don't know if everyone in America can become a millionaire, but I think that more or less everybody can earn a decent amount and have an average standard of living if a person knows how to work and isn't lazy.

I know there have been sociological surveys, studies that have shown that among the unemployed and the homeless there is a large percentage of people who don't want to work, who aren't completely healthy psychologically. And really you could say that here we also have unemployment. Everything on earth is relative. First of all, we have people we call *bomzh,** vagrants, homeless, people who don't work anywhere. Different kinds of people are included in those groups. There are criminals, people who are hiding to avoid alimony payments, alcoholics,

---

*The Russian acronym for "without a specific place of residency."

people who have had something unfortunate happen in their lives and just want to bum around, there are hippies, and so on. They've just started to write about the fact that this exists here.

And another thing about homelessness. You can't always call the conditions Soviet people live in "having a home." The standard of living is higher in your country, and the apartments are better. Here a lot of people live in communal apartments and in dormitories. If you showed Americans the way a large percentage of our population lives, they would say think that it was just a kind of flophouse, a slum, the kind of place homeless people live in in the USA. This is reality.

Unfortunately, our society tried to build itself according to the principle, "We are going to live the way we want to, not the way we can." For us that was the most important goal we set for ourselves, and it's not always an achievable one, no matter how beautiful it might be. We didn't know it couldn't be achieved, and that led to violence. We have to live in a way that is possible and solve the problems that exist here by means that are within our capacity.

ORGANIZING YOUTH:
INFORMAL GROUPS AND THE KOMSOMOL

"Informal youth groups"—that's become quite a fashionable term these days. They're very diverse both in behavior and convictions. At first their names referred to various groups and tastes in contemporary music—the *metallisty* (heavy metal), the *volnisty* (new wave), *rokery* (rockers), and of course, a group that disappeared a long time ago in the United States, hippies, punks, and so on. They're still popular here. I've had a lot of contacts with hippies, and there are a lot of things I like about them. But the word "informal" has become much better known in connection with the politicization of our society, in terms of political positions and outlooks. Now there are very specific political "informal organizations." There are many groups and popular fronts that have been quite successful in the Baltic regions and practically share power with the official authorities, for example, in Estonia. They resemble different kinds of clubs—people gather there for various reasons, united by their political views. There are elitist groups, where only intellectuals gather, and there are large mass movements. An ecological movement has grown too and become quite widespread in the Baltic and in Russia as well, because that's a problem that really does affect large sectors of the population.

I deeply admire the ecological movement, and, for example, I would gladly participate in the activities of a popular front, although in general I think it's best to remain independent. Of course, I'm glad they've emerged; it's both good and interesting that these groups exist, both rightist and leftist. I would probably be a leftist.

Now we have Pamyat [Memory], an anti-Semitic organization that is in general against anybody who is different. I don't think we have to quickly disband or arrest those people, but I think that as soon as we have a state based on the rule of law,* these groups will have to act within the limits of the law. In our criminal code we have an article that prohibits any kind of propaganda aimed at creating discord among nationalities, so I think that some kind of legal measures are justified.

There are also extreme left organizations, such as the Democratic Union. I've read their leaflets. Their position is perhaps not always the most rational. They speak out against the Party authorities, against a one-party system, and for them without a doubt the ideal is the model of the Western political system. They are skeptical and have doubts about everything going on here, even glasnost. I don't think anything is wrong with this—it's a completely natural phenomenon to have movements developing here both of extremists and more moderates.

If you walk along the Arbat† at any time of day, within fifteen minutes you can meet people from the most divergent tendencies, starting from the Democratic Union all the way to Pamyat. They discuss political problems, cultural problems, musicians play on guitars and violins; you can walk up to the wall and read the leaflets pasted up there from various groups, newspapers from the Baltic republics. It makes you think of Hyde Park. On the Arbat you can also talk about anything you want to, and the militia is pretty calm about it all.

We also have Pushkin Square, where there are rallies much larger and more organized than the ones that take place on the Arbat. Everything on the Arbat is much more spontaneous, and unfortunately the police and internal security forces can break up those meetings. There have been incidents when they've broken up rallies of the Democratic Front when they committed some illegal action, and they put them on trial, even though no long sentences have been imposed. I don't think anybody got more than fifteen days, but the fact is that it happened,

---

*The demand for a "state based on the rule of law" has been a central issue and rallying point of the reform movement. Laws on freedom of speech, freedom of the press, and so forth, are being proposed as part of the movement for a "state based on the rule of law."

†The old Arbat, in the historical downtown area, was blocked to traffic and turned into a pedestrian mall of stores and cafes. It has since become a major social and political center in Moscow. The Arbat mall is one of the improvements associated with Yeltsin's tenure as Moscow Party leader.

and they beat up people. A friend of mine who isn't a member of the Democratic Front was there, and he was taken away in a police van. They kept him for twenty-four hours awaiting trial, and only his knowledge of our laws got him out of there—he got in touch with his lawyer and he didn't receive any sentence, although if he hadn't known our laws he might have been fined or gone to jail for fifteen days.

So you see, the "informals" aren't completely free, but if you walk along the Arbat, you can hear them criticizing Gorbachev and Ligachev, cursing various members of the Politburo and the government; they curse everybody and nobody stops them. I think that's really good.

There used to only be one view of politics here. The way they used to treat people who thought differently—all of that is over. The informal groups, the dissident movement, they used to get a sentence for what they did, or get sent away to prison camps. Now none of that is connected with any kind of risk to their personal freedom; it has all become political activity.

After all, the most progressive people's deputies we elected, about fifty people, are basically from informal groups, and they are going to have their faction in our government. And that is an official organization! In these cases, the line between "informal" and official has become a little tenuous. They are still involved in the same activity, but they've become official. Still, in general the main characteristic of the "informals" is their independence from the authorities. They're independent in thought and in action.

I myself am a member of the Komsomol. Of course, I had already stopped harboring any illusions about that organization when I joined it, and I joined for a specific reason. Here, to this day, when you fill out an application form, there is a question: Are you a member of the Komsomol or not? This influences things to some extent, although probably not so much anymore, but it did when I joined. I had purely practical considerations. I won't make up any excuses.

I consider the Komsomol as it exists now to be one of the bureaucratic organizations that nobody needs. There's a lot of talk now about what the Komsomol should do, but the Komosomol can't do anything but try to think up things just to preserve itself. Because the truth is that it's worthless, and people join it for the sole purpose of getting into the university or to be in a certain crowd, but it's not a serious political organization. And in general I think that any serious political organization cannot have a mass character—and there are several million Komosomol members here! It's not possible for several million people to really have such similar views!

And what are the Komsomol's prospects? I'm not saying we should disband it, although maybe that really should be a first step. The Komsomol has several advantages that other informal youth groups don't have because the Komosomol isn't a grass-roots organization, just the opposite, it's much too formal, and in order for it to be effective, well, you can call it whatever you want, but it needs to be organized on a grass-roots basis. The Komsomol has been given some power. It is financed. And it doesn't refuse that money or that patronage. Although I do think that if the Komsomol would begin to do something serious, it would actually lose that patronage. But for now it is nothing more than a formal organization and there are people who believe in that, but I myself can't take it seriously, I can only laugh at what the Komsomol is now. Youth organizations have to be organized on a grass-roots basis.

I'm so unconcerned about the matter that I wouldn't even consider leaving a principled move. Going there and placing my membership card on the table and leaving that organization is absolutely meaningless. My sister, on the other hand, would have joined the Komsomol in the late 1970s or the early 1980s, in the period of stagnation. She didn't join the Komsomol—the only one in her class at school who didn't, although they put a lot of pressure on her and tried to convince her. She didn't join as a matter of principle, because our family at that time had a lot of contacts with dissidents. The dissident Orlov was a good friend of ours, and at that point they had put him in a prison camp. But she got into the university and they tried to convince her to join there, but, thank God, it didn't affect her fate.

Young people do have a lot of problems here. I think the problem of drug abuse exists but to a much smaller degree here than in the United States. Personally I've never come across it. But I have come across people who sniff gasoline. I haven't met those kids in school, but I've come across them at our dacha. It's become the latest rage—sniffing. But I wouldn't really say that the problem is that serious or widespread. You can probably find out about these kinds of problems from PTU students, because personally I'm in a certain circle of people, so I haven't really haven't come face to face with them.

RUSSIANS AND AMERICANS, SOCIALISM AND CAPITALISM: "THE WORLD HAS CONTRADICTIONS"

I've seen the television bridges with America. They're interesting. Thank God I've had the chance to talk with Americans personally. But for the majority of our population, and to some degree for me, too, the television bridges are really the destruction of certain kinds of stereotypes that exist and that have been cultivated by our propaganda. Or perhaps just the opposite—the disbelief in our propaganda created its own kind of stereotypes. Naturally, I'm probably not free from that myself. At times you don't feel satisfied with what the Soviet participants say. Sometimes they tell the truth and sometimes you can tell they want to show another country that we're doing better than we really are. For example, on one television bridge one of the Soviet women said that she never stands in line. And I know the television station received a lot of letters saying, "Just show us one woman who never stands in line!"

For so long they told us that everything there was bad, but people who actually went there saw that your stores have everything in them and that your people live much better than ours do.

I could agree with the point that not everything is fine in America and it's not almost paradise, and not everything they tell us *isn't* true. But look, when they tell you over and over again that there's unemployment in America and you get the impression that unemployment is the only thing that there is over there and that black people have a very hard time, when that's all they talk about and there's no access to an opposite opinion, and then you or your friend goes over there—although of course that happens infrequently; they don't let many people out—and then our tourists come back from the States or from other countries with huge suitcases full of things that are all scarce items here, of course a disbelief in official propaganda emerges, a great disbelief, and a person ends up going to the other extreme, which I consider less dangerous than believing that everything in America is bad. It's better to believe everything is fine in America, although I am against any kind of extremes. But this is probably a question of people's ability to think independently and to always be free of propaganda and understand that there is a thing called dialectics, the world has everything, it has contradictions, it's not all black and white.

I've been fortunate enough to have had contact with Americans, and there's a lot more information now in the press about your country. The average American, it seems to me, is much less politicized than the average Soviet. Perhaps this is because the average American is less dependent upon politics. When Americans come here, the first thing we do is start to ask, "What do you think about perestroika? What do you think about Gorbachev? What are your elections like in the USA?" The Americans' answers are lively enough, but I would hardly say that those are the questions that interest them most. But actually, ideally, that's the way it should be. I think that when a person doesn't get involved in politics it's a sign of a certain state of well-being. I think there are two things that can kill everything that's alive in a human being—daily life, the kitchen and all of that, and politics! They force you to spend too much time on them.

When a country is governed in the most part by the economy, politicians and politics have to submit to the economy to a certain degree, and politics become far less important. In our undemocratic, monarchical conditions, it's extremely important who the king will be—if he'll be good or bad. Now we have a good king who is doing something absolutely strange for a king—he is undermining his own power and trying to form a kind of democracy.

It's difficult to compare our leaders, because Reagan* is America and Gorbachev is the USSR. They are both important political leaders. Gorbachev is undoubtedly an unusually important figure because he took such a burden upon himself, and it's very rare when someone from his milieu begins progressive reforms. It was easier for Reagan than for Gorbachev because there he had a developed country with a good economy that can take care of itself. I don't think an American president could work in our extremely difficult conditions.

If we take the average American schoolchild, you have a wonderful tradition there that older students are supposed to earn money for themselves. And they try to spend it without consulting their parents. There simply is no opportunity around here for schoolchildren to earn money for themselves, although it would certainly be desirable. And— of course, this might be a stereotype—Americans value money more and are more attentive to the problem of how much they earn, to their careers. Here in this country, for certain reasons, it's possible not to work but still get your pay. In the USA you have to work to earn money. That's not bad! An American is supposed to go to college, or university, get a profession and earn money, have a family. Then there must be a car in the family, if I'm not mistaken. People who are well off try to get out of the cities and live in the suburbs in two-story houses.

There's something else—this might or might not be a stereotype— Americans are people who have a very narrow field of specialization, and outside of his own profession the American turns out to be not very well educated. When American schoolchildren showed up in our school, it turned out that none of them knew Somerset Maugham, an English-speaking writer who is well known here. Even though they were educated people they didn't know who he was!

I think in general that we have two approaches to education—American and Russian. In Russia at the beginning of the nineteenth century,

---

*George Bush had only been in office a few months at the time of this interview, and Ronald Reagan was better known.

perhaps even earlier, education was valued in and of itself, regardless of what one could get out of it. People tried to get into the *gymnasium* or *lycée*, and it was considered very prestigious. Our schools are still based on this. Unfortunately, most of the knowledge we get isn't really necessary later on. But in America, from what I know, people have a wide choice and the opportunity to study whatever is most interesting to them. Concretely.

I don't really remember the Marxist definitions of capitalism and socialism that we studied in class, even though the characteristics Marx gave are already outdated. After all, you continue to change as well as we do. The phenomena of what we call capitalism I would consider to be: freedom, a highly developed economy, of course, minimal limitations and restrictions—although I think there are restrictions in the areas of ecology, finance, and laws against monopolies—freedom in politics, democracy. Basically, I have a positive impression of that system.

And what is socialism? This is a question that is torturing everybody now, because there are articles discussing what it is we've built so far, what it is we wanted to build, and saying that in many ways it was utopian. It's not realistic to have a system functioning in this way. Our history is evidence of that. In order to build socialism one would have to ... well, in general we had a totalitarian government and an absence of democracy, repression, and very few pleasant things. We're headed toward a complete breakdown, and that is why one could say that there is no socialism.

In general I am against ideals. I think that humanity really likes to set ideals for itself and then tries to achieve them, but setting up a goal is the easiest thing of all. The goal of building socialism might be the best in the world—the idea of equality and well-being for everybody—but the real question is how to achieve it. This is what Dostoyevsky wrote about—nothing good can ever be created through violence, and here there was violence, and therefore we were not able to create anything good.

I think that things have to develop more naturally. When capitalism developed, it didn't set itself these goals, but here there was this goal—building communism. And nobody knew how to achieve that goal.

MEN AND WOMEN

It's true that women have more difficulties than anyone else here because we live in a society of shortages and women are the ones in charge of housework. In America you just go off to the supermarket and buy something that can be cooked up quickly, in five minutes.

Our women are truly great women, and yours couldn't keep up with them. A woman here spends eight hours at work, takes care of her children, does the shopping, and stands in long lines to buy things, the most basic things, and then she cooks—and of course you spend unthinkable amounts of time in those lines. Our women carry around huge bags, walk around with such tired faces; they come home only half-alive. So the major burdens fall on their shoulders. But it depends somewhat on the family. If the husband is a good one, he helps. Still, women are traditionally the ones in charge of housework. It's so hard to do housework here, and it all lands on her. A good husband helps with the housework and understands that if he doesn't it will be very hard for the woman alone.

In this matter I personally have some patriarchal ideas, and I think that the woman should take care of the kitchen and the housework more than the man should, even though the man should help out. I just don't really believe in emancipation—that attempt to achieve equality between men and women—because there are certain natural functions that determine every person's character, and I think it's completely natural that a woman should take care of the children and men should be the breadwinners and try to support their family. For women that is not the most important thing. The man should try to take care of the family's material needs. And a woman, if she wants to, should work. There shouldn't be any obstacles in that sense. Of course, in that case she will just have a heavier load, but . . . Perhaps my ideas are old-fashioned, but this is the way I think about it.

I have this idea of the nineteenth century—although of course this probably applies more to aristocratic families—where men were truly the stronger sex and women the weaker. Women were lovely and men would protect them and take care of them, get enraptured over them. And this emancipation, well, some of these demands end up in absurdities—you can't kiss a woman's hand because that lowers her dignity. I think that's absurd.

Raising children is primarily a woman's responsibility because she's a mother; she's the one who gave birth. There's a Russian saying, "When there's no father, a child is semi-orphaned, but when there's no mother, a child is completely orphaned." It seems to me that a mother should take care of her children, even though a father's role is also important. A mother should be able to spend an hour and a half each day educating her children and a father twenty-five minutes. This is a completely natural process. It's all related to the conditions of our daily life, and after all, a woman generally is the one to maintain the home and keep the family together. That's the way it turns out. And it's bad when it doesn't. If the home breaks down, I would tend to blame the woman for it more than the man. Working out problems depends more on the woman than on the man.

There is a sexual revolution going on here. I can't say that I favor it. Attitudes toward girls, and girls themselves, have gotten much freer. Different ideas about honor. In Russia, especially among the peasants, it was always considered a life-long shame when a young girl had sexual relations outside of marriage. Now it's gotten much freer; we have the problem of teen pregnancy. Of course we certainly don't have the kind of sexual freedom you do. Perhaps it's a natural process, but I don't really like it.

My school has special characteristics; most of the students are the children of intellectuals, let's say it's a privileged school, so they are pretty strict about these things. Girls can't even wear makeup to our school; the principal prohibited it. This isn't the case of all special schools, but in ours there is a tradition of a certain kind of behavior, of general culture. Somebody from an ordinary school or a vocational school could tell you better than I could. I have a friend studying in a trade school for the arts, and it's much freer there. Intimate life begins there at a much earlier age.

Traditionally in Russian culture, talking about sex is considered totally improper, especially among adults. Young people are freer of course. Many people here blush when you talk to them about this. Just talking about it! Adults here are very conservative about this. There is a sexologist here, Igor Kon, who is considered the top expert in this field. He writes that we're paying the price for being so sanctimonious, that we're totally ignorant in this area, we have completely primitive notions about it. Of course we need to talk about it, but for some reason it's considered completely indecent. Discussions about sex here are still in an embryonic stage. If they show a bed in a film, if they show two people in a bed in a film . . . Once on a television program on the differences between erotic and pornographic films they showed completely harmless clips from films. They even showed a spicy moment from Fellini's *Casanova,* and did that create a tempest! They got so many letters, such indignation! One of our satirists, Mikhail Zhvanetsky, speaking about the film *Little Vera,* said it was the "first Soviet sexual act." It really is as if that sphere of human life didn't exist! They're just beginning to talk about it now.

In my case, I am the one who started talking about it with adults, not they with me! They're less free than I am—in conversation, in any case. But I wouldn't say that my parents are conservative. I know of parents who, the minute conversation starts about that, will say, "What? You talk about that with children?"

My sister has her own firm convictions about this, and perhaps she has had conversations with my mother about it. Kon, the sexologist, wrote that there are channels of communication about this between mothers and daughters, because it's related to medical issues for young girls, but young boys only get their information from the street.

A PATRIOTIC TOUGHENING UP

MAXIM

Fifteen years old. A worker. He left school after the eighth grade and has not completed his secondary education. He is taking a training course in a culinary school in order to become a chef.

Maxim is hard to pin down. He agrees to come to my dorm to talk, but several times he doesn't show up. When we meet again he is apologetic and promises to be there the next time. Eventually we finish the interviews, but it takes months.

Maxim is blond and handsome, a combination of boyish shyness and grown-up seriousness: he is already a working man! At first he finds it strange that I want to interview him, would find his ideas interesting. He is quiet during our initial talks, blushes now and then, doesn't quite know what to do with his hands, looks away, down at the floor, when I ask him something difficult. But by the third time we meet, it's clear he's been thinking about our previous conversations and how he would like to present himself to me. During our fourth and final conversation we talk for hours. He even offers to bring a friend of his, one of the "unwashed Arbat hippies," to meet me, so I can interview that kind of Moscow teenager. Unfortunately, this meeting never materializes.

When I left school after the eighth grade, at first I wanted to go to the Merchant Marine Academy in Leningrad, but there were too many hitches for me. At the end of the school year I had a concussion, so I had to take my final exams in the fall. Right at the last minute, literally, I fell out of a tree and got a concussion. I was laid up in the hospital when everybody else was taking final exams. So I had to take them in the fall and didn't get my papers in on time—you had to get your papers in early to the Merchant Marine Academy. So I thought, "Where else could I go?" I wanted to go to vocational school to be a cook, a chef on a ship. And then I got this good opportunity to go for a job as a chef in Moscow. I wanted to go because there was a good teacher there. He's

MAXIM

spent a lot of his life abroad, and he knows how to cook, and generally he's a good teacher.

I work in the restaurant complex belonging to the Hotel Moskva.* I work as an apprentice cook in the Stolichny Restaurant. I like the work a lot—if I didn't like it I wouldn't have gone there. Like any work, it requires your attention, even though sometimes you get tired. But I really do want to work. No work is awful when you want to do it. I used to like cooking at home, not just preparing the food but making it look good too. I went to work in a restaurant because in a cafeteria they usually serve already-made plates. In a restaurant you design the plates yourself so it looks nice for the customer, and you get pleasure from having prepared such good-looking plates.

My parents are satisfied that I'm working now, because even though I've only started working very recently, I can already help out some with the cooking at home. It's useful for me as well as for them and doesn't take up much time, so I've still got free time. I work only four hours a day. That's how it is up until you're sixteen here. I work from ten to two, and then I have the whole evening free. The rest of the day and the whole evening. And since I don't have to get up early for work, I can go to bed late.

My mom's thirty-four now. She works as a men's hairdresser in a hair salon. She was born here in Tyoply Stan.† She went to school here, she graduated from the tenth grade and then went to vocational school. After she finished school, at first she worked as a hairdresser; that's what she wanted. Then she went to a different vocational school, one for business, and worked as a salesperson. She worked in sales at Men's Fashion, downtown somewhere. But it was no good there in the store, and in any case, she wanted to work in her own field, so she found a job as a hairdresser. She's been working as a hairdresser for five years already. She really likes that job, she says she doesn't need another one. Even though a hairdresser here makes very little, measly pay, she says: "No matter how little they pay me, I still like this job." She makes about one hundred rubles. Those are minimal wages, that's how it is here, unfortunately. She works every other day. One week comes out to three days, the next, four. All in all, Mom likes her work. She's bored when there's no work.

Dad's older than Mom. He's thirty-eight. At first he played hockey for Dynamo (in Riga). He was serious about it. He lived in Riga three

---

*A major Moscow hotel and restaurant, and therefore a prestigious place to attend culinary school.

†A neighborhood in southeastern Moscow.

years. He was a first-stringer for Dynamo from 1970 to 1973. Then he got into a lot of different institutes, but he left because of training, never graduated from any of them. Then he started going to Gubinsky Energy Institute. For oil. Then he went to MAI: the Moscow Energy Institute. He also got into the institute for physical education and sports, but he left early for training because the teams were making their picks and there was no time to study. He graduated from vocational school as a supplies buyer and worked as a supplies buyer in the Prague restaurant. He worked there probably five years, then he left there, too.

Now he works for a neighborhood health and recreation complex in Lefortovsky—that's a district with a lot of dormitories for the foreign students from the Moscow Energy Institute. They have everything there, a cafe, public baths. He's in charge of one of the groups there. He does pretty much the same work as the workers, but he has overall responsibility for everyone. They provide the services there—people come to the baths and you have to give everyone good service. And when someone's out sick, then he has to do their job himself; sometimes he has to work as the cashier. He's got many professions combined. Who wouldn't take something like that? And he thinks that any work is honorable. Any work. But all the same, of course, I don't know, he didn't go ahead with coaching. . . .

He really loves hockey, of course. It just can't be that he doesn't regret it. He watches all the hockey matches, his team. He only gets worked up over his own team. So that's that. He didn't become a coach, that's just how it worked out. That's the kind of man he is, if something happens to him, he keeps it to himself, he doesn't talk about his problem so as not to bother anybody else. He doesn't want anyone to think something's going on with him. When it's really necessary to talk to someone, to get help, then he will; but just, you know, to talk, he never does. He keeps quiet. He doesn't make out like he always feels bad. But maybe he does feel bad about it, because when he was playing hockey they were his best years, he was really young. Probably he does wish he was a coach now. He still worked at it after that, but just a little. It's just been about a year now since he stopped playing. For a while he worked as a sports instructor at a stadium near our house. He coached the youth team there. But it's so . . . It's not a very good team. And then it didn't work out there anymore. Now he earns about 180 rubles.* . . . He also works every other day, like Mom. It's just that while my sister was

*His parents' total income of 280 rubles a month (the average worker's salary is 250) for four people means that Maxim's family is quite poor, particularly given the general increase in prices over the last few years.

little . . . that's why he took that job, so he could work every other day. In general, I share Dad's opinion that well . . . any work is considered honorable, whatever it may be. So in my eyes, Dad's just fine.

The only problem in our family is one that other families could have too, the problem of living space, an apartment. That's the only thing like that. We live in a three-room apartment, but we share it with two other families. It's a communal apartment, and we have only one room for four people. One of our neighbors in the apartment is never there. He doesn't keep anything there, just an empty room. And the other one is a woman with a child, a really small child. When I come home, I can't do what I feel like because my parents might not want me to do something or they make me show them what it is. And even if I want to have friends over, you know, where would we sit? We just wouldn't fit in one room. Mostly I stay at my grandmother's. My grandmother lives alone, in her own apartment. So I'm with her. At least I eat there so as not to be in the way at home and so that everything's all right for me too, because in our communal apartment you come home, you want to take a bath, and your neighbor's in the tub. And you're sitting there after work; it's not that you're dirty, it's just that your situation is . . . unpleasant. It's the same thing with the stove. You want to get dinner ready and it's taken; you can't just shove them aside . . . so you sit and wait. There's always someone around. They haven't solved the housing problem around here yet. Of course it's better to live separately! Mostly I live at my grandmother's. Grandma and Grandpa live together and you feel free around them.

As I said, my parents and sister and I have one room for the four of us, and our neighbor has a child. My parents went on vacation somewhere and I was studying and working . . . I had to get up early . . . and that kid runs around till late, you can't get to sleep, and then you finally get to sleep and you want to go on sleeping, but he gets up at seven or eight in the morning and starts to run and scream. . . . He's got something to be happy about. And that's it. You try to fall asleep then, your head starts to ache. We've been on a waiting list for seven years already. It's awful! It's good my grandmother doesn't live far away.

LEAVING SCHOOL

I wasn't very interested in studying when I was in school. When my sister comes home, even though she's still little, I don't know . . . she just sits down and can do lessons for days on end. She gets all A's. As for me, I was never like that.

At the end of the eighth grade somehow I started to have more friends. Sometimes I just didn't go to school at all. I had already made up my mind to leave and go to work. Otherwise I would have stayed on and studied. Of course every citizen is required to complete a secondary education, and I'm setting myself up in night school now. Selection for night school will be in December. I'm arranging to go to a night school for working youth. After work lets out I'll go study, for three years. You get an education. You go there only twice a week and you get a full secondary education.*

At first, school was very interesting, but then my attitude started to change as the years went by because my opinions never jibed with the teachers', and it's useless to argue with your teachers. That can sometimes end very badly; the teachers start to regard you unfavorably. And if they start to regard you unfavorably then the progress you make changes. School was fun until about the sixth grade. . . . I didn't have so many friends then. Of course I had my small circle, but pretty much they were school friends who sat down to do their homework right after school. Then sometimes we'd get together in the evenings, go out, when we were still little. We'd go home and go to bed early. But then I got to know older kids. Sometimes we'd stay out real late and didn't get enough sleep for school. I came home late. Of course I had problems with my parents for coming home late, but my attitude toward school had already changed. I didn't have the time or any particular desire to do my homework. I'd think on the way home from school, "I'll get home and do my homework," but then someone would call, or I would run into someone and that was it. My mood for the whole day, regarding homework, had changed. I would go to the movies with someone, then on to somewhere else, just to hang out. Then I wouldn't have time to do my homework. The next morning I would get bad grades again in school. In the end, when I got to the eighth grade, I understood that you could just behave well: don't cut class, don't fight with your teachers, and basically everything's fine. I finished the eighth grade. If the teacher says anything it's better just to keep quiet. So I did. When I had a conflict with a teacher I tried to keep quiet and just not tell the teacher he wasn't right when he wasn't. A lot of school kids finish school that way, because once you start to say anything in protest, relations change, because the teacher is already an older person; he's already been through life and here you have children just starting to try out their voices. Basically, you can also understand the teacher. During

---

*Maxim is actually a dropout. Secondary education is supposed to be universal and compulsory, but by the time Maxim and I met for our last conversation, he still had made no moves toward enrolling in night school and indicated that he had no intention to do so in the near future. He felt that he had no real need to finish his secondary education.

a whole day he can get really tired. There isn't just one class studying with him but many classes during the course of the day. So that's what happens. In my opinion it was better to keep quiet, because it isn't anybody's fault.

I didn't know where to go after eighth grade. I didn't think about it. I don't even know how to explain it. I just didn't have any ideas. I set myself the task of finishing eight years of school and studied as well as I could. As with everybody, sometimes I didn't study my lessons and sometimes I cut classes too. My grades depended on how I studied, because there are things you want to learn. Generally speaking I liked history. I always got good grades in history. I used to take part in the History Olympics. We would get together with other districts, other schools. History was the only class I liked. You find out what came before: a few years ago, a few hundred years ago, a few centuries ago. It was all very interesting. I liked the sixteenth and seventeenth centuries best. That was such an interesting time. Peter the Great! I liked Peter the Great as a leader and as a person. He had enormous strength of will; he only slept four hours a day, the rest of his time he gave over to work. He made a city as beautiful as Leningrad. I love those structures, all along the Neva! A beautiful city, gorgeous. And Russia's cultural level became significantly higher during the years of his reign. Mostly there were only Russians in his government, but after his death foreigners became representatives and ministers. Peter the Great brought about a major strengthening of the Russian fleet. Then he won back some lands that had belonged to Russia long ago but had been occupied by the Swedes. He hacked open a window to Europe, that is, during his rule Russia was able to communicate with other countries; it developed its commodity circulation, solidly. . . . It was a prosperous country.

Our week of practical work at culinary school isn't the same as in a vocational school. . . . In vocational school, basically you study and work comes second. Here it's the other way around. Practical work experience takes first place and learning from books is secondary. We study, but we don't get a secondary education. This isn't called a vocational school, but rather an enterprise offering on-the-job training;* you get strictly professional experience here. In our enterprise, where we work, there are people from all the restaurant complexes in Moscow, from all over the place: from different restaurants, cafes, and other institutions.

---

*The distinction is significant. Vocational schools are mandated to provide young workers with a secondary education in addition to giving them training in a particular trade. The school where Maxim studies does not offer academic coursework, and it is not supposed to be a substitute for a vocational or general academic school.

People are all different ages, some come after military service, some come right out of school, after the eighth grade, and there are older people. But they only take people who really want to be here. It's not that people don't know what they want to do so they become cooks, because only those who have the desire go there.

You go there and get processed for work, not like in vocational school. In culinary school you're studying for yourself. In school you don't have much responsibility because your parents still answer for you, but here all the responsibility is yours because this is work. It's entirely different from a school or a vocational school. . . . In school you were completely sure they would pull you through, that in the eighth grade they would give you good reports and good grades. The ones who didn't want to study got pulled through. It's not going to be like that anymore now: starting this year, they're not going to pull you through anymore; whoever wants to study has the right to study, whoever doesn't can go and work.

Now I'm in what's called Courses for Upgrading Professional Qualifications. It's an intensive course and after it's over you can work as a grade-three cook. That's the cook who does the lowest-level work, I don't mean work that's dirty, he just does what's easier. He works with the machinery: juicers, meat grinders, mixers. Lately I've been working the smorgasbord, pouring out the drinks and preparing them to be served, and in the appetizer department I prepared the ingredients to make salad. The salad itself is made by a cook of a higher grade. We've made soups: *borshcht, shchi,** other soups. We've done all kinds of slicing. We've sliced the components for dishes and prepared ingredients for borshcht. And for *solyanka*† too; we had to cut special cubes. We cut up ham, meat.

I have my last exam in August. I'll pick a card like at all exams and it will tell me to prepare three dishes. I'll have to prepare those three dishes, and when I make them, they'll confer the title of grade-three cook on me. I'll start working immediately. Actually I'm doing the same work now that I'll be doing then, but my salary will go up and I'll have a grade. Now I get fifty-two rubles a month.‡

We have a trade union at work. Let's say I got sick; depending on how much I'd worked, I'd get paid, sometimes even half my salary. You get sick and receive your salary. Trade union assistance. And if you've

---

*Cabbage soup.

†Russian soup made of meat, sausage, and various vegetables, including sour pickles.

‡This is notably higher than the student stipends at a vocational school, which average between twenty-five and thirty rubles a month.

put in a lot of time you get your full salary. The trade union offers free stays at Pioneer summer camps, free transportation, and free trips to a spa during vacation, too. I feel workers should have that. Plus the trade union does a lot of active work—Party work—and they send people to competitions and to rest camps on days off. The trade union defends workers' rights.

I pay 10 kopecks a month in dues, and when I work full time it will be a little more. But I don't regret it. Let's see, if they take 10 kopecks from my 50 rubles now, then they'll take 30 kopecks from 150; I won't mind even if it's a ruble.

Another reason I went to work was because I was going to go to the Merchant Marine Academy. I love the sea and ships, but I spent the whole summer in the hospital and didn't get to fill out my application. So I didn't go anywhere. I didn't want to waste time, so I went to become a cook, because now after the army I want to work as a cook on a ship. I've been on ships; I have a friend in Sevastopol and I went to visit him. He works as a captain's assistant on a big ship, and he took me along with him, for a week or two. I really liked that. In the summer I always try to get to the sea.

BECOMING AN ADULT:
THE ARMY, WORK, AND RESPONSIBILITY

I want to serve in the military. I think that your character is strengthened in the military. There are completely different conditions there, not like in civilian life. There are intensified sports activities, you have to get up in the middle of the night, maneuvers; in general, a person changes there. It's a patriotic toughening up. A soldier defends the motherland and when he comes back to civilian life he comes back strong, he comes back through all his trials and all the sides of his character should be stronger. They have sports activities there and political training, and those military conditions sort of temper you. I believe you have to go through military service. I want to test myself, to see what I'm capable of. I want to go into the navy. First of all, I really love the sea. Secondly, you serve longer in the navy;* you have to hold out longer. And I just like the navy. You can get toughened up like a man there; that's good.

A lot of people don't want to serve in the army. I don't understand people who don't want to serve. They're mostly society's castoffs, splinters. That kind gathers on the Arbat, walking around singing songs

---

*Three years rather than the two years required in other branches of the military.

about how you shouldn't join the army; they run away from the army. Of course, it's bad to have to leave your loved ones, those close to you, but I believe it's something you definitely have to go through, even if it's only to strengthen your character, to be tougher.

I think that if the pacifists want peace they shouldn't be fighting against the army but against something else, because as long as there are people who want war, the army will exist. And there are people like that. When they no longer exist, then there won't be an army and there won't be wars. But there are people who want war. I don't even know what to call them. There are people who need war. War doesn't come because someone gets offended and then there's a war immediately, but instead to win new territory and resources. When there aren't such greedy people who want other people's riches and land, there won't be any more war.

Still, only those who want to should go into the military. I do think we need a volunteer army. If you want to, serve, if you don't, don't. For now men are being remade, even if it's by force! But personally, I believe you only become serious after the army. I had this friend . . . before the army we'd walk along the street and just laugh. Well, he was just home on leave, and now he thinks before he talks. The army strengthens you physically and morally, and I believe it's just valuable to be there. Even if it's just two years, it's necessary.

The navy's three years. I'll be a cook in the military. I can fit in everything there: cooking and the physical regimin and the training. I think that after that I'll be more serious. I'll get through my childhood. Now I still feel like going sledding sometimes. Childhood's like that— you have snowball fights. And I haven't met any adults . . . well, only very, very rarely do they have snowball fights or go sledding. And I often feel like going sledding! And I'm almost always in a good mood. I don't have many worries yet, and the ones I have are just at work. It's like that for almost all children. Later on in life they'll have a lot of responsibilities, and they'll be more serious too. There's family, responsibility for children, for your wife, how you can earn more.

When a person starts to work he develops a sense of responsibility. When you study the state pays for you, but on the job you're working for the state and for yourself. So it comes out to be your personal money. You earned it yourself; no one gave it to you, you didn't just find it. You can get really tired at work, it's very hot there, but then when you come home you take a shower and you feel like an honest man who's put in an honest day's work. You can eat in peace, go somewhere, or go for a walk with a friend or a girl. At school we kids flew out the door at the end of the day as soon as the torture was over.

When the bell rang for the end of class, everybody shot out like bullets. But you leave work calmly because you know you've done what you had to do.

When I was in school I had an unbelievable amount of free time; I even made more for myself—I cut classes. I did all kinds of nonsense: we hung out, we were rowdy, sometimes we wound up at the police station. And now that I've started to work, it's not that I don't have time, but I don't want to waste what time I have; you want to go somewhere. . . . I try to go to the movies or to hear music. There's no time left for just wandering around.

At first I studied well, in a special German school, almost no C's. But then I started hanging out a lot and there was no more time left for German, because to study well I had to stay at home. Once I just had to try it—I cut once, then a second time, and I became freer. I started to miss a lot of classes and couldn't take everything in anymore. I became a worse student and I transferred to a regular school so they wouldn't kick me out. I just hung out with my crowd, guys a year or two older. We'd go to the movies or just sit around somewhere and talk about things. In general we didn't do anything. In the mornings they don't show too many films, so we'd go to the cartoons. We had a lot of excuses: we said they let us out early, or that we were going on a class trip. . . . There were times when the police would take us back to school; we were in our school uniforms. They'd come up to us and ask why we weren't in school, and you'd say either you were sick or they had let you out early.

Sometimes we fought among ourselves, with someone from our neighborhood, not the ones we were hanging out with, just someone else from the neighborhood. There were a lot of reasons why. Somebody stole a girl or insulted someone; that's why we fought. But we only fought with our hands. I was only at the police station twice. My parents knew about one time. One evening we were sitting in an entryway and it turned out some girl had gotten killed there. And they said we did it. And two days later—I was at home asleep, it was during vacation—they came to our house; I was at home with my sister, my parents were at work, and they took me away. They took me out with my hands behind my back and into the patrol car. And my little sister was home all by herself. They took me to the police station, sat me in a chair, and started to interrogate me. They asked me what I had used to beat her with and said my friends had all confessed. I said I didn't kill anyone and hadn't even seen her. They showed me a picture of this woman. Then they said she had survived. She was still alive, even though at first they thought she was dead. So once they called us in and told us not to go anywhere, that they would call us, and they never did call. Everything just quieted down. They held us about four hours that day. My little sister called Dad at work and told him and he came home right away. I told him everything. He understood, of course, that I wasn't guilty. Then nothing happened; they didn't call again. Dad forbade me to come home late; he said I should start getting home earlier. One time they picked me up and then let me go. They could see we weren't really doing anything, just being rowdy among ourselves. It was late and they let all of us go.

I don't think I need the ninth and tenth grades. You don't do anything in particular. When it didn't work out for me to be accepted anywhere and I'd already applied to the Merchant Marine Academy, I wanted to make a joke and went to the school principal and said that it didn't work out for me anywhere and seeing as it was already the end of September I'd be coming into the ninth grade after all. She got so scared her hair stood on end. And when I told her I was just kidding she was so happy. . . . I don't want to go to college or anywhere. I'm going to work. Maybe later on I'll understand that it's important to study—we have as many night schools as you could want. I have a friend who went on to the army without finishing his secondary education. He became an officer, and he's taking the exam now. For now, I don't have the strength to work and keep studying at the same time.

Right now I'm not involved with the Pioneers or the Komsomol, but with the working class . . . you work and are useful to people and it's not bad for you either, it's a pleasure because it's interesting there. You cook and make everything look pretty and you're a worker too; they have a lot of privileges: free trips. You can get travel passes, and there are day-care centers for those with children and nurseries and Pioneer summer camps. But I didn't decide to come here because of that. I didn't know any of that then. I only found out when I started working here, and I started here because I like to cook and because you can get on a ship with this profession.

Right now I don't really pay attention to people in the governing organizations. I spend more of my time with the working class. There are a lot of workers here. I don't come in contact with Komsomol and Party activists. We have Komsomol members at work, but I'm not planning to join. I'm not interested in that. It's not that I'm not sure, it's just that I don't know what real help the Komsomol can be to the State. *Real help.* I just don't know. And I think the State has more need of concrete help: work . . . and these meetings, gatherings. . . . They have Komsomol meetings during working hours. I just can't understand that. They take people away from work for some meeting, just to talk about something. If they really want to talk, let them stay after work, or before work. You shouldn't have meetings during work! It was the same way in school. Instead of class there'd be a meeting. It's better to have to sit through class and listen than to go to those meetings!

PERESTROIKA

The basic thing I've noticed about perestroika so far is the cooperatives. It's true there are some cooperatives like those parasitic fungi that grow on trees and only drink out the sap; they only put out garbage. I respect the produce cooperatives. They have good produce there. Then the leasing and brigade contracts. Cost-recovery, self-finance, economic accountability—all that.* It's good.

But still, even though here, in principle, people are supposed to be equal, there are several strata in our society. Now that we have the cooperatives, some people work there while others work in a factory, and they all do the same work, but the ones in the cooperatives get a lot more money. And because of that we are seeing the development of poor and rich here. In our country, that is not supposed to be. From the very beginning it was decided that everybody should be equal, and it should remain that way. But there are always some people who are richer, and I don't know why.

Then there were elections for people's deputies; that was also interesting to watch. There were crowds of people at the subway station listening to campaign speeches. We didn't have any of that before—you came, threw in your ballot, and that was it. Now you elect whoever you want. During the period of stagnation everyone closed their eyes to illegal actions. The higher governmental bodies didn't want to see what was going on in the country. There was a lot of bribetaking and corruption, and everybody stole from work. The only people who lived well were those who were dishonest.

Stalin destroyed a lot of good people: a lot of leaders, marshals, military types. But Stalin won the war and for that you have to give him his due. If it weren't for him, the war would have been lost. People followed him like a god into war. They wrote that when there weren't enough planes or tanks for the front, Stalin called in the executive in charge and told him that if the equipment wasn't ready on time then he'd be shot. And they gave a measly amount of time. But he [the executive] got it all done. At a time like that, that's good. For some

---

*These are all part of the economic reforms aimed at making enterprises responsible for their own finances and making it more difficult for unprofitable ones to survive.

things people need fear to work. Because nowadays you're not afraid to take things from work. . . . But where we work, for example, everyone's afraid of the inspector and no one takes anything. That's also a kind of repression.

Personally I don't take anything from work. Maybe it's because I've only first started working. I haven't gotten used to it yet. I'm afraid of the chef. He's such a respectable figure that you just . . . if you do something wrong or badly, he can make you wash the pots, he can make you work every day, not every other day, but every day. He's mad at me for some reason now and I have to work every day. I only have one day off: Sunday. That's also terror.

But it's in the interests of all workers now that nothing disappear from the plant. It will be their loss. They're not financed by the State; they have to make their money back.* So actually, nobody's taking things from our place now.

I would like the country to become freer somehow. Of course a lot of restrictions have been removed, but it would be nice if the borders were at least open. According to what the people who have traveled to America or West Germany say, life there is really interesting. If you have money, if you've earned it, you can buy a car at sixteen and get a license to drive it. Here you can drive only at eighteen.

I don't really think I'm a free person, because if I were a free person I could go wherever I wanted, but that's not possible here. I'm free only within the borders of the Soviet Union. And freedom means complete freedom of action, when you do what you feel like. You don't have to work if you don't want. You want to work, work—you don't, don't. You don't bring home any money then, but nobody bothers you. You want to study, study, you don't, you don't have to. We don't have anything like that. Here they start to scold you right away: Why aren't you working? We have a statute on parasitism; if you don't work they can put you in prison. It would be interesting to know if they have that in other countries. Do you have a statute on parasitism? Do you put people who don't work in prison? We have people who just don't want to work. Someone has the resources to get by, but they can put him in prison for that!

Another problem that has to be solved is the problem of food. Here if you come home from work and want to make yourself something to eat, you have to drag yourself from store to store and look for something, even though you don't know if you'll find it or not. In my neigh-

---

*Another reference to reforms that make enterprises responsible for their own losses and profits.

borhood there's a lot of *limitchiki*,* people who come into Moscow by bus to buy things. They're occupiers! They occupy the stores! They come from Ryazan, Kazan, Orel, from the provinces, the periphery; they come like starving masses! After they've been there it's useless to go into a store—they buy up absolutely everything, butter, cheese, sausage. And I get to thinking, look, they're the ones who are producing all of this stuff, so why don't they have any? That's not right! They should at least be left with a little!

And it's not just having all the food, but it should be quality food, without nitrates. That's the most important question. Just recently I was in Kankovo, outside the city. I ate fish and drank some water from the river and we got sick. I was in such bad shape I couldn't walk. My head started to really ache at work and they told me to go to the doctor. I went and they told me I had chronic acute gastritis. I asked what from and they told me from an infection that was in the water and from the fish.

There's also the problem of transportation. They should produce more individual means of transportation. People can be on a waiting list for a car many years. And public transportation is horribly crowded; it's really hard to ride. It's stuffy in summer; you get all sweaty. If there were more private cars it wouldn't be that way.

I think we have to follow the examples of a lot of different countries. We shouldn't pollute the environment. They say that in America there are a lot of national parks—like a whole country. Everything's clean. And we have almost none of that. Take the Volga, an age-old Russian river . . . or the Yauza, which flows through Moscow. Peter the Great went down it. There's a place there where he put together his first regiment. . . . If I were a Party leader or general secretary, for example, I'd build a monument on the spot where that regiment was organized, because the whole Soviet army began from that. And right now there are cars, warehouses, and garages on that spot, and the River Yauza is solid metal through and through. Twenty-five percent oil in that river! Everything's really polluted. And all the nature around it is covered in dust and dirt.

---

*The term *limitchiki* generally refers to workers who live in the outskirts of Moscow, attracted to low-paying temporary jobs by the hope of obtaining a Moscow *propiska*. Here Maxim may be referring to the people who come to Moscow from the provinces in order to buy goods that are unavailable in their own towns. An estimated 2 million people pass through Moscow daily for the sole purpose of shopping, and there is considerable popular resentment toward them among Moscow residents, who say that they buy up food intended for the city's inhabitants. An ordinance was passed in the spring of 1990 that required people to produce proof of Moscow residency in order to purchase food in Moscow stores.

We have to create the kinds of conditions in which people feel good. The kind of mood you're in is the way you'll work, and every person who lives in the Soviet Union and loves it will feel glad if everything is good. We have to foster patriotism. There isn't any now. Nobody praises the country now, but there was a feeling of patriotism under Stalin. Everyone loved our motherland, and for some reason we don't have that now. We won the war even though Germany was stronger and better armed because everyone was for the motherland and for Stalin, and we made it to victory. We don't have that now. Something to die for. Right now, in general, everything is kind of strange.

What happened was awful, but I'm in full agreement with him [Stalin] that he fostered a feeling for the motherland. I myself don't have that kind of feeling now. And I don't know how such a feeling might come up in general. I don't know how to explain it, but there isn't the right moral atmosphere now. At the moment I have some kind of . . . I just don't care somehow. You work and that's all. Nothing's interesting. I don't need anything. The main thing is that no one hang the "parasite" label on you. You do your work and that's it. I live as I please. I don't bother anyone and no one bothers me. Of course I don't have a feeling of patriotism!

Look, we have organizations of Nazis here now. I'm neither a Nazi nor an activist in the Communist Party. Not a Komsomol member. I'm not interested in either one. I simply go to work and that's it. Quietly. None of them has managed to interest me, not those who are against Soviet power who stand around shouting, and not those who go around saying, "Long live the Komsomol!" I'm just an average guy. I work quietly. And somehow or other I don't suffer from that. I don't go to any meetings, which only take up time with nothing going on but talk; I can go to the movies when I have free time, or to the park. I don't waste my free time on nonsense.

I go to church, but it's not so much that I believe; I've been baptized and I wear a cross; so I believe what's to believe. I go and listen. Grandma took me to communion, like washing my sins away; the priest reads the prayers. I went by myself recently. The old ladies there babble something or other and their babbling is supposed to cleanse you if you go there to church. So it's just that it washes your sins away. I like it, it's beautiful there. I just go there for myself. And then I think that everyone should live peacefully and that's what they preach, not to fight. I think that's how it should be. Mom goes sometimes, I don't know about Dad. He's also been baptized, but I don't think he goes, only very rarely.

I'm not particularly happy, but sometimes . . . there are moments of happiness, of joy, like when you go out into nature for example, a river there with a campfire, a starry sky, everything is peaceful and you don't need anything, you forget about everything. No worries. Now that's great! But otherwise . . . I don't know.

I'm sort of counting on perestroika now, that it will change something. I still can't come to terms with the fact that all kinds of good materials are just lying around on construction sites. They break them, shatter them; it's ugly to look at; it's harmful and a loss to the state.

MEN AND WOMEN

Women have equality with men now. They work just like men. They've started dressing like men, they have the same hair styles. Of course they're significantly different from earlier times, when they only wore dresses. At the beginning of the twentieth century they all pretty much wore dresses, but then after the Revolution began . . . At first they wore overalls, then they started wearing pants on a daily basis. Basically I believe that this is a normal occurrence because with time anything can happen. In Scotland, for example, the national dress for men is a skirt. So why, if men's national dress in Scotland is a skirt, shouldn't women here be able to wear pants? It's a normal occurrence.

When girls grow up, the only way they're different from boys is that there are girls who become more serious because they have to become mothers and to think about future generations and can't behave so casually. The ones I know are still young and all behave like they did in school . . . hang out, relax, mostly they go to discos, and for some reason, I don't know why, I just don't like it. I go very rarely, only when I'm in a really good mood, if someone invites me. Otherwise I never go. I don't like to. A lot of them try to spend as much time as possible with that crowd. Before it was good. You'd go to the park with a girl, stroll down some long alley almost till morning, walk along the embankment. . . . Now everybody goes to discos. It's not because I don't like the noise, it's just a wish for something else. . . . You go there to meet up with someone. But I don't want to do it that way. I want to meet in some other place, even in a subway station. If I'm with a girl, I'll go if she wants to, but I like listening to music at home better. It's more interesting. Because at a disco there are all kinds of shrieks, different kinds of groups: heavy metal, punk. . . . None of that really interests me and that's why I don't go. I've never cared much about either punk or heavy metal. It's not that it's bad music, I just never had the desire to listen to it. Punk tunes aren't bad, I like a few of them.

I've had a lot of girlfriends, but not just one who I loved and made me not want to look at anyone else. That hasn't happened yet; maybe it's just too soon. I've had many girlfriends and they're all different. One of them works in the Komsomol organization; she's so strict, she's nice, but her character . . . I don't know, she was like a stranger to me. I don't like these Party and Komsomol meetings. I don't even know why, but it seems like somebody is always screaming at all these meetings and I like quiet; I don't like to argue with anyone, insist on something if it comes up. . . . Well, it's just better to keep quiet. Everything was so strict in their organization, and the way she dressed . . . she didn't like to wear pants. And another one was just a regular girl who dressed like everybody else, she was fun; it turned out she fought with her parents, tried to stand on her own. But not that other one. To her, her parents were on a pedestal; she'd speak with them using the formal "you." And me, I can't talk to my parents that way. It's what I'm used to. If something comes up I don't like I can tell them and they discuss whether to do something about it or not. Sometimes we wind up having arguments if I really don't like something and they insist on their way, but mostly we can talk it out peacefully. I think I relate normally to my parents; they don't get offended and I don't get angry with them. But for her, she's done strictly whatever her parents have said, since childhood. Even if you don't like it, you still have to do it. I never had to go through anything like that. There was the one girl, if her parents asked her, told her to stay home, she did, didn't go out, and I knew another who, if she didn't want to stay home and if she thought it was still early, say about eight o'clock, of course she'd go out, she'd make them let her go. And the other one, if they said to her, "Stay home," she stayed. She was doing her homework all the time, sat there till it was done. That's a good quality, but a lot of people don't have it now.

Everyone has the right to work where and how he wants; it doesn't depend on your sex, it depends on your mental abilities. But for all that I think that everyone should work wherever he wants, I'm against my wife working and against women being in politics. I don't think that's women's business, and I'm against the fact that a woman has become the ruler in Pakistan. It's not that I'm protesting against it, it's just that it somehow doesn't sit right in my head, that a woman would be in politics. I believe it's not women's business, but men's especially. Basically, women are softer than men, kinder, although sometimes women are much braver than men. But their goodness can very often do them in, and if a woman is ruling a country, the smallest mistake because of negligence, her purely feminine goodness might make her feel sorry for someone, and then that might turn out to go against her. I think that's wrong. As for my wife's not working . . . You see, you come home from work, all tired out, and she's not there, let's say she gets home from work later. Right away you have this gloomy mood for the whole evening. As it is you get home from work in a bad mood, but if your wife's home and everything's clean and she's not tired . . . Women's work is in the home, although I don't have anything against it if, say, on my day off, it'd be a pleasure to help out with the cleaning. But basically I believe that women should do women's work and take care of the home. You see, before girls were taught household work from childhood, but I know a lot of them now, those around sixteen or seventeen years old, who simply can't cook and somehow . . . I don't know any who are particularly handy when it comes to cleaning the house or who are good at doing things around the house. There are very, very few like that. Man is the strong sex, you see. He should bring home his pay to his wife so that she can keep up the house and support her husband, and then you'll have a good family. This is the main reason couples fight: here the husband's come home from work and his wife isn't back yet, so he sits and worries, imagines all kinds of things; the wife gets back, the husband's come home from work tired, he hasn't made anything to eat, and the wife gets home, she also wants to eat, she's also tired, and she still has to make supper. Women get very tired; they work at home and on the job too. In general I'm against a woman working.

There are many cases when women have turned out to be braver than men—during the war when the women didn't turn over the wounded partisans, even though they sometimes really suffered for it. They were beaten and tortured. There were only singular instances when a woman went over to the enemy's side and betrayed the motherland, while many men during the war left to join the Nazi police. I can't even imagine it. Let's just say they didn't like the policy, the course the Party was taking, let them just go to another country, if you don't like it, leave, but you have to treat your own people humanely. They even joined the Nazi police once they were in the other country, and then they started to torture people from their own villages, to mock them. Not one woman went over like that. Many old women were superstitiously against Soviet power but hid wounded partisans all the same, for the sake of the people. Zoya Kosmodemianskaya, for example; they tortured her, but she didn't say a word even though she knew they would beat her, she had a choice. If she had talked, she'd be alive today. They killed her brutally. A woman isn't answerable for herself alone; she has more responsibility placed on her because she's responsible for her children. Whatever kind of child she might have, an invalid or deformed, he's still the best to her. She won't let anyone hurt him. A mother always loves her children more than the father does because she suffered all the pain giving birth to the child. Sometimes she even loves her child more than her husband.

But women shouldn't be in the army. Because a woman should always remain a woman. She should be beautiful, shapely, soft, and she could become coarse in the army; a woman and a machine gun are entirely different things. Boys should have strong characters; women should have strong characters but their bodies and in general ... Women couldn't serve in the army and be soft. You always have to yell and be harsh there, and for a woman ... A woman must remain only a woman.

A woman here works at her job and then comes home and starts to work again. She has to run around to the stores with a child. That's how it is now. My conclusion: a woman shouldn't work. If she wants to work then let her work and raise the children and run around to the stores. If not, then she can just raise the children.

"IT'S TIME WE REALLY BUILD SOCIALISM"

YELENA
Sixteen years old, ninth-grade student

Yelena is tall and elegant. Her long hair flows freely; she is almost always wearing a skirt or dress. Her movements are delicate. She smiles and laughs quietly, pulls her hair away from her face, but never ties it back. Her soft manners are deceiving: in debate she can be fierce. One day I see her arguing with several of her closest friends. "Strikes?" she says loudly, as if incredulous. "How will strikes solve anything? It would help more if people would do something at work!" No one agrees with her, but she doesn't give up. "Okay, go ahead, strike!" she continues. "Bring the economy down to complete ruin!" One of her friends retorts, "How much further could you bring it down, anyhow?"

Yelena tells me that this year has been one of the best for her. She is coming into her own. Her family received a larger apartment and moved, and she transferred to a new school. She decided she had to make a quick adjustment and lost no time developing a new circle of friends. They're inseparable, even when they argue about politics.

Next year I'll finish tenth grade, and hopefully I'll be accepted into an institute of higher education. I'll probably go into a teacher training college, into the history department. It's hard to get in there, but I'm going to try. You have to know a lot to be accepted.

I'll graduate and get married. I can't really imagine what my husband will be like, but I have thought about it. It's impossible to say concretely, "Oh, my husband will be like this or like that." I really appreciate the qualities of honesty and kindness in men. Loyalty. As far as the structure of the family, I think that a husband and wife should both manage the family equally. But in my family, for example, my mother manages the housework. My father only does things once in a

YELENA

while. You might say that my mother is the head of the family. But in my family I would like all responsibilities to be divided equally, even though men at the moment are not at all the type to do housework and they're childish. And really, even if I wanted to, I couldn't trust a man to do the housework. He wouldn't be able to. Even though it really does depend on a person's character, there are a lot of men now that simply can't do housework. And when I cook, I don't like anybody else to get involved. I like being in the kitchen by myself. Of course it would be nice if my husband would be the same way. But I've only met one man, my cousin, who loves to cook, and he knows how to do it, and he does housework. He's the only man I know who does. I haven't seen that anyplace else, and mainly women are the ones in families who manage the money and who have the last word. If something has to be decided, it's usually the woman who decides. But women of course try to divide that equally—not just, "I said that, and that's the last word."

My mother is a very independent woman, and, for example, if we're going to go someplace or take vacations, well, usually she does try to decide that together with my father, but usually it ends up the way my mother wants.

She works and all of the housework is on her shoulders. Of course she gets tired. I try to help her with some things, but not with everything. She doesn't really trust me to cook very often. She cooks and washes the clothes. I'm the one who cleans the apartment most of the time.

My parents work the same amount, and they come back from work together. Usually when my mother comes back from work, she goes right to the kitchen to cook dinner without even changing clothes. She usually spends evenings after work in the kitchen, and my father spends them on the couch. My father gets tired, his work is hard, not in the physical sense, but morally. He works with people, and such people . . . they're hard to work with.

Both my parents work at an electronics factory, but in different departments. My father works where they produce televisions and my mother where they make radios. I don't know how they relate to their work, but when they come home, they don't have much of anything good to say about it. When they talk to each other about work, they basically make unflattering remarks. Really their work is sort of strange. Now, for example, it's the end of the month and they come home very late, they leave early in the morning, but the way it turns out is that at the beginning of the month at work they don't do anything; they don't have anything to do, but toward the end of the month they have to catch up to the plan, and then they start coming home late. But that's the way it usually is around here as far as regulating working conditions goes, and I don't like it. I don't know how they feel about it, but for the most part they come home from work and they curse it up and down. In my opinion a person should work in such a way that he doesn't complain about it and regret it.

My parents, for example, and many other people as well, I think, just say that they have a lot of work and that they're tired and don't have time to do anything. I don't think that can be called apathy; I think that's pessimism. They blame everything on work, it's always work, work, work, and on Sundays they don't want to go anywhere, maybe they'll go to the movies, but they won't go out walking or leave the city; that's too much for them. And we start to get used to that, too, but I don't like that way of being. I think people should be just the opposite. People spend their whole life at work, on their business, they have absolutely no time. But I think if they really wanted to . . . a person shouldn't spend his entire life sitting in one spot, watching television in an armchair. I can't imagine doing that. Although I don't know how my life will turn out, at least I will try my best not to end up sitting in one spot. I only have one life, after all, and it seems to me that we have to try our best to see as much as we can, to learn as much as we can about what is going on around us, and not only in our country—although we should at least see that. I haven't been any farther than the area around Moscow. And I really want to travel around this country, not to mention seeing how people live in other countries! But it all leads to the same question—in order to travel, you need money.

It's mainly young families that are dying to travel, and they can't because young specialists get paid a ridiculous amount, 150 to 200 rubles. So it's a paradox, because when people have already worked a certain number of years they get paid more, and then they start to spend that money, not on trips, but rather to buy a car, a dacha, furniture, a cooperative apartment,* which is very expensive. And then when they've gotten everything that they need—their car, their dacha, their apartment—they begin to live quietly and they don't feel like traveling

---

*Most apartments are built, owned, and distributed to people for a minimal rent by the government or through state-run enterprises. It is possible, however, to purchase a cooperative apartment. These apartments are built by cooperative housing associations and are bought, at a high price, by people whose current living space is below the standard allocation of square meters per person. (This figure is set by the government and varies in different cities depending upon housing needs and availability.) There is usually a wait of at least several years to purchase a cooperative apartment; despite the prohibitive price, there is great demand for them. The waiting period for a state apartment can be far longer.

anywhere. When they start to get money, the desire to travel has already gone. It's a real pity.

They don't actually tell us to sit at home and not go anywhere. Perhaps it's just that children, no matter what their level of awareness is, simply copy their parents. In other words, no matter what their awareness, children become the same kind of people as their parents. That is really very sad. I think that every person ought to have something of his own, but the way it seems to turn out is that they copy their parents and become the same kind of people. If parents don't take their kid anywhere from early childhood, don't ever take him on trips, the child gets used to this, and he doesn't care about anything, isn't interested in anything. I don't want to live quietly.

A lot of the way my future turns out depends on me, but a lot of it depends upon my husband. I don't think that the most important thing is running after wealth, after a car, a dacha. I would like two or three children. Probably two. I'd like my husband to earn enough so that we could live well, so we wouldn't have to worry about economizing. But probably that's not possible, especially in the first few years of work. Young specialists get miserable wages.

As far as housing goes, even though they're saying that by the year 2000 every family will have their own apartment, somehow I don't really believe that. On every lamppost you see there are notices about young families looking to rent an apartment. It's very hard for young people to get apartments—an entire forest can grow before you'll get one! And in order to buy a cooperative apartment you need a lot of money. It's very hard for young families. I don't know how it will be in five or six years. We'll see. They have to build more housing.

Personally, in the future I would like to be free, completely independent of my parents financially, and actually, in all ways. Never to depend on anybody financially. And there is another kind of freedom —independence in views and convictions, but that is not so much a question of politics as it is of character.

I don't think my parents are completely free. But I do think that they say whatever they want to, everything that is on their minds, in their souls. I think they are fairly free people. I see this from the point of view of what is going on in general. The situation in this country has changed, and all people have started to feel freer, and I think my parents have as well. But at the moment I am more interested in these new political things than they are. They seem to be pretty critical of this new information. I try to find out more than they do. I don't think that there are things that I know better, at least when I talk to them about today's political questions they are able to offer enough information, and sometimes they disapprove of what I say. Just like that, no matter what evidence I have.

I would be happy if I had complete financial independence. A job you love, that you go to as if you were going off to a holiday, and not with thoughts like "curse this place," wanting the factory walls to just come tumbling down. The truth is that I can't imagine this, because I haven't seen a person who really gets pleasure from his work. Really, I haven't seen even one. I look at my own parents and I don't know how they manage, although in principle they chose their own work, and perhaps they liked it at first, but now ... They come back from work irritable, tired, there are always unpleasant things happening there, and at work the bosses are always coming around as if they were owners. They make them work second shift and stay until late evening, showing the bosses what kind of shape the factory is in. And after that they come home angry and tired, and in a bad mood, and there is no joy, either. Of course all of those daily worries, the stores, getting food and clothing, ruin a person's good mood, and once you've been pushed around in the store and yelled at by the clerks there, you come home in a bad mood and you take out all the frustrations that have accumulated on others. People shouldn't sit around at home, they should travel with their families, their children, as much as possible.

GENERATIONS

What's going on now should excite people. They can speak out, say what's on their mind, express their positions, and now that we have this opportunity we mustn't let it slip by. But people of our age right now— well, there is really very little we can do; we still know very little about this life of ours.

We're preparing ourselves! We're beginning to think differently for ourselves. As it turns out, teachers are playing a very small role in this. Our teachers are there only so that we learn their subject, and that's all. I don't know about my parents. I do talk to my father about what's going on, and he thinks that if what's going on now doesn't just wither away and develops further, then maybe we'll be able to say that our government isn't completely rotten. But he thinks that his generation can't really change very much. They've gotten used to it, they grew up in such an atmosphere of silence, and it's the most difficult for them to make a transition to a new life. It seems to me that we are the ones who have to prepare ourselves for something different.

I don't think my parents will be able to live a different life. They don't have the necessary consciousness. They were taught in a certain way and they learned it well.

Look, if a person was stealing—let's say the director of some factory—now he's hiding himself behind a burst of enthusiasm and he's begun shouting on every street corner "Perestroika, how wonderful it is!" and at the same time he keeps on stealing. In other words, you can't make him over. Perhaps that's pessimistic, but that's my opinion. If a person was an honest person, he'll remain that way.

It seems to me that a little paradox has appeared here. In the past, people got by on sheer enthusiasm. The Chinese railway that connected China and the Soviet Union was built by young people on sheer enthusiasm. Then the people who built it were simply arrested and accused of espionage in the 1930s. Now we have an opportunity to tear down the old ways, start over again, but there's no enthusiasm anymore.

This is a serious problem, trying to raise people's enthusiasm. We've never seen anything like what happened then. People lived to do something, to build. With the years that enthusiasm grew dull, and it's still dull now. It's gotten to the point that people simply don't want to do anything. Particularly young people. They don't care about anything, they aren't interested in anything, they don't give a damn about any art exhibits, only strange rock concerts. Now the most important task—and it's very complex—is to raise people in such a way that enthusiasm will once again appear. Although of course I don't know—there has to be some reason for it to appear. Even if everybody agrees that they would like to raise the level of enthusiasm, it won't happen by itself! But I don't think all has been lost.

Look at the earthquake in Armenia. In the very first hours voluntary brigades began to form and people went there to try to sort through the debris. For some reason it seems that people's best qualities come through when there is a disaster. It's a shame of course that that's the only time when they do. Look at Chernobyl. On the one hand, there was the most horrible kind of negligence on the part of the workers of that station, but on the other hand there was absolute patriotism on the part of those fire brigades. On the first day of the disaster the chief of that station took his own children out of town in his own car to their relatives and didn't warn anybody, and the general evacuation first began on the seventh day, even though in the papers they wrote that they were evacuated the day after the accident. That turned out to be false. Such a tragic event—how many children died, how much land, almost all the land in the Ukraine, has been ruined, and in Belorussia as well.

On the other hand those firefighters were young people, most of whom have children, new families, and still they went into the fire, knowing that there was radiation there, and they were exposed to radiation and so many of them died, so many film directors and cameramen

died as well. They didn't spare themselves. And the construction workers who went in to lay cement under the foundation so that the radiation wouldn't sink in further . . . It's strange—you only see these kinds
of relations between people when there is a tragedy.

The enthusiasm didn't disappear, it exists, but those same firefighters who threw themselves into the flames—what is there for them
to do with themselves in peaceful times? Their fire station is basically
inactive, and they have nowhere to channel their enthusiasm. Even if
they're burning with desire to do something, in peaceful times, in our
situation it's hard to get through all the bureaucratic apparatus, all the
red tape.

So on some level it's a question of bureaucracy, not enthusiasm.
Because what can one do with that enthusiasm? Let's say a group of
enthusiasts wants to organize an expedition to the North Pole. Just to
organize it they need equipment, among other things. And to get all of
that you have to get such a number of documents and go through so
many bureaucrats, the enthusiasm is simply lost. Most enthusiasts are
young people; they have a fire within them. Young people want to do
something, in essence they have a kind of fervor. And when these
young people are faced with such a lack of confidence in them, when
they have to collect such an immense number of papers, when absolutely kind, sincere desires meet with totally opposite sentiments—one
person wants to adopt a child and the other says that in order to adopt
you have to assemble certain documents, and if they can't do it they
won't be able to adopt. This is all very difficult to restructure, this way of
thinking, this way of life; we have become so accustomed to it that
getting away from it isn't possible. It's so difficult, it will take years. But
enthusiasm, in my opinion, is eternal. In hidden forms. But it's hard to
cleanse ourselves. Look at our schoolmates. Nobody will even go out
on ski trips. They all want to stay home and watch television! It comes
from our parents, this is the way they've raised us, in peace and quiet.
We stay at home and watch television, we don't want to go anywhere,
we just want to sit quietly and be left alone, and this also dulls our
enthusiasm. We're used to closing our eyes to everything and not paying attention to anything. And that's the way we are going to raise our
own children.

PERESTROIKA

This is where perestroika begins: people simply have started to reflect
upon our past and about things they didn't question before and didn't
know. Before they used to shout about how everything in the Soviet

Union was fine and somewhere in another country things were bad. Now everybody understands that's not the way things are; things aren't as simple as they used to say.

No matter which direction you look these days, the picture is pretty sorry. Our economy in any sector of production is in a deplorable state. Take industry, for example, all you have to do is simply stop in at a grocery store. We in Moscow are in a state of horror when we go into the shops, but if you compare us with other cities in the Russian federation, things aren't so bad here. Moscow is actually very well supplied because at least we can manage to buy some things, but in other places people have ration cards for meat; they get half a kilo of sausage per person per month. I don't know how to explain that to an American: *one half-kilo of boiled sausage per person per month.* There are terrible articles being written now by workers from other places who stand at their machines, eight hours at an open-hearth furnace, big strong men, and they get half a kilo of sausage a month. They simply don't get any more meat. The meat situation is really bad in other places.

Look, it turns out that there are some regions in the Russian federation, near the Ukraine, southern regions, that send us all they produce—grain for bread, meat, milk—and they themselves are left with nothing and go hungry. I don't know how that happens. I know this because I have relatives who live in those kinds of cities, and when I go there to visit them I am horrified by what they have in their stores. If there is anything, it's only in the cooperatives. Sausage from the cooperatives, canned goods, three times as expensive. And people buy it! It's very hard for ordinary people to buy things there now. But at least those cooperatives save somebody a little bit.

The cooperatives have been a mistake in perestroika. We've already understood that without cooperatives our industry is going to have a hard time. They already passed a law on individual labor, but before those kinds of laws are passed, they should think through what might happen because of them. The principle of cooperatives now is that they are supposed to compete with each other and above all with government enterprises, but the way it's turned out there's no competition, just outrageous prices, and the quality is certainly not improving. So now we've ended up with cooperatives that don't actually compete with the government, as well as a market and rackets and everything else imaginable to boot! For example, we have the Rizhsky Market, a center for all kinds of shady deals where things got to such a point that not too long ago there was a roundup. Usually there's a lot of business there on the weekends, and one weekend they sent several police squads and they went around and inspected everybody. The result of that inspection was that they arrested half of those wheeler-dealers. There was speculation going on all over the place and a whole mafia of cooperative members. It turned out that in order to have a stall at the market they didn't pay the government for permission but ended up paying other cooperators! There's a special cooperative that distributes the stalls in the market, so in order to sell there, people had to pay an enormous amount of money. A lot of them didn't want to pay, so they went there without permission and just sold things without having a stall. The police found a lot of that kind. Somebody was selling more than a hundred copies of *Children of the Arbat* right from his car. That's fashionable literature, about the personality cult.

I saw a television program and then my mother told me about an eye doctor who is the best in the Soviet Union, S. Fyodorov, who founded several clinics where they feel that they have already begun to live in socialism. They live wonderfully! They operate on the system of cost-accounting. A nurse who would normally earn 80 to 100 rubles a month earns 400 there. A nurse! And accordingly, a surgeon there gets 800 rubles. They live wonderfully, and the atmosphere in the clinic—there's no quarreling, gossiping, everybody cares about their work, they do wonderful operations, and they already created mobile units on airplanes, they go to Africa to perform operations. They're going to do this on ships. Fyodorov did things the way they're supposed to be done and was able to do this in our difficult circumstances. If all of our enterprises would live and work using cost-accounting and care about the result of their work, things would be fine around here.

GLASNOST

I was at a rally yesterday for the first time in my life,* and the most important thing is that it was an unofficial one in which very many

---

*This demonstration, in spring 1989, was one of the first spontaneous mass demonstrations in Moscow. It took place shortly before the March elections of candidates for the Congress of People's Deputies. The issue was the formation of a government committee to investigate possible wrongdoings of Boris Yeltsin, precisely at a moment when it was clear he would win a majority of votes in the Moscow race. The establishment of the committee invoked popular wrath, and this demonstration drew a crowd of thousands who marched from Gorky Park through downtown Moscow, where people assembled in front of the Moscow City Council. Yeltsin went on to win more than 90 percent of the votes in the election.

good and bold ideas were expressed. But my first impressions were not very good. That rally went on for two hours, but everything was clear after five minutes. Most of the time went to shouting, "Yeltsin! Yeltsin!" "Down with the Committee!" and so on. That mass of people staring into the mouths of those speakers made a bad impression on me. And the mood of that crowd was such that if anybody had said anything against Yeltsin, even one word, they would have torn him to pieces. If they would have told them to storm the office of the Moscow Council, that crowd would have stormed it. Of course I'm glad the meeting happened, and even though there were some real firebrands there, people basically behaved themselves well and eventually dispersed peacefully. The police behaved well. I'm for this way of expressing oneself, because other ways don't lead anywhere. That's already been proven, by history, by everything. So probably this is what's necessary. But people would spend their time more usefully at work.

They've really been after poor Yeltsin. I remember Yeltsin from when he was mayor of the city. They took him from that position, but he managed to do quite a lot for Moscow, little cafes appeared, little stores, they constructed the Arbat pedestrian area, they rebuilt parts of the city, and they got rid of him. And that got people upset. They got rid of Yeltsin—and people already loved him—and now they've formed some commission, and then he was nominated as a candidate [for people's deputy] and they've formed a committee again, using the names of some anonymous workers, and when they tried to verify those addresses it turned out they didn't even exist. How vile! Our leadership should be ashamed. Once again they won't get to the bottom of this and give us evidence about who is guilty. So much for truth in the newspapers!

A lot has changed in these four years, even if only that we can say whatever we want and not be afraid. That rally we were at yesterday shows that. People gathered unofficially, nobody was hassled, and the Moscow Party leadership—the most bureaucratic organization in the city—said nothing. The fact of that meeting is evidence that we have achieved something. Both in the press and on television they broadcast and write about things they would never have talked about before.

But still, so what are demonstrations? We had a demonstration and nobody said anything, not in the press, not anywhere. Have a demonstration, don't have one! It makes no difference. True, basically it's a big step, if people begin taking to the streets. It used to be that we shook our finger and said, "Look at the West! All their demonstrations, and they keep breaking them up!" Now basically the same thing is happening here. So far this has aroused great interest in me, but I don't have an opinion yet. I have to find out what demonstrations really are. And then there are all these groups—Pamyat, Memorial,* one defends Stalin, the other just the opposite. . . .

I think that lately here they have started to tell the truth much more in the press and on television, about things we didn't know before. We've learned about the personality cult mainly through the press; they print a lot of materials about it. I collect articles on it, and I have a whole packetful, mostly on the personality cult. I think they're right to pay a lot of attention to that, but they're writing very little about the 1970s, about the 1960s. We know that those were years of stagnation— but we know very little about it concretely. And then the material about our history is sometimes full of contradictions. What we are reading doesn't mesh with what we hear, what they teach us in our history classes. And we have no idea how to begin to approach this material and get through it. Recently we had a lecture on "A New View of the Pact between the USSR and [Nazi] Germany" that was signed in 1939. There was an article about that in *Literaturka*,† and we heard that the man who wrote that didn't use our archives—they were mainly German archives. He used Goebbels's diary and our newspapers from those years. Yesterday there was an article in *Literaturnaya gazeta* not only about that pact but about the situation in the country in general before the war. They write about 1937 to 1946, mainly about the re- pression, and about the situation here before the war. Our historians are stubborn about not wanting to admit that there were mistakes, simply fatal mistakes made before the war.

They've been showing the election campaign on television, how they're elected first at the workplace. They've been showing all their yammering— I don't know what other word to use to describe it—all their fights and

---

*Pamyat is a Russian nationalist group that has been at the center of considerable controversy. Ostensibly founded to protect historical monuments in the Russian Republic, its anti-Semitic nature became clear shortly after its creation. The fact that several promi- nent writers were among its leaders caused great dismay among pro-perestroika forces. Recently, Pamyat's activities have intensified and become much more violent and openly anti-Semitic. Memorial is a group of pro-reform academics and intellectuals devoted to the de-Stalinization of Soviet society. The organization's main goal is the full disclosure of Stalinist repression and the public exoneration of its victims.

†The diminutive name for *Literaturnaya gazeta*, the official newspaper of the Soviet Writers' Union. Even before the period of perestroika and glasnost began, *Literaturnaya gazeta*, one of the favorite publications of intellectuals, was known for its critical views and articles.

scandals, they interrupt each other at those meetings, get up on the podium so they can start talking themselves, and slander the person who just spoke before them. This doesn't make a very good impression. It's good they're showing it to us, but I don't like the way it's happening.

What I'm learning affects the way I think about my country, but it's hard to say how. The fact that they're talking about all of this is good. The most important thing is for them not to stop talking about all of this now. On the contrary, everybody should be given access to archives and documents.

It's hard to determine now what really corresponds to the truth because we can't form our opinion even about one lecture now, or one article in a newspaper, because they all contradict each other. It's very hard to form an opinion. We have to dig deeper.

I'm counting on the success of perestroika. I want to hope for it. . . . But when Khrushchev came to power he put an end to the personality cult at the Twentieth Party Congress, and it seemed as if it had become possible to say anything, but then, gradually . . . well, now they're starting to say that there were two Khrushchevs, the one that emerged at first and then another one, after a few years in power. Everything began to be closed off again, people weren't allowed to speak the truth. It seems to me that nobody knows yet why that happened. Perhaps power ruined him. This is why I am cautious about our present perestroika and how it's going to end up. Of course I hope perestroika will triumph, but just hoping isn't very much. I don't think my parents believe it will work. They don't say that, but I can feel that they don't believe it will be successful. Four years have already gone by since Gorbachev became general secretary, and nothing here has changed in our economy.

At home, the minute the news program *Vremya* appears on the TV screen we always watch it, and any time Gorbachev is on we watch him too, but not the way we did during his first years in office. We've already stopped taking it so seriously, and I think he talks a lot. Of course, it's clear why . . . but still, he should talk less. He needs to demand more. Our people are such that if you don't demand anything from them, if you allow them everything, well, you could end up destroying everything good, destroying what's begun. And I don't think he's very demanding.

But even if they are saying that perestroika has its shortcomings, basically everybody is getting swept up in it. They're being inspired by what's going on now here. That's probably the right thing, because the process that's going on here now might really be able to change our lives quite a bit. And they're starting to show us that life needs to be changed, even though I think we knew it before and saw that there's nothing in the stores, we saw that and we didn't need newspapers to tell us that we were living poorly.

SOCIALISM

I don't know right now what socialism is. Look, Marx and Engels developed an idea—the principle of socialism: from each according to his ability, to each according to his need. We certainly don't have that. We've started now to restructure and build everything over from the start. I don't know what we're going to end up building!

I cannot say precisely what socialism is. But I imagine it to be a society where there is true equality. As it turns out, there's no real equality here now. Our constitution says that all citizens are guaranteed equality regardless of their social position, but we're a long way from that. It's not that way at all. And it seems to me that it should be!

For example, someone who works in a ministry gets special privileges, clothing, and an ordinary worker doesn't have that and he can only buy what he finds in the shops. I don't think that's right—the worse the conditions of a worker's life, the worse he will work. And that worker is the one who feeds and clothes that person who works in the ministry!

We've started to look much more at ourselves from a critical perspective. Americans are starting to come, many to share their technical knowledge, from various companies. Lenin said something about how we needed to learn from capitalists, and now for once we've decided to do just that. Really learn, to work, above all. We've stopped viewing other countries as if we don't need their help, as if we ourselves were capable of building communism.

I think we do have to learn. And we've decided for now not to build communism. I don't think it's possible to build communism. At the moment, in this country, that's impossible and unrealistic. Because what is communism? In the first place, it means people have complete trust in each other, and from each according to his ability to each according to his need. And if you look at the kind of people we have nowadays, you see it's impossible. Maybe someday, but not for a long, long time.

I guess it's time we really build *socialism*.

SEX: "THEY TELL CHILDREN FAIRY TALES"

In our country there are no sources of information. In other countries they have special books on sex education for first-graders, and as they grow up children are quite at ease about it. Here even people my age don't have these sources, not to mention those in lower grades. They tell children fairy tales, that they found them in a cabbage and things like that. At our age we find out about this [sex] from underground books, retyped, rewritten by hand. But there aren't sources that are available to everybody. We have a class in school called the Ethics and Psychology of Family Life that is supposed to prepare us for future family life, but the way they're teaching that course now, nobody needs it. It doesn't give us anything. They talk about what a young man should be like, what a young woman should be like, how we imagine our future husband, and I think we know all of that by ourselves, and anyhow, we talk about it a lot, among ourselves, so I think that class is unnecessary, at least the way they teach it now. And the way it should be taught is a big question.

They're talking now about lifting restrictions on pornographic films, but I don't think that will lead to anything good. People shouldn't be sanctimonious about it, but opening all the doors and lifting all restrictions won't lead to anything good either. I don't think we're ready for that.

THE WOMEN'S QUESTION

The women's question is really complicated. If you go into a store, for the most part you see women standing in line to buy sausage, and you'll never get out of there without having somebody scream at you. Or in a collective that's mainly female, for some reason, they don't understand each other, especially the women, and there is such anger, somebody is always mad at somebody else. Perhaps there are problems at home, in the family, arguments, and they've gotten used to blaming everything on fate, or placing the blame on another person. A woman in my opinion should be delicate, tactful, but our women aren't very different from men. And women should be kind. A woman after all is a kind and loving being. But now you don't meet up with those kind of women who are truly kind, delicate, or sympathetic very often. I don't know what's going on, but it seems to me that for the most part women are bitter. About somebody or something. I don't know why.

There are some who think that women shouldn't be involved in politics. The only woman I know of who really participated in politics was Alexandra Kollontai, and that was a long time ago; she participated in the Revolution and after the Revolution she was the first woman-diplomat. A woman has to be really talented and intelligent to participate in politics. But I don't think women really have a place in politics. There are intelligent women, but they're not in politics. I don't think it's a woman's business. It's just accepted here that a woman is a housewife, and politics is serious business, and the responsibility is great.

Becoming a Worker:
Dima, Lyosha, Alexei

Dima, Lyosha, and Alexei are all friends. They live in a working-class neighborhood on the outskirts of southeastern Moscow and in their free time participate in an amateur choir of Russian folk music run by the Ministry of Vocational Education.

They love being together. They insist that our initial interviews be done as a group, and they invite me to Alexei's house to talk. On the map it seems as if their neighborhood, Tyoply Stan, is quite near Moscow State University, where I live, but they are afraid I will get lost if I go on my own. We agree to meet at a Metro station near the university, and from there they will accompany me. When I get there I find a group of seven teenagers from the Russian folk music choir. It is a cold January day and we end up taking a long, complicated bus ride, transfer to a second line, and walk quite a distance between the buildings of a massive apartment complex. They point out their favorite cafe as we walk along; the waitress, Auntie Nadya, has just returned from a trip to the United States. The cafe is closed or we would stop in to say hello. Next we walk through some woods; it is true I would never have found this place without their guidance! The air is remarkably fresh and crisp as we walk; it's hard to believe that this neighborhood is part of a metropolitan area of more than 8 million people. We stop along the way because they're carrying cameras and want to take pictures of me, of each other. Afterward, they start tossing snowballs at each other and run around, laughing. I'm not quite sure what to do so I wait for them to finish and we resume our walk. They seem at ease with me, and each one of them wants to be a tour guide, often all at the same time. It's hard to follow the conversation.

We arrive at Alexei's home, a two-room apartment with a large kitchen in an old four-story red brick building. There are several similar buildings clustered near his, and we're surrounded by snowy woods; it feels like a quiet village. We are greeted by his grandmother. His parents are abroad, which is why his house has been selected: we'll have more privacy. His grandmother leaves. Alexei and his friends prepare tea, and we sit together in the living room as the afternoon grows dark. As we talk we drink tea, and eat jam, cakes, candies, and fruit.

They tell me that their neighborhood has a bad reputation and is full of crime and recite a little rhyme about it, which they claim anybody from Moscow has heard at least once: "Better two years [military service] in Af-gha-ni-stan than to spend even one week in Tyo-ply-Stan!" It's hard for me to believe that this quiet, snow-covered, parklike area could be so tough. However, during the months I am interviewing them, both Lyosha and Alexei are victims of muggings quite close to their homes.

In late winter Lyosha is approached by a group of young men, about his age, who decide that they like his 1950s-style trousers, which he has carefully searched out in a used-clothing store. They order him to take the trousers off and hand them over, or else they will take them by force. He obeys, hoping to avoid physical harm. But it's quite cold outside and, as he later tells it, "They took pity on me." One of the boys gives Lyosha his own pants, which of course are not nearly as nice or unusual, but he makes it home without freezing.

Alexei's experience is worse. He leaves the house listening to music on a Walkman, a scarce and highly coveted item in the Soviet Union. His parents have brought it back to him from abroad. He is approached by a group of young men older than he who demand the Walkman. They knock him to the ground and beat his head against the pavement. Alexei suffers a concussion and is hospitalized for two weeks. When I see him after he leaves the hospital, he is worried about what his parents will say: it is clearly a great risk to walk out of the house in Moscow wearing a Walkman, and he should have known better. People have been telling me that this type of crime is on the rise, but these are the first direct experiences of this kind that anybody I know has encountered.

After our first meeting at Alexei's house, Dima, Lyosha, and Alexei decide to continue the interviews and come to my dorm at Moscow State University once every week or two. They insist on coming as a group. I conduct interviews one at a time. The other two take another tape player I have and go into the second room to listen to music. They are particularly fond of Suzanne Vega and seem to ignore the louder tapes I thought might interest them more. I make sure that I always have something to offer them for tea, Soviet style—it wouldn't be right to let guests go unattended. I buy great quantities of pastries at the buffet downstairs in the dorm, or candies if I find any for sale that day. They eat mountains of sweets, demolish whole cakes and cookies, drink gallons of sugary tea, and then go out into the hallway for a smoke, in some ways still boys, in others, already men.

They ask me questions about prices in America, styles in America; once they ask me if I have a husband, and then if I believe in women's emancipation, "or something like that."

Always respectful, trying not to show their amusement at my sometimes odd formulations in Russian, quite patient, they strike me as being much gentler than their American counterparts.

DIMA

BRINGING A LITTLE
BREAD BACK HOME

DIMA

Seventeen years old, vocational school student

*Dima is modest and quiet. He takes my questions very seriously and likes
the idea that he is helping me to finish a project. Still, it makes him
nervous. Unlike most of the other teenagers I have gotten to know, he never
stops using the formal* vy *(you) when addressing me.*

*Dima keeps his hair short and a little punk, to keep up with his
friends, but he doesn't really seem too interested in clothing or style. He's
an outdoorsman; any free time is spent working out at the family dacha or
going off to the woods with friends. He's always in a good mood, and
when he comes back from a weekend at the dacha, he always describes his
time there with the same word:* Prekrasno! *Marvelous!*

I was born in Moscow. I finished the eighth grade in school, and then I
entered a PTU,* where I've finished two years. Now I'm in my third and
last year. I'm learning to assemble radio-electronic equipment. My profession is a pretty serious one. It requires a lot of concentration.

I live with my parents and my brother. My mother was born in the
Ukraine in the city of Drogobych. She finished school there. Now she works
in a central scientific research center as head financial inspector. She
counts out the wages of all the workers at that enterprise. She's been
working there for three years. Before that she worked for the KGB—the
Committee on State Security. I don't know what she was doing there. She
didn't talk about it. I've seen her at work now—she sits at a desk in front
of a big pile of papers. She counts out people's wages. They bring her a
paper and she gives the worker his money. She has a lot of different papers.
They send them off to other ministries. Actually, I think her work is boring.

*Vocational school.

My father finished two institutes—he has two higher education de-grees. He graduated from an electronics institute and the aviation insti-tute. Now he works at a mechanical engineering design office designing new airplanes. He's chief designer there. He likes his work. He's been there around thirty years now. I like my father's work. He has a lot of friends there, and he has a job that has more responsibility. Everything he does is new there.

My father advised me to leave school and go to a PTU. He told me that the PTU was a good one, and a person needs to have a profession. My father wanted me to finish my secondary education and get a profes-sion at the same time. My mother was for it, too.

I was really lazy in school, and English just wouldn't come to me. I didn't like English and I kept getting D's. Then I went to the PTU and I started getting B's. Perhaps the teachers were different. The teacher in school was an elderly woman and very demanding, she was mean, and the way she addressed us schoolchildren, well, I don't know. She'd ask you a question and if you didn't know the answer, it was, "Sit down, you get a D." I didn't like all those D's, and my parents yelled at me, and maybe because of that, on principle, to spite them, I stopped studying. She yelled at me a lot, and maybe it was because I didn't understand and I stopped doing homework. It was hard. And she kept giving me D's. But in the PTU we have a young teacher, he reads books and magazines to us in English, and somehow I started to think that I might really need to use English in my life, to communicate with people, and English is considered an international language. Or maybe I've just grown up. I remember that right at the beginning, in the first year, he spoke a lot in English to us—and I wanted to be able to do that too!

The teachers in the PTU treat us well. We greet the male teachers with a handshake. They're cheerful. Our teachers are all good people. I like them all. In school, discipline was much stricter. During our lessons we all sat there and kept silent, listening. It's freer in the PTU, some-body throws a paper airplane . . . that kind of behavior. The teachers don't pay much attention to it. And in school, God forbid, any paper airplanes, or you hit someone. Straight to the principal! In the PTU it happens pretty often—the teacher says something and the kids are busy with their own things. Of course at school they're preparing you for an institute of higher education. In school they make you do homework and they don't do that in a PTU. They basically don't even give you homework. Very rarely—basically only in the first year.

In school you can tell they're preparing you to go on to get a higher education because, for example, during a class a teacher asks you, "Dima, what are you going to do with your life? Are you going on to college or are you going to go and learn a trade?" And if you say you're going to learn a trade, he'll start asking less of you. This is how it happens here—whoever gets at least a B on the exams after eighth grade goes on to the ninth. And whoever gets a C goes to the PTU. They suggest to the ones who get good grades that they keep on studying.

I can tell the difference in the way the teachers relate to me in the PTU. They ask less of me. In every class. And the teachers are not as good as the ones in school. In school the teachers knew their subjects and they knew they had to graduate you with good grades. And they make the curriculum harder. In the PTU the curriculum is much easier, and it's easier for me to study. So I'll finish my secondary education and learn a trade, and the teachers are easier than in school. In the PTU they don't ask you questions very often, and if a teacher does ask you a question, you know he won't call on you again for another month.

In school I didn't know what to do because I had homework, but I wanted to hang out. I like being in a PTU because I have more free time. I have a lot of free time after class. I either go to the movies or I hang out with my friends on the street. I have downhill skis, and sometimes I go with the guys to ski. I go with some friends of mine who live in my building. Or we go to a cafe. Pretty often. My favorite place is an ice cream cafe near the Belyayevo Metro station, and we know the waitress there. We call her Auntie Nadya. She just took a trip to America.

In school we had literature more often than in the PTU. In school we had to write compositions at home. We would write for two or three hours. And here they talk to you about literature much more simply. In school they tell you about everything, from A to Z. And in the PTU they tell you what's in the textbook and that's all. We copy the compositions right from the textbook. In school they took the textbooks away from us, and we read the work and had to write a composition from our own memory. They really demanded much more from you in school, made sure you learned more. In the PTU nobody really thinks about anything, nobody thinks, "He cribbed from the textbook." You just find the right word and that's enough. It wasn't like that in school.

I really couldn't stand studying in school. I got C's and D's. I wanted to finish as quickly as possible and get out and work. Even in school I wanted to find some kind of work in the evenings. I simply didn't know where to go. And I didn't think about my classes. So my father advised me I might find a good base enterprise—one that's connected to a PTU and trains young workers—near my house and go to work there. It's a pretty clean trade. Being a milling-machine operator or a lathe operator is physical work, but in our trade you sit and you wear white robes.

You don't have to use a lot of energy. So after the eighth grade I turned in my documents and went to the PTU. My mother felt good about it. She said, "Now you're going to be a working man! You'll bring a little bread back home!"

Actually, in school the first few years were good—until third grade. Up to third grade, primary school, we had only one teacher, and then as we got older we had different teachers for the different subjects—mathematics, Russian, literature, physics. It got harder. In the first years after school I just stayed at home with my father and mother and did what I was supposed to do. And then I started to have some new friends and I wanted just to hang out with them, and then the conflicts began. At school I sat in the classroom trying to catch flies. I talked with my friends. I was already bored by school. As the years went by, things got worse. It got hard for me to study, and the teachers thought I would have problems in the future. And then my home room teacher told me I should go to a PTU and finish there. It would be easier there. That was in sixth grade. But somehow I managed to get through the eighth grade, and then I left. I could have kept on studying, but I myself didn't want to. There was space in the ninth grade; they were even taking kids from other schools into the ninth grade. But I decided enough, I made it through eight years and now I'm finished studying; I want a different life, I want to get out and work a little. I like physical work more than mental work. I'm satisfied with my decision. I think I'll need my trade in my future life.

The kids in a PTU are different, and their problems are different. In school things were kind of simple. You went out just a little bit, went to the movies once a week, but in the PTU . . . We go to the movies, we go out dancing, to discos, and a lot more often. In school there were smart girls, more modest, and in the PTU they're the same way we boys are. They don't want to go on studying through tenth grade. They go to a PTU, where everything is easier.

But I would like to get into an institute of higher education (the MIREA, or Moscow Institute of Radio Engineering, Electronics, and Automation). I'll study for another five years. If I have a higher education they'll take me more seriously at work. And you know what they say—Live for a century, and study for a century. In the PTU I'll get my secondary education. Maybe the situation in school just wasn't right. The teachers already knew what I was like. I had already separated myself from them.

My father will help me get into the institute. I'll find more serious work if I have a higher education, at a large enterprise. Something technological, where there are designers. Maybe I'll become a technician. I guess with time you begin to understand that without studying you won't get anywhere. You have to study.

FINDING MY PLACE IN LIFE

I'm going into the army, into the border guards. I'm going to serve in the northwest, next to the Finnish border. I just found out about that now. They called my house and told me to report to the enlistment office. I'm glad because the border guards are the best part of the army. There's a lot of responsibility. I'd like to get into the institute now, but there's no way I could do it now. In order to get into the institute I'd have to take additional courses, and I only have three months left before my birthday and the end of school.

I'm not going into the army to prepare for war but rather to prepare myself for my personal life. And they prepare people there to fulfill their duty in the moment of need. In general I am for peace, but I'm ready to defend the motherland if need be. I'm for decreasing the size of the army. I have a friend who was affected by the reduction. He served five months and then he came back.

I don't want to go into the army. But it's a duty. According to the constitution we have a law about universal military service. I would rather go right into an institute now, but the way it turns out is that I can only enter an institute after I finish the army. And two years is a long time. I think a volunteer army would be better. That way you would know you were serving your country and you would be getting paid for it. I don't know, I guess I'm going to prepare myself to defend the motherland. Because, God forbid, a war begins, I'll already be a soldier.

My parents think that young people should serve in the army. They tell me I'll become a man. They know I don't want to go; I told them. They said, "Go ahead, try to get into an institute that has a military department.* If you get in, good, and if you don't, you'll go into the army." It's not that they want me to go into the army, but they understand that I have to. They know a person has to serve in the army, and that the army makes you a man. In the army boys become defenders, professionals. They also would like me to have a higher education. And they think the sooner I get it the better.

I think the army should become salaried. All youth are for a salaried army. This way a young person could earn money, and if he didn't want

---

*Military service is obligatory for all young men in the Soviet Union. However, if a young man is accepted to study at a university or institute of higher education that has a military department, he may fulfill his military service by attending weekly classes there rather than by being drafted into the armed forces. One example of the growing discontent with obligatory military service occurred in late 1988, when students at Leningrad State University held a successful protest demanding that attendance at the military training courses be voluntary.

to go to the army he could either keep studying or get a job. I would go, but at least I would have had a choice.

In two years, after the army, I would like to enter an institute, to get a higher education, or else I'll go to work in a cooperative repairing televisions.

I would like to have good friends and to find my place in life. The friends you have—that's who you are. Your place in life is your collective at work, in school. People I respect. And my friends respect me. In the collective people relate well to me. For me the collective is my friends, who can understand me, help me in difficult moments, who love me, respect me. And I love and respect them.

Later I'll get married. I don't know if I'm going to continue studying or if I'll start to work, we'll see how things go. I'll take time to spend raising my children; I want to have two. We have to continue the species! I would like my wife to be pretty, intelligent, and kind. With character. She has to know how to control herself, be collected, not like girls now who smoke and drink. She should feel that she is the mother of her children.

I'll work in my trade—electronic equipment. I'd like to work in a cooperative because they pay more there for your labor.* I really like working better than I like studying. I've been doing this since childhood. I've always helped out at home, and outside, on the street. At the dacha. And one works to support the family.

I want to have children, and they have to be educated, so that they turn out smart. I think from childhood you have to spend a lot of time with them, teach them foreign languages. And make sure they are well developed physically.

I think it's up to me to get what I want in the future. Nobody is going to help me continue studying or working to keep my family going. All people live by their own efforts. All people have to raise their own children. That's what I think. The collective plays a role, of course. It can give direction toward making a correct decision or give advice when differences arise. We'll see what happens.

At the moment I'm not very free, as long as I'm still at the PTU. The teachers are above me. I don't feel very confident in myself. They tell me, "Do this, do that," until you've learned everything you'll keep getting assignments, from all sides, from different leaders. I don't have one specific boss, but I don't feel very free at the moment.

But on the street, of course, I can go wherever I want, even though

---

*The growth of cooperatives has created new alternatives for vocational school students. Many PTU graduates have marketable skills, and cooperatives can offer at least two or three times as much money to their members as a state-run enterprise can.

there are a lot of things you're not supposed to do. It makes you feel uncomfortable. For example, a person decides he'd like to have a drink, but he can't. It's not acceptable. You have to follow the rules of accepted behavior, and there's a lot that you're still not allowed to do here. In society. There are things I'd like to do, but I keep myself in check.

I don't think there is one single person who is free. Nobody has complete freedom. My parents aren't free either. They're not free at work, or in household matters, family matters, and in the summer we have a lot of responsibilities at the dacha. So nobody is able to live in such a way that they can spend entire days resting. If you want to live well, you have to work a lot. You have to be able to earn a certain amount. You have very little free time. You have to work a lot, and only then can you rest.

I can't say that I feel totally happy. Sometimes when things are going my way I feel a sudden happiness. Like when a girl tells you she loves you. But my happiness is going to be when I finish the PTU! I want to be free as soon as possible.

PERESTROIKA: WHICH WAY?

There are big changes going on in our country. I think that glasnost is getting rid of all the leaders who don't do their job in production, directors, dealing with them at Party meetings, talking about their faults, about absenteeism, about discipline. In general dealing with production. Talking about those who are producing flawed goods and those who are producing well. Raising all of these questions and discussing them. Talking about what we're doing in this country. We have to talk about our losses.

When "Comrade Brezhnev" was in power, we had the period of stagnation. Everything was neglected, organized at the lowest level. Bureaucracy, and nobody cared about it. And now, with glasnost and perestroika, they've gotten much stricter about everything, and people have started to have some conscience about doing their work. But nothing in my life has changed. Perhaps just that, in the PTU, they got rid of the old director and put in a new one. The old director didn't do anything for the school, he just sat around and gave orders, but he didn't do anything to keep the school going the way it should. I think the people from the ministry got rid of him. And now we have a new director, a real solid man, and he's keeping things going. Discipline has improved and the teachers have started to reorganize themselves. It used to be that they just showed up and didn't care about anything. But now they've really started going after students. Now you go into the classroom and you feel that there's a working atmosphere. Especially in our special subjects, connected to our trade, and mathematics and literature.

I used to think that Stalin was a great leader, that he wanted victory, that he did everything for the people. I simply didn't know that he was capable of treating people, Soviet people, so brutally. His own brothers. And now I'm learning about this, and it feels really terrible to know that such people existed. A Soviet person and he acted like a fascist! I feel sorry for those people who had to live in Stalin's time. There were so many intelligent people, who knows what they could have done for the Soviet people, how many discoveries they could have made! And Stalin wiped out so many scientists, professors. This has to be talked about, so people know about it. I don't think people knew. There were those who guessed it was going on. But they were afraid of the repression. God forbid you might say something about Stalin—that would be it for you. But it's useless to lie to the people, because the people see everything. You can't hide anything from the people.

I think perestroika is in action here. But the only thing is that I don't know in which way! Meat has disappeared! But not only meat has disappeared around here. There's no laundry detergent, and now there's no cheese around either. I don't understand this. My parents are disturbed. They say that we have such a large economy, but where all of these things are going to nobody knows. Everybody has their own opinion. Some people say they're sending meat someplace else, maybe to other countries. Or it's lying around somewhere. I don't know why there's no soap.

Who knows if perestroika will be able to change these things in the near future? Everybody is talking about this, and everybody has a different opinion, and a different mood. Perestroika is a struggle for quality, for progress, discipline. At every factory there will now be control over the quality of production, every worker will have to work the same both for himself and for society in general. I think that this way the number of people coming to work at factories drunk will decrease. Now they're going to adopt some penalties for this, hold discussions about it, and get it under control. Not the way it used to be.

With time, everything changes. I think that little by little everything is going to appear. The thing is that the Party went after all areas at once, and if everything were done slowly, first livestock farming, then meat and milk production, then the heavy engineering industry, well, then I think they could get things in order. But perestroika took on everything at once, and that's why I think it's going to take a long time.

I do think that the Party is partially to blame for the shortages, because they should have solved the problem of getting the very basics to the people. The food industry. The most important things for the people are lacking. The necessary basic goods. Now they've gone after everything at once, and there aren't enough finances for it all. Enterprises that aren't fulfilling the plan have to be brought up to speed. And agriculture is behind too. And now they've gone after the food industry, so that things will be all right and there will be sausage, and meat. But this is why they should have tried to do things slowly.

At my factory people have started to work better, and they show up late less often than they used to. We do piecework. Now if someone wants to go get a smoke, he'll think twice and he'll have to make some kind of plan for himself to go smoke less often. Our boss talks to us about this all the time. He talks to us about production. That we have to increase productivity. Fulfill the plan. Our department has a commitment, and everybody tries to overfulfill the plan.*

I think young people have a role in all of this. Let's take agriculture, for example. In general people now are leaving the countryside and moving to the cities. There aren't any people left to work there. If it continues like this and everybody leaves for the cities, who is going to work there? This is why we have to get young people to move to collective farms. There's nothing terrible about doing this, working in a village. And now on the kolkhozes they're contracting out to families who want to lease land and become farmers, and they get good money, their yearly income is very high; they're helping the government. So this isn't bad. What's bad is that people aren't going to work in agriculture. I myself have other plans. I want to get into the Electronics and Automation Institute. But there are other people who are really drawn to nature, who love animals. They simply like to do that kind of work.

I would like to join the Party. I would like to be like my father. He's a Party member. Above all, the Party is supposed to defend the motherland. Communists are heroes. At any moment a Communist is ready to defend the motherland from its enemies.

I've been in the Komsomol for two years already. I think a Soviet person should be in Komsomol, should go through all the different

---

*The centrally planned Soviet economy works on the basis of five-year plans, which set production quotas. "Overfulfilling" the plan means producing more than the set quota. This method of production has been criticized for its overdependence on central planning and neglect of local needs as well as for its emphasis on the production of quantity rather than quality. For Dima, as a young worker, the essence of perestroika is improving productivity, and fulfilling the plan remains a very important concept to him.

levels. He should feel some kind of responsibility to help the Party and to help people, to help younger people.

A Komsomol member has greater responsibility to his motherland, understands his obligations better, and isn't indifferent in difficult moments. He should help the police, people in trouble, all of that is his responsibility. And if he has faults, he should correct them. I think being in the Komsomol helped me overcome some of my faults. I used to skip classes and I wasn't well behaved. I hung out in the streets and got into some trouble. I used to get into fights. My friends and I fought with guys from other places. And when I joined the Komsomol, that was the end of that. I finally understood I might end up in trouble. A lot of our guys ended up being taken in to the police, and they dealt with them there, wrote letters, found out who you were, and if you weren't a Komsomol member, they wouldn't really bother you, but if you were, they would send a letter to the organization, and they [the Komsomol] had different steps for dealing with it, even being kicked out of the Komsomol. So I got to thinking. . . .

I am for socialism. Under socialism, I have everything I need, and I can get a job wherever I want. I have a large choice of interesting places for me to work, and I'll find one and go there. I don't know how long it will take us to get to communism, but I do think we will get there. Socialism is when people try to do more because they are doing it for themselves, because as much as you work you will receive. We don't have exploitative factories. Here you work for yourself; however you work, that's how much you'll get. It's all in your interest. Nobody is going to oppress you. In capitalism people in a country own their own factories and plants, they hire workers, and the capitalists get a lot of financial gain from the labor of the workers. Workers get a miserable wage, and the capitalist makes a lot off of this; he gets a lot of capital from it. That's how I understand capitalism.

I feel good about Gorbachev. Positively. Because you can tell that the country has taken off in the right direction. If we're not moving toward communism, we're certainly headed toward socialism. People will have enough, as much as you give, you will receive. Things will be better.

"IF I COULD JUST MEET
THAT ONE PERSON . . ."

LYOSHA

Seventeen years old, vocational school student

Lyosha is long-legged and thin, looks as if he is still going to grow a lot taller. Over a period of three or four months he changes his hairstyle several times, until he gets a result he's pleased with: short-cropped and punkish, a few spikes somewhere on top. One of his ears is pierced, and he's pleased when I give him a peace symbol earring brought to me by a friend from the States. Every time we meet he is wearing it.

Lyosha is shy and finds talking about himself difficult. Everything personal makes him blush, from telling me that his parents are from the provinces to relating how he manages to find stylish clothes. He sits on the edge of his chair and leans forward, his palms planted firmly on his knees, tapping one foot nervously. He finds the idea of interviewing him curious, wonders why I find talking to teenagers interesting, but he enjoys it. When he talks, he doesn't rush; he is thoughtful and wants to be sure that I've really asked what I want to ask. He is gentle and polite, and even when he finds my Russian funny—when I make a mistake or my pronunciation seems odd—he struggles not to smile, turns his face away from me so I won't notice.

I'm studying to assemble radios in a vocational school. This is my third year, the last. Just half a year left. But after that we still have another two years of "army life."

I like my history class in the PTU very much. I adore history. Chernyshevsky* said, "A person who doesn't know history cannot love

---

*Nikolai Chernyshevsky, a nineteenth-century writer and radical critic whose works are included in the standard literature curriculum. Chernyshevsky strongly believed that art and literature must serve a social purpose.

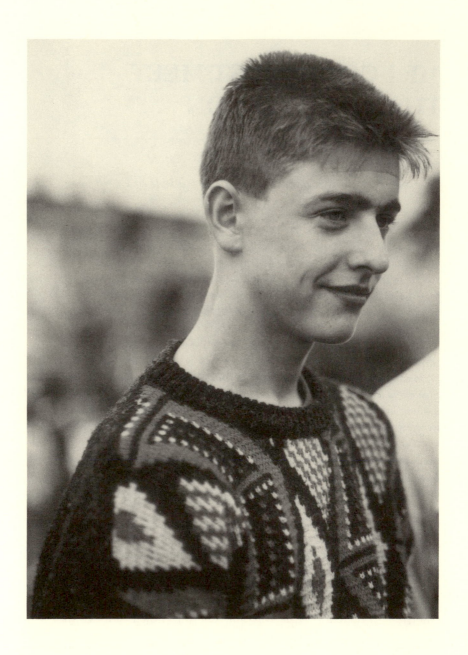

LYOSHA

his motherland." You have to know it, especially since there's not only
the Soviet Union; other countries have a history too. In my opinion, to
live in a country and not know its history is something horrible.

I'm satisfied with my decision to go to vocational school, but I want
to study further. I'll either go to a technical school or to college or to
MIREA (the Moscow Institute of Radio Engineering, Electronics, and
Automation) or to a design office, also at the institute.

My mother was a pastry cook. She worked in a bakery; they made
those cakes, pastries, sweets and spices. She also graduated from grade
school and vocational school. My parents were born in Ryazan, not
Moscow. I was born here. Somehow everyone here is drawn to Moscow.
The capital! My mother graduated from the eighth grade and vocational school and then came here, Dad too. At first she worked at a
textile mill . . . where they make fabrics, textiles—light industry. Then
she switched to this work, but she's retired now. She has a slight disabil-
ity, her heart isn't quite right, not quite, her health has given her a little
bit of a bad shake. I liked her job more than anyone because all little
kids love sweets!

My father works as a machine operator. It's like . . . basically my dad
is like a road worker; he drives along in his snow sweeper, you know, a
tractor. He's a machine operator with a lot of different skills, so he can
work on a variety of equipment: graders, bulldozers, that's what they're
called here. He goes on business trips a lot, so he works in a lot of
different cities. He also finished eighth grade and graduated from vocational school. He was in the virgin lands; he dug up virgin soil. When
they were developing the virgin lands, he worked there—there was a
movement here in the 1950s: they built new cities, factories, where
there had only been empty space. They plowed up the earth. He
worked in Kazakhstan. He likes his work. He was just fifty this year, a big
celebration, and he doesn't regret anything.

My mother's retired but she still tries to earn a little extra money.
She works as a guard at a factory, in the boiler room; they come at night
just to keep an eye on how it's running. But you know, she says it's not
the same. Maybe it's just that she's not used to it. She hasn't been
working there long, maybe a month. She decided to take on a new job
because I'm growing, after all, and don't work yet. I also have needs;
she's got to put something on my back. All that costs money. Our
pensions aren't very big, like an allowance, not much. So you know, she
went to work there to hold up her end of the finances. Mom always
does everything at home; when guests come, the table is always full.
She's very professional at that; she's a really good cook. As far as the
home front, Dad does the repairs. We also have our own garden plot—

not a flower garden, but a place to grow fruits, a vegetable garden. I help Mom as best I can, and Dad too. I go shopping for her, clean up when it's necessary, when she just can't do it, the lighter work, like dusting the apartment. I help Dad dig.

My sister works. . . . She's twenty-two. She's five years older than me. She works as a technician; she has a husband and a daughter who's already three years old, my niece.

My parents are happy with how they've led their lives and they're setting me on the right path too. But they also haven't gotten in my way, in the way of whatever profession I choose for myself. Of course they would like me to go somewhere more . . . not to the university necessarily, but at least to technical college.

When I left school they said, "If that's what you want, then go ahead," because they can't order me not to leave school after all. Right? They say, "If you like where you're going, that's your business; you're choosing your own career in life." After all, I might have been making a mistake, right? Somehow or other they gave me a little push in the direction they thought best. In general they're not sorry now, and neither am I sorry that I left to go where I'm studying now. In general I like my profession too; I don't have any complaints about it. A career in radio technology is pretty interesting.

A worker works and an intellectual also works, but a worker's labor is less complex than an intellectual's. An intellectual does mental labor and a worker physical. Mental labor is more complex. I want to do mental labor; it's just something I have in my heart. I feel it, that's all.

It's easier for someone who's studied in a vocational school to get into an institute [of higher education] if he wants to; in all our vocational schools they'll advise him where to go study and write letters of recommendation, and he's given certain advantages in the entrance exams. Not many want to though. But those who do usually succeed; it's much easier for them than for those who went to the ten-year school.

If I get into a technical college, I won't go into the army.* It's very advantageous to me from the point of view of time; I won't lose two years. I'll be graduating from the technical school already and other guys who went into the army will just be applying for their first year.†

My teacher at the workshop [at the PTU] is a very good person; I've never met such a good person. He has the best of hearts. His goodness

---

*The school Lyosha wants to enter has a military department. Students can fulfill their military service at the institute rather than going into the army for two years.

†Lyosha was not accepted into an institute before being called up for military service; in late June he reported for duty.

makes me feel ... In vocational school if you don't do something just so, they scream at you, but he speaks calmly; you don't even feel comfortable snapping at him. We got used to having everyone yell at us: our parents yell, they yell in the PTU; it's like something's wrong for him to be so calm. ... When I was little I thought I would never hurt my child or raise my voice to him. But I've understood. ... Of course I'll try to be softer, but it would be better not to yell at all. I don't know how to raise a child; I just can't imagine it yet. First I'll finish studying, then I'll think about it.

The thing is, good people aren't treated well here. Here's an example. We have two teachers in our school: one is evil, mean and evil; everyone tiptoes around him. If he says something, everybody jumps. And there's another one who isn't capable of yelling at anyone; they behave terribly toward him. They don't go to his classes; they snap at him. They know he won't do anything to them because he's nice. It's not only teachers; there are just people like that. My friend Alexei, for example, you can't hit him because you know he won't fight back. But there are evil people who come with their fists ready to help them get what they want. Everyone's afraid of someone like that; whatever he says, goes. That's what they do. It's only in fairy tales and books that they say if you're good, people will be good to you. It's not like that in life in my opinion.

Most of my spare time I spend doing folk arts; I sing in a chorus of Russian folk music. Rock and all these directions the young people are going in get more publicity, which is probably why I didn't want the other to be forgotten. I like that it's something from long ago. Generally we sing because, for example, you get upset about something during the day and you go there and feel refreshed. Rock is something new, well not entirely new, but these are songs from the depths of Russia. I'm not saying that I only like folk music; I listen to rock with pleasure too, which I like, but all in all, I much prefer folk music. When I sing folk songs, I think of the music itself, while when I listen to rock, I have extraneous outside thoughts in my head; I can daydream, relax. ...

I have probably not been happy yet. Maybe I'm just unlucky. I don't want to say I'm unfortunate, but I'm not happy. To be happy is to have a lot of joy, but I haven't had any special cause for joy, very, very rarely, you could even say never. Maybe it's funny, but I'm not happy. If I could just meet that one person ... That's really all I need right now. ...

THE PTU

Generally speaking, I had wanted to go to the energy industry's technical school. That's at Gorky Park Metro station. I even went to the preparatory course. But then I didn't like it. I imagined the kind of work it would be. They graduate technicians for atomic energy stations, hydroelectric stations. I went to see and I didn't like it.

In the general ten-year school they only have an academic program, and this way [the PTU] I'll graduate with the same thing.* This is what I was thinking: "If I stay in school, I'll study for ten years and I'll be left with one free year.† It'll be a do-nothing year to just hang out, and I'll have to find a job somewhere." Well, I thought: "That just won't be right. I won't have a trade. But if I go to a vocational school that free year will be kept busy with studies—and I'll get the same education and a trade to boot."

What I didn't like about regular school is that they're ready to call your parents right away; at the least excuse the first thing they do is call your parents. No question can be resolved there without your parents. In the vocational school there isn't any of that. You feel that you're responsible there. You answer for your own actions. They look upon us as adults in the vocational school because it's as though you're going to work already. It's easier to make contact with the teachers in vocational school. Also, you feel yourself, I don't know, to be a worker. And they also know that you're not a child, but an adult already preparing yourself for a working life.

The academic subjects are for our education and the vocational subjects prepare us for the factory—here we have more strenuous preparation. They give us more, because after all, it's a vocational subject, for some it's for their whole lives. They demand a little bit more because it's in their interest. If I go out to work and do a bad job, they'll think what kind of a teacher did I have. That's why they try to give us more, so we'll know more.

All our teachers are young now, and the principal's young. When I was in my first and second year they used to talk a lot about perestroika; now, I think, they're doing something. Before, we were supposed to get a complete secondary education. And that was like a trap. Even if we didn't want to, the teachers just dragged us along. It's not like that now; if there's a subject you don't want to study, you'll get an unsatisfactory grade, but they won't try to force you to get a good grade; they'll be strict with you but they won't pull you through; if you want to do well, study yourself. That's related to perestroika.

Before, we weren't studying, just playing the fool. Now, for example,

---

*Like all vocational school graduates, Lyosha will have a secondary education diploma in addition to learning a trade.

†Before being drafted at age eighteen.

if you have D's in a couple of subjects, the teachers don't have to struggle or waste their time; if someone doesn't listen in class, for example, or is distracting and keeps the teacher from teaching, they take his papers and process him for the factory. Say he finishes his first year, he's dismissed at the beginning of the second, and he'll have to go to night school and get a job. Now, if you want to, if you feel it's necessary, you'll study; but a lot of them don't want to study, they have no use for it, although in time they'll understand that what they're doing is wrong; but the teachers, in the final instance, are no longer required to pull someone through. If students were failing, getting D's, the teachers used to ask them what and why. But it's not like that now. If you don't want to study, please, be my guest, go to work!

We're doing our practical work now, and every month they pay us up to twenty, twenty-five rubles; I save some and keep some. I work as a radio assembler; our workshop makes cables to connect one tape recorder to another. I solder. Most of our solderers are women. The men work mostly on the cables; there are a lot of operations and our work is mostly mechanical: we put in screws, do installations, and they just sit and solder. All that has an effect on the eyes. It's a little bit boring. I've constantly got a screwdriver in my hands and am turning screws. It would be very boring and uninteresting to do that all my life. I don't imagine I'll be doing that all my life; I don't like it. I don't think anyone stays on in that job. Maybe they move to other workshops where there's more interesting work. They'll work with radio components and parts. They make radios, tape recorders; the work is more varied. It's not the same thing every day. One day it's one thing, the next day another. My work now is very monotonous; all I do is turn screws; of course I don't like it! I don't know, sometimes when you really get to thinking, you wonder if, well, in choosing to go to a vocational school, that maybe, on some level, you did give up something.

CHANGE: "ALL WE HAVE IS GLASNOST"

In my opinion we only have perestroika in words. I don't see anything in actions. Speculation has even grown. There's nothing in the stores. Everything has literally vanished, disappeared somewhere. Everywhere the storerooms are plenty full. If you go into the storeroom of any shop, you can find anything you want. And if it's not in the storeroom, then it's hidden somewhere better. There's nothing on the shelves. This is an artificial shortage; I mean someone's created it.

I don't see perestroika yet. There's only talk and what will come of it I don't know. There hasn't been anything substantive in reality yet. So

they're standing in the subway campaigning . . . notices are stuck up
everywhere; things were stuck up before too, but now they come up to
you to "talk with the people." It's a little unusual. But all of that is just
words; in action there's nothing. That's just it; all we have is glasnost,
but no action's being taken. . . . Well, maybe somewhere there's something going on, like the cooperatives . . . that's just a side effect. Maybe
it's even up to us, the young people. If we all got together and went . . .
maybe they'd give us some satisfaction. . . .

Maybe you don't feel it because there's still so little of it; I haven't
noticed. All the problems in the consumer industry, in trade, I want all
that to change. Basically that's our most complicated problem now.
They talk about it everywhere, on radio, on television, everywhere.

I don't want there to be these problems. I want everything to be on
the shelves. When I get to the store I want it to be . . . Well I won't hide
it, I also have some acquaintances. . . . In the hair salon, when I get
there they wait on me right away without waiting in line, like an old
friend. That shouldn't be, even though I'm flattered that although
there's a line I just go in and go straight to the chair. But sometimes *I'm*
the one in line, not in the hair salon but, say you're standing in line
somewhere, for apples, for example. Say the clerk has only ten kilos left
and everyone's buying a kilo and I'm the tenth one in line, but then
one of their people comes along and buys that kilo without waiting in
line, so nothing's left for me. Really, it's annoying. But I do the same
thing sometimes!

I, for one, haven't bought anything co-op made. Not a single thing.
For example, take food, you also want better quality. But the prices are
very high there, maybe not that high, but not within reach of everyone.
Prices are pretty high for everything they make. So these stone-washed
jeans turn up and you want better quality, but a lot of them make them
so that after the first washing you can't even look at them; you can't tell
what they are, pants or . . . rags. And the price, of course, is not low.

There are problems everywhere, in every area: agriculture, at the
factories . . . everyday problems, the ones I personally come across. And
I don't know, but for some reason we now have ethnic hostility. It
wasn't like that before. It wasn't that things were better during the
period of stagnation, but I never even heard anywhere that anyone
would want to leave the union. There was never anything like that.
There are fifteen Soviet republics and all are brothers and sisters. If, for
example, a Georgian, an Armenian, and an Uzbek came [to Moscow],
you looked at him like you would at anyone else, but this problem is
very acute now. The ethnic problem: Nagorno-Karabakh, Armenia,
Uzbekistan . . .

I do think Gorbachev is outstanding. For example, he's solved a lot of problems in international relations. You see, we have two contradictory systems: the Soviet Union and the USA. And there was constantly propaganda; America ran propaganda against the Soviet Union and the Soviet Union against America. So when Mikhail Sergeyevich* got down to work he started to fix international relations and he achieved that. If you look at what's happening now—high-level talks, meetings on disarmament—the situation has become better now; we've already forgotten that propaganda and we're trying to find out more not only about America but about other capitalist and socialist countries in general. It's true they'd already been telling us a lot about the socialist countries, but as for the capitalist ones . . . About the countries, the people, how they live. Maybe we didn't know much before, but now there are different television programs, space bridges, and once or twice a month we see American programs for a few hours. We have a show, *The International Panorama,* where they also tell us briefly about the most important world events. So Mikhail Sergeyevich has raised this question well.

There wasn't much interest before, but now you really want to know. Before everybody wanted to go to America, but basically it wasn't because they wanted to see but because everything was cheaper there; you even have casual clothes, which we have very little of. If someone goes to America, they expect him to come back fully dressed. Or if you say, "I went to America," everybody just oohs and ahs. There is still some of that, of course, but now we just want to have contact with Americans, with the English, the French, just to make contact. Actually I've gotten to know some Americans.

GLASNOST: "NO ONE KNEW THE HONEST TRUTH"

Last year we didn't have our history exams in school because of the repression, because of the disclosure of the cult of personality. We studied that cult of personality as it was written about in the old textbooks: "Stalin, hurrah! Brezhnev, hurrah! Everyone, hurrah!" We won the war under Stalin; under Brezhnev we outstripped everyone in milk production. But in the end it became clear that we're a people with a bad past; I mean, it wasn't all good; there was bad too. It's even possible that if Gorbachev had been governing the country in 1975 we wouldn't have had Afghanistan and a lot of other problems. And we would probably be living better now. Only ten years ago. Gorbachev's been in for only four years; in 1975 it was Brezhnev. You can't say that they were

---

*Gorbachev.

deceiving us in our history lessons; to some degree they were deceiving us, of course, but those very same teachers . . . they were also being deceived; no one knew the honest truth; only a small circle of people knew; it was all buried in the archives, inaccessible to simple people, and now this . . . freedom of speech, glasnost.

I have yet to meet a person who always tells the truth. I can't imagine how such a person could live in our society. It would be very hard for him. I don't know, but it seems to me that would be a difficult life. Even if a person tells the truth but adds a little to it, you already don't have the truth. It's already a little white lie. Usually, when they tell us the truth here, no one believes it, and when they tell us untruths, everyone believes it. That's probably how it is every-where.

THE ARMY

Well, I can't judge everybody who would benefit from being in the army and who wouldn't. We believe here that if someone goes into the army, he should be changed afterward, both physically and in the sense of discipline. But it's just that there are people who are already physically fine and who have the kind of personalities they should have, and the people around them like them. In my opinion they don't need the army. What they teach in grade school, elemen-tary military preparedness, should be enough. But whoever has a weak character and who's physically weak needs the army, in order to change his character and strengthen him physically. In general, that's something a person has to determine for himself, whether he needs the army or not. If they said here, whoever wants to go, go, many wouldn't..

I probably wouldn't go into the army if it was voluntary. I don't have such a good impression from the stories of those who come back. And I just don't want to stop my studies now while my head is fresh. After the army I will probably have forgotten a lot; it's simply easier now. I don't know about anyone else, but me . . . My character, of course, is not entirely ideal, but it's not so bad either; I'm physically pretty well devel-oped too.

YOUNG PEOPLE

Young people have quite a lot of problems, and they're all pretty seri-ous. But probably they're mostly related to how to spend your time, because a lot of young people don't know what to do with themselves during their free time. They don't know what to do, how to keep themselves busy. Also, a lot is related to clothing, because what they're making now, I don't know how to say it; well, the clothing they make doesn't satisfy us; the co-ops are making some things now, but that's beyond the means of young people. That's also a not-so-unimportant problem. And in general, it's our lifestyle.

Some neighborhoods have a sports complex; if you live there, for example, you can always find something to do, but if you live much farther away, it's not convenient time-wise. . . . I would solve the youth question by having more sports facilities; there's a demand for that. Everybody wants to have something to do. Often even if there's only one particular facility and you don't like it, you go anyway just to have something to do. I don't think the discotheques really solve young people's problem, only that during the times when the discotheques are open you'll find fewer of us on the street, but I don't think it helps because a lot of drunks come to the discotheques and more fights probably take place there than anywhere.

We have kids like those in the film *My Name Is Harlequin.** They were only pushed to it by life. The kind of kids who do that stuff, it's a kind of mini-business for them. They take something off somebody and sell it. The ones I've run into have just been pushed to it by life; they have no money. All they know is that you can take something from someone weaker, sell it, and have money to spend. Not long ago, they took my pants. I consoled myself with the thought that at least they didn't use physical force, that I was still in one piece and unhurt! I don't feel good about them. Maybe you can understand them, but it's hard. A lot of them are driven to it because that's how they were treated when they were weak. They learn to fight just so they can survive that evil, but then they start doing those things themselves. It's like an addict, they try it once or twice and then they just start to like it. Then they just can't live without it. And if they see a weak person, and if there are a lot of them, they go ahead with their dark deeds.

Frankly speaking, the majority of the punks have a few screws loose, it seems to me. I've heard in their songs they sing they're not satisfied with how we live now. I don't really know, it's just that a lot of people our age think that if you're punk, then something's not quite right up there. To some degree I think that and to some degree I don't.

I'm not a punk; this is just a hairstyle. . . .

---

*A recent film that focused on a gang of rough youths involved in robbery and crime. One of a number of new films focusing on crime and alienation among young people, *My Name Is Harlequin* caused considerable controversy due to a graphic rape scene.

SOCIALISM AND CAPITALISM

I'm for socialism because it's a system where I know I'll never be without work.

Probably Soviet people differ from Americans above all because they're two different systems: socialist and capitalist. Two different policies. America has what the Soviet Union doesn't and the Soviet Union has what America doesn't. Different political systems. I don't know much about politics, but as for domestic problems, in the consumer industry, for example, if a person in the Soviet Union has money, not a lot, an average amount of money, he still can't be sure that he'll be able to buy anything. He is not assured of that. And it seems to me that probably in America, if a person has money and he knows how much an item costs and he has enough, then he can go and buy it. That's not always possible in the Soviet Union. We have shortages.

MEN AND WOMEN

Girls are a lot freer now than they were before. For example, you can't even compare them with how it was in my mom's day. They used to be very, very obedient to their parents. Especially the daughters. And now, well, it's less like that. They're more talkative probably. When a boy and a girl get together, he thinks about how they should spend their time, where to take her. You know that's also a problem for young people: where to go. There aren't so many places. The majority only go to the theater when they're studying in the ten-year school. Otherwise it's the rare one who goes to the theater. They try more to go to discotheques. If a girl's got a guy, she probably trusts him to make those decisions because boys should be more attentive, so they have to amuse or entertain the girl.

The ideal girl should have a good personality, not be a lazybones, and be beautiful. I have a girlfriend. She's beautiful. Her personality's not bad. She understands me. If something unpleasant happens to me and I share it with her, I know she'll understand me. We see each other every day; we tell each other things: how my day went, how her day went. We think up where to go: skating, to the movies, to a discotheque. She studies in a technical school for teaching; she wants to be a preschool teacher.

A woman probably needs to pay more attention to the home, to running the household, while a man works and earns money. A woman should work and attend to the housework. It's different in different circumstances; not everyone's that way; some live on the basis of equal rights, but basically, more often women work on the job and at home and men work on the job and rest at home.

Before, when I was younger, I helped Mom a lot. I washed the dishes, straightened up the rooms, not just my own. So, for example, when Mom went out, was invited to go visiting, I did whatever she asked me, whatever I could. Dad only does the physical work around the house: he does repairs if something breaks. In the future I'm going to have a family and I want my wife to have a good character, to take care of the housework; of course I'll help her. You know, sometimes I look at my mother and I feel so sorry for her. She's a human being, too, you know, and she gets very tired. She comes home with big bags of groceries and there's still plenty of work to do at home. I almost never see her having free time. In the evenings she sleeps with one eye and watches television with the other! Dad comes home from work and lies down right away. I'm going to help out in my future family, so there'll be time to have a personal life and not just work. I'll do the heavy work; take out the garbage, put the rooms in order, clear away my own dishes. To make it easier for her.

GENERATIONS

I'm only home rarely now; I come home in the evenings and study for exams. There's not enough time; I talk with my parents, but very little now. They only ask me where I've been, all of that, how things are at school. For now I don't talk with my parents much.

Of course, they teach me something. But I try to explain to them that we don't live in the country, but in Moscow, and that when they were growing up things were different. That's why they're surprised at my behavior so often. It's like young people here are much freer. We're very active. Very. . . . Our behavior is, well, a little wild.

Before, when my parents were growing up, they had closer relations with their parents and they agreed with them on almost everything; they listened to them. But it's no longer those times, and we don't listen to our parents so much anymore. For example, if I needed to go somewhere to some party, before, before in the countryside, if your mother and father said no, then you obeyed them. But now you try to find some way to talk them out of it, you plead with them. . . . Parents were kind of stricter before; you listened to them more.

If they ask me to stay to help them with something, most of the time I do. For example, if you're seeing someone off to the army, it's accepted as a kind of custom that you have this kind of party where everyone gets together and you drink tea. If you don't go, it's like insulting him. You see. So how do we usually see someone off: we usually stay there till morning. My parents are usually against that a little; come home, they say, ". . . And you don't come home; you stay till morning saying goodbye." Like all parents, they yell at me some.

My parents were raised in a different atmosphere; they know less than my friends now. How can you say it—they have life experience, but as for what's going on now, often they just don't understand it. First of all, they weren't brought up in Moscow. Where they come from it's completely different. You know, it may be one country, but everywhere it's different.

If I'm talking with my parents and I have something personal, I can't say that to them. I just know that they won't find it interesting. It may even irritate them. It's so easy to understand that. They're not living in these times; they might not understand it properly. That's why I can't always tell them the truth. I have my own personal business; I don't mean friendship with a girl, but, well maybe. . . . Well, just some personal business that has little to do with them. And they may just not understand it or take it the right way. And I don't know how they would react to it. That's why I don't always tell them.

This is probably because they were living in another time. They lived under Stalin, under Khrushchev, and under Brezhnev, and my parents are from deep in the sticks, from the country, and all of this is beyond them. Maybe they had more fun: the concertina and balalaika, songs, clean air. They just had different problems. A city person has completely different problems compared to country people. There are a lot of problems here in the city; you don't know where to go in your free time, the problem of clothing . . . but there you can go around all summer . . . one pair of pants is all you need for the whole summer. And as for the problem of free time . . . If you don't have anything to do you can go down to the river, mushroom picking in the woods; there are a lot of things you can think up, but I think you can always find something to do there. But here, if you want to go somewhere you have to dress well, and there are those conflicts when I don't tell my mother the truth. For example, I went and bought something from someone, a quality item, like they don't have in the stores; I bought it from some guys I know. So I bought this thing from them and if I told the truth about where it came from, Mom might just not take it right. "What is this, how could you do this?!" So I said that it's made in our country. But they'd figure out that it wasn't made here, not just because there's foreign writing on it, but because of the quality they'd figured it out, so I said someone I know went abroad and brought it back. I don't know, in their eyes it's anti-Soviet. They were young during the period of stagnation and the idea was that we have everything we need and don't need anything else. There were slogans like that. Among young people, if I say this item is such and such, they'll understand me. But Mom won't. You see, Mom looked askance on this sweater I'm wearing now. She told me she'd buy me a better one or make me one like it herself.

When I bring something home they understand that it doesn't cost what it used to cost; before, the most expensive shoes cost twenty-five rubles, the best shoes; there were a lot of them and they weren't that expensive. There just isn't anything now. Sometimes when she goes to the store—she goes out very infrequently—she's also surprised; there isn't anything there! They hadn't come across this before; I was just . . . it was possible to get everything in the store, you might stand in a line or two first, but you could buy anything. My parents were indignant that there were lines, of course, but they submitted to it because you could buy things. But now . . . I never used to buy things from other people, but now purchases have to go through five, ten hands because you can't get anything in the stores. So I buy something from someone. They understand that now, that you can't get anything anywhere—they don't want their son to look bad either—which is why they don't pay any particular attention to it now. This sweater costs 160 rubles. If things were normal it would cost 70 rubles; that's what it cost before when they were still lying on the shelves; if I tell Mom it cost 160 rubles, why I just don't know how I'd tell her. So I don't tell my parents the full value; I tell them this sweater cost 110 rubles; Mom thought about how you really couldn't get it anywhere for less, and she gave me the 110 rubles; the other 50 I paid out myself.

ALEXEI

"ALL THAT MILITARISM DOESN'T ATTRACT ME"

ALEXEI

Seventeen years old, vocational school student, learning carpentry

Alexei looks different every time I see him. His hairstyle changes; by spring it is cropped quite close to his head, no more than half an inch long. Sometimes he wears antique clothing; once he shows up in old Red Army cavalry pants that look like they belong in a museum. Another time he puts on suspenders. He is full of questions and spends as much time asking me about the United States as I do asking him about his life in Moscow. He's not at all bashful, brings presents, talks freely, and is totally at ease looking through my shelves and desk drawer, searching out cassette tapes of American music. He brings me recordings of Soviet music he thinks I'll enjoy and carefully writes down the names of the groups and songs on the case so I'll know who and what's important in Soviet rock. A week or two after giving me a tape, he asks me what I think of it. If I don't seem too excited about a group, he suggests another one I might like more and makes another recording for me.

I live on the outskirts of Moscow. My neighborhood is almost the same as the rest of Moscow, except that here there's more green and more fresh air. I live with my grandmother, and with my parents, when they come here. They're in the Republic of Burundi now, teaching in the university there—cartography, advanced mathematics, Russian language. They've been there eight years. My sister lives in the building next door, with her husband and daughter.

My mother is forty years old. She got a degree in Old Church Slavonic at the university, and now she's teaching Russian to young African students who are getting ready to come to the Soviet Union to study but don't know Russian. They learn Russian there so they can come here and study, and then go back and help develop their country. She knows Russian better than many people, and in just a few years she was able to learn French perfectly; now she speaks wonderful French, and English.

My father finished the Engineering Institute. He did graduate studies and taught for a few years there. Then they sent him to the Republic of Mali to work. He worked there for four years and returned to the Soviet Union. And then they invited him to work in the Republic of Burundi. He teaches at the university there. He's forty-seven years old and speaks French with a pure Parisian accent.

They miss me of course. They write me, send photos, tell me about their life in Africa. I haven't been with them in Burundi, but I lived for two years in Mali. I was still little then, around six years old. I have some photos somewhere—I'm sitting on the bank of the River Niger, with my black friends. I'm the only white one among them.

I miss my parents. I stayed here [in the Soviet Union] because I have to finish school. I can't study there; it's all in French. I saw them in the summer; they come here for the summer. We go fishing here, around Moscow, or in other places. We went to Kazakhstan. So I've only been with my parents in the summer lately. They write, about once or twice a month. We don't talk on the phone—it's expensive. They're coming back from Africa soon, to stay in the Soviet Union. But for now I'm teaching myself how to live an independent life. It's simply that my parents aren't here—and I'm more independent.

I think my parents have a wonderful profession. Each person has his profession and each person likes his profession. But me, for example . . . I don't know. Every year I have new interests. First I want one thing, then another, so I throw myself all over the place, pull in all directions, rush around, and don't manage to accomplish anything. But I still hope everything is ahead of me. That way I'll still manage to get an education and go to work. In general, my plans are to finish my current studies, go to work, and then go on and study further while I work. Go to college and work.

Around two times a week I work with a musical group. We sing Russian folk music. A year and a half ago I heard about it. I went to see them, to see just what it was. I liked it a lot, and I started going. I met the kids from the group; that attracted me more. At first I went because I wanted to learn how to sing and develop my ear, meet the people, and take part in their concerts. I started taking part in the concerts half a year after I first got there. We rehearse three times a week from three to seven. Four hours.

I love music a lot. And all music interests me except hard rock. Recently I've even started to like classical music. When I listen to Russian folk music, I lose myself in thought and imagine my own past. Somehow it's alive in me, just not fully developed, and when I listen to it, it completes me and I can meditate serenely about anything. I can think. About my life, about what I still have to do. What I haven't done, what I passed up. Like when I left the technical school.*

I didn't listen to folk music before. I wasn't interested and only heard it rarely, but now I like it a lot. I don't miss a single concert on television of any folk group. And I go to concerts in theaters and concert halls. Somehow it completes our people. A people without folk music isn't a people but just a . . . it's hard to live without that kind of music. The source of our creativity is in that music. It's a sort of native music of belonging, the same as literature or the history of your own state. About life in ancient Russia, historical songs, for example about the Pugachev rebellion.†

About my future. I don't want to go into the army. I want to get an apartment, to live in that apartment with my wife. There should be stores nearby. All the shortages should disappear, and stores should have everything I want to buy in them. In the store and not on the street. I want my wife to know how to cook. I want to communicate well with her. I want her to understand me. I have an ideal, a model girlfriend right now. I go visit my ideal almost every week. That's at the other end of Moscow. It's a long ride; it takes almost two hours. It's true that it's probably impossible to find your complete ideal, but she's the only girl I trust now. A regular girl. She's tall. I don't know, she's ordinary. She understands me. It's just easy for me to communicate with her.

I want to find good work. Any kind of work as long as it's good and you can make a good living. Not one hundred rubles. It's impossible to live on one hundred rubles now. A pair of jeans alone costs one hundred rubles here.

If I take an active interest, if I look, maybe I'll find what I'm looking for. I don't know what is and what isn't up to me; I just don't understand that yet. For now, at least I need myself. I don't know yet who else may need me in the future. I want to find a good job so that society will need me, so that I can help the state in some way . . . so that everything

---

*Before entering vocational school, Alexei studied one year in a technical school and then dropped out. Technical schools are much more prestigious than vocational schools.

†Emelian Pugachev, a popular folk hero, led a peasant revolt from 1773 to 1775. His army of Cossacks, Tatars, and runaway serfs took over parts of the Volga region, occupied the city of Kazan, and declared the abolition of serfdom. The revolt was defeated and Pugachev was captured by the forces of Catherine the Great in 1775. He was taken to Moscow and beheaded.

we need will be in the stores. So they ask someone, "What can you do for perestroika?" He doesn't say anything. He doesn't know what to say. All we have to do is say all together, "I can work for perestroika with all my heart." Let's say they ask that shoemaker from the shoe factory, "What can you do for perestroika?" He doesn't say anything; he doesn't know what to say. And yet we don't have enough shoes! He could do his job well and produce good quality footwear that doesn't fall apart the day after you buy it and that looks more like good shoes than tarpaulin boots. We just need to do our jobs well: each person's labor supports the work of the next one and all that taken together is something like perestroika. You just have to work from your heart, not just sit there and look busy.

Studying is good; it just hasn't worked out yet. I got used to not doing anything, to sitting around with my hands folded without thinking. Now I want to but I can't. I want to go to college, but I don't have the knowledge of math I need. My whole family, my sister, my sister's husband, and all my relatives are engineers, members of the intelligentsia. Of course I will be too. But I have to understand what work is in order to be an intellectual. To go to college I have to study first, master some trade first. I'm not mature enough now. When I feel like studying, when I'm drawn to my math books, I'll know I'm mature enough. I'm still not mature enough to study further. I'd sooner work for a while and then go on to study, because it's never too late, and I don't feel like it just yet. I'm still thinking about what profession to choose from the ones you can study for. I'd even sooner go study to be a subway engineer after I graduate from my vocational school. Then I'll have two fields of specialization. My profession is such a good one and will come in handy in life. It's one of the best professions you can have for the home; you can do everything around the house.

I have a huge desire to visit other countries! I'd go anywhere! Just to go. Even to Czechoslovakia. I'd go . . . well, anywhere, to any country. I want to see landmarks and museums to find out about their history. I want to come into contact with people, to get to know them. To learn more about the country, to stroll along nighttime Broadway, for example. I'd even visit Finland. I'd go anywhere with pleasure if they'd just let you, but they don't! Everybody wants to travel, but not everybody does. More than anything I'm concerned about communications with other countries. In every sense of the word. In the sense of trade, of working out relations, so that foreigners would come here more often, so that we could have more exchange.

My parents are Communists. Communism is belief in the future. Communists are in the vanguard of all the people; they're role models who set an example for everyone. During the war, the Communists were always the first to give their lives for the motherland. A regular soldier might not have been able to go forward into certain death. Maybe that's why when the Germans took our people prisoners they always said, "Communists step forward!" because the Communists could spread discord among the prisoners; they would have set the people on the right path, taught them how to struggle against the Germans even as prisoners. I know that Communists struggle to make things better, not worse. Communists struggle to make things better for everyone, not for just one part of society, but for everyone.

I don't know right now if I'll want to join the Party. For now I don't see the need to. When I grow up, in another ten years or so, then maybe I'll want to. My parents are in the Party, but so far I don't want to; I don't see any point to it yet. It will depend on how my life works out. My dad is secretary of the Party organization of teachers in the Republic of Burundi. Mom . . . I don't really know; she also has some kind of leadership position. She also plays some active role in the Party.

BECOMING A WORKER

I left high school on my own, just like that . . . just up and left. I went to study somewhere else. I thought, I'll finish school when my classmates will only be graduating [academic high school]; I'll have a profession already. I only have a little further to go and I'll have both a profession and a secondary education.

School just doesn't interest me much yet. I was a straight-A student until third grade. Then I became less and less interested in everything and started to cut more and more. I kept on cutting until the eighth grade and then went to a technical school. I had been getting C's in a lot of subjects already by eighth grade, so I decided to try a technical school. I passed my entrance exams and spent a whole year getting B's. But toward the end of the year I got tired of going there. It was very far away, at the other end of Moscow. I got tired of traveling and started over again in a vocational school. I did my first year again, a second time.

In school I just got bored with those teachers. I felt that maybe I'd have a different attitude to my classes someplace new. I thought: "I'll have more new friends. And more plans. I'll save two years because I'll have a profession and a secondary education."

The vocational school has technical subjects. The teachers treat you as more grown up. They don't think of us as little, as first-graders. The workload is more agreeable to do because it's new. Only they digest everything for us in vocational school, and they don't give homework, like in the regular school. They don't give homework in the vocational school because they know no one will do it. Very rarely. For example, they'll give us a paper to write. I wrote a paper on astronomy a semester before I had to. And now the semester is ending, but I've already got an A for the year. An A for the year already! I've already made all my grades for the whole year! Now I'm completely free from astronomy because I have an A for the semester, for the year, from all my papers and all my independent work. It all takes longer in regular school; they give lessons in school and they give you homework besides. And that's such a pain; it's so boring to stay at home doing homework when everyone else is out having fun. At least I managed to cut classes no less than two months over the last year. I love cutting classes; it's my passion, especially in the spring. In the spring I practically never go to school. I come for one class and then I leave. They criticize me for that, of course.

I chose this vocational school because it was close to me. It's just that for a year I traveled a long distance, so then I thought about finding somewhere a little closer. It's a ten-minute walk for me to this one, and it took me an hour and a half on public transportation to get to that other one. An hour and a half to ride to the technical school and ten minutes walking to the vocational school! That's why I chose the vocational school. I think my parents are satisfied. They told me themselves, "If you go to a vocational school, you'll work. You'll be a working man. You can master the higher sciences afterward." My parents say, "Go to a vocational school; study to be a worker. Then you can work while you go to college." They want me to get a higher education. But in the PTU I've got a profession and a whole group of new friends. I have old friends and new friends because my school friends are still my buddies and I've added new ones. That's how I am; I love making new friends. I'm always meeting new people in Moscow. So that's how it is; I went there just so I could meet people, have new friends.

My parents advised me to study carpentry. My great-grandfather and grandfather were carpenters. That's a good reason. He could put together a cabinet like that without using a single nail! But that was a long time ago, before the 1940s. That's what he did, and he told me, "Maybe it could work for you too; maybe you'll have a talent for it. And at the same time you'll have a profession." I'll work as a trim carpenter in construction. I'll put in window frames, cut out holes for locks, put in doors. Sometimes I'm sorry I left school, of course. I'm sorry that I left, that I lost the opportunity to have a higher position than after graduation from vocational school. But basically it's fine. Really, it's okay this way. I'll be a worker, not a manager.

PERESTROIKA, SHORTAGES, AND SPECULATION

I think Gorbachev is a wonderful person, but he's made mistakes. For example, he had prohibition for alcoholics, which almost doubled the price of vodka. My uncle's an alcoholic; the day the price went up, he couldn't stand it and died. I don't know whether it was a coincidence or not. Gorbachev raised the prices and that's why there are more drug addicts and the like. They started drinking glass cleaner and fatalities rose a lot; they didn't go down. Crime started to rise. Now he's had time to think it over and he said, "Okay, have your vodka. . . ." And the other problems, it seems, have eased up. What can you do, they always drank and they always will drink; it's probably in the blood.

The main thing is that it all started with Gorbachev; without him, we wouldn't have any of this. But now everything will follow, even without him, because the people have learned to live openly. He made contact with the people, met with them; he goes out among the people; he knows how to talk to people. He goes to factories and talks with people. It's true that before he gets there they paint everything, clean everything, and make it look nice, but mostly he relates to the people and talks more openly about everything. He's the father of our native perestroika. With his help, maybe the consumer industry will pick up.

I saw a program on dentistry in the Soviet Union. We have free medical care, but it's not worth anything. Even if it is free. For free they do it badly. I just dreamed . . . I would give all my money just so we could have inexpensive, reliable medical care, because our Soviet technology, excuse me for saying this, but they drill rocks with the same drills they use on our teeth. That's why I'm so afraid to go to the dentist.

And the problem of shortages. You can't even get soap in the Soviet Union right now; you could say everyone's walking around dirty. It's embarrassing. Everything's become difficult. We've started to have shortages of so many things now. The cooperatives have started doing this sort of work, but they ask a lot of money because almost nobody buys from them, only people with a lot of money they don't know what to do with shop there. And young people don't have so much money, only what Mom and Dad give them. . . .

Sugar will probably disappear by summertime; there won't be anything to make jam with. Our light industry is really undeveloped, and it's hard to buy anything of good quality. Soviet sneakers are frightening! You don't play sports in them; you would break your legs. That's why everybody's running after imports. Everybody's trying to grab something fashionable. It's not so much that it needs to be fashionable as foreign, because those things are much more comfortable. We haven't even gotten as far as being able to wear what we make.

The problem of fashion—we don't have anything to wear. I, for example, try to stand out from everybody else; I wear what no one else wears. Everyone is surprised and then I notice that later, first one, then another of my friends starts to follow my example. I get my clothes in my grandmother's and grandfather's closets, in attics. There was a lot more concern about quality work before. We were building communism before, and now it seems we've become disappointed in that. . . . Now we're not building anything. The same with the movies. We have a lot of classic films. American films—classics of world cinema—and they didn't release them here because there was too much sex. So what's sex? Why, it's classic! And you can't cut out what's classic! That's why they didn't release a lot of classics. Now they've started to release them some, and they cut less. Otherwise, a film usually runs two hours and here they show just one hour. So there you have it.

In the Soviet Union it's impossible to get a cassette. A regular cassette that used to sell for nine rubles now costs up to thirty rubles. A lot of people go running around looking for cassettes.

Crime is increasing. Maybe it's a kind of protest and maybe it's just that young people are getting dumber than before. Just as an example, they stop someone on the street and take his boots or jacket off him. They can do that. Because you can't buy it, and if you can find it for sale, then it's not for the kind of money you could afford. They couldn't earn as much as that and that's mostly why there's crime. Where are they supposed to get that kind of money from?

Speculation is a very important issue. I don't think speculation will disappear until we have everything on the shelves. Probably there's speculation only in the Soviet Union because only we have such shortages. The small percentage they raise the prices in the secondhand stores is also speculation; it's just state speculation. And probably it's only called speculation in the Soviet Union; in America, for example, it's called business. It's not about selling lipstick on the street, but about the fact that there isn't any! It's the state's own fault! When we have everything, there won't be speculation. We shouldn't round up the speculators and send them to jail, because new ones will take their place anyway. We should develop our industry in just those things they speculate in. Speculation is a sign that something's lacking. It's hard to say whether speculation is good or bad. It's just that if someone has more money, he can permit himself to buy something more expensive if he needs it. So speculation is like an index of what we don't have. They should look at what's being speculated in and produce those goods. There are less fruits and vegetables since perestroika. It's impossible to get caviar. We're lacking a lot of things. The people's demands have grown, but the supply of goods hasn't.

Maybe under Stalin there was caviar and sausages and there was more meat, but now there's very little of all that and it's worse quality. More chemicals. Everybody wanted things produced faster, more meat to be available, and that's why we don't have any now. Everything should have been done in proportion and then there would have been enough for everyone, for all time. There was a campaign here at one time: Brezhnev said to produce more meat faster. The peasants were neglectful; that's probably why we have less of everything we eat. If they'd been working their own fields, had their own homes, they would have tilled their own fields and turned everything over to the state and the state would have distributed it to all the stores.* We would have had everything and everything would have been inexpensive. As it is now, they come to Moscow from the country to buy whatever's left.

We have to give everyone land now; whoever wants to can be a farmer on his own land and raise cows, for example. But it's come to the point where nothing's left and the countryside's emptying out. All the people live in the city, although it's true a few have started to go back. But that's not enough. There has to be private property to cultivate everything. Take potatoes, they don't harvest more than 50 percent for the market, and then whoever lives in the country gathers the rest of those potatoes to last them all winter. But if they were working for money, they'd harvest every last potato. The same thing with the calves they fatten up for meat. They don't care whether they're thin or not, but if they were their own, the better the meat, the better for everybody. They'd feed them until they grew into big bulls.

GLASNOST

I think they're telling the truth now because, first of all, I remember some of the things I'm reading about in the papers, plus the things I hear going around fill in the gaps between the things I'm being told. It's like there's a staircase that's missing some steps and it's hard to jump over the missing steps, but then the supplementary things you hear going around among the people sound like those missing steps so you can learn everything from that staircase exactly the way it was. Most

---

*Agricultural reform is one of the key issues of perestroika. Long-term land-leasing arrangements give people the right to work land rented from collective and state farms. Reformers believe that cultivation by small farmers will increase productivity.

of the time there aren't any false steps. The people know everything. They kept quiet . . . they were afraid.

People complement each other. Each knows his piece of the puzzle. Now they're saying that a lot of soldiers are missing in action in Afghanistan. Their names are being kept secret; they're trying to hush it up, to sort of write it off. But people are taking it up now; the mothers have organized some kind of group and they're going to search out those who were left behind as prisoners in Pakistan. They're going to try to get them out of there even if it costs a million, even if we have to give the last shirt off our backs, we'll get them out of there. We'll bring them home.

For half my history class now I get information about how things were, and for the other half of class the teacher reads the paper and talks about what she knows from her own experience. We're interested in what she can tell us, how Tupolev made his planes. Under Stalin, all the scientists were put in jail so that they'd make their planes there rather than at their own will. Tupolev was kept under house arrest so that he'd invent planes. Who knows, maybe he wouldn't have invented as many planes, or maybe he would've invented more.

I've only recently started reading the papers; these problems didn't interest me before. You see, I have a book: *USA: 200 Years—200 Wars*. That's what I call politics! Maybe it's some kind of propaganda; they say how bad it is, the USA fighting all the time, although we also make war, but that's not talked about. We were in Afghanistan; I don't remember what other country we were in: Poland, Hungary, and not that long ago. We also make war, but we fight more to defend ourselves. We help friendly countries, but that's still making war.

I'm a member of the International Peace Committee, and I should be concerned about whether there will be peace or war on earth. With the committee's help I meet with others; it's interesting to be in touch with people who live in another country. They have the same problems we have. They're also trying to stop the arms race, and so on.

What kind of policy is that to spread rumors about each other? In our papers America is always talking about the contemporary Soviet threat, saying that the hammer is about to fall; that's propaganda right? So they said that America talks about the Soviet military threat, but that's the same thing we're rumoring about America. It was all related. In 1984 our propaganda was no less developed than in America; they wrote all kinds of things about the CIA, different caricatures. But it's no longer like that; we have a freer attitude now.

I'm very concerned about whether I'm going to have to fight against others. I'm very worried about that, because I don't want to. I think about it every day.

There was an incident in Armenia [after the earthquake]: the French were digging out this old man and he came out of his cellar with his hands raised; he thought a war had started. People think that war could break out at any minute. They could drop an atomic bomb; you think about that all the time. I'm against war in any way I can be; I'd give everything if only there wouldn't be a war. I mean that seriously. A lot of people would die. Because a war wouldn't be with bows and arrows but for real, with chemicals. It would be the end of humankind; nothing would be left.

I don't know a single person now who doesn't want to visit America. I know that for a fact. We know very little about your country. Before, my impressions came only from the newspapers: the CIA, killing with pistols, violence, sex on every corner, selling weapons, guns, to children in the stores, shooting in the schools, incidents like that. . . . But we have that here too, the same thing. It's true they don't sell weapons here, but we still have them. They just didn't talk about it before, and now they've started to talk about weapons, the rackets; someone stole 100,000 rubles from some cooperative. But now that I've started to meet Americans, to get together with them, I look at them and they're just the same kind of people as we are. Exactly the same. They don't differ from us in any way at all. I pictured them like in the newspapers before. . . . I can bring you clippings; there are some about the CIA, Rambo; Rambo's such a parasite; he's against the Soviet Union, against Soviet Communists; he kills them. But the first Rambo was against America! He's a Vietnam veteran, like our Afghan veterans. First they show American helicopters slaughtering; the anticommunism only starts later.

I don't think the Soviet Union has an enemy. Before, but not now. Not America. No one considers America an enemy, only the most inveterate army officers, only the guys with the epaulets think about how there might be missiles of some kind, but the simple people don't believe it; even the soldiers don't believe it. Absolutely not. I'm for America.

The world has changed. Who wants to make war if it means the end of the world? There have already been so many disasters. . . . Chernobyl, earthquakes; this isn't the time to fight; this isn't the Middle Ages, when people killed each other for gain, to eat the bread of whoever you killed; everyone has bread now, and what more do you need?

THE ARMY

I'll go into the army in two years. I'm seventeen now, but I should have a one-year deferral because I lost one year in technical school. I absolutely do not want to go to the army. I just think I'll lose the best years of my life. The army doesn't attract me; I don't know what to do there. Of course I won't get anything out of it. All that militarism doesn't attract me. Weapons don't interest me at all. Just the opposite; we should get over it as quickly as possible. Then there wouldn't be any weapons or wars or borders. . . . Moreover I am absolutely against guys going into the army. Against it.

If I didn't have to go into the army, I'd get married at nineteen and start a big family; I'd study to be a subway engineer; I'd work and go to night school; but this way I'm just losing two years.

My parents tell me it's better if I go into the army, that I'll get stronger there. They served together, here, not far from Moscow. But I don't want to, I don't want to be involved with the hazing of newcomers, and so on. . . . But I have to. Maybe they'll think something up for the army over these next two years; maybe they'll make a volunteer army. In two years' time. If they have the chance to, of course, but it's not likely.

THE MODERN YOUNG MUSCOVITE

Young people used to listen to foreign music before, but now, because of glasnost, Soviet rock is coming along and they've started being interested in our groups. Soviet pop music isn't very developed. Before it wasn't permitted: you can't listen to this, you can't listen to that. . . . But now it's allowed: go ahead and listen! Our Soviet music is only beginning to develop.

From eight to ten in the evening there's simply nothing to do. You're not going to sit home and watch television when there's nothing worth watching. Mostly you go outside, but there's nothing to do there either; everything's closed. So you begin messing around from having nothing else to do. Some young people run around the streets in chains. The way they dress is unbelievable; probably they do it as a protest against the Soviet Union's poorly developed consumer industry. Probably against the fact that it's hard to buy anything now.

Everyone I know wants to know about America. Maybe because you have a lot of good music and your consumer industry is highly developed. And even though American young people are a lot like us, we lag behind them a lot, even in clothing. We lag far behind in the level of our development, psychologically and socially. The way we dress . . . we walk around sad, with fallen faces, in sweatsuits. We all look alike; what I like about America is that nobody looks like anybody else. Nobody wears a uniform like soldiers. Everyone wears his own clothes and doesn't look like everyone else. There's a choice; you wear what you like, but here there's no choice. Everybody here is wearing felt boots now. Everybody resembles everybody else. Moscow young people: you can describe them by their clothes. The guys are in sweatsuits, the girls in berets, that's it. In caps like these. And they all have perms. That's a must. They're as alike as test-tube babies. They wear either jeans or boots from a cooperative, nothing more!

NATASHA

"THERE'S NOTHING A RUSSIAN WOMAN CAN'T DO"

NATASHA

Sixteen years old, ninth-grade student

Natasha is well known in her school. She works as a classroom assistant with second-graders, and she is always surrounded by them. They crowd around her, talk, laugh, cling to her, don't want to let her go.

Tall and thin, neat and proper, Natasha has a reserved sort of energy. When she talks to the second-graders, I see the teacher in her emerging. She is friendly and open, hugs her second-graders, has a lovely smile, but her words have a purpose. She thinks carefully about what she says to her charges, how she presents herself.

When I interview her, she lets me know that she is taking time off from a very crowded schedule in order to talk to me.

I'm in a special class in my school that's for those of us who want to study at the pedagogical institute. I've wanted to be a teacher since the first grade. As long as I can remember I've dreamed of being a teacher, even though there were times when I also wanted to be an archeologist or a political scientist, even a criminologist, working for the police, with fingerprints, well, as a specialist. But all these nine years, while I've been at school, this dream of becoming a teacher has always been at the back of my mind. I don't know, it seems like teaching is the job I'm best suited for, the one where I can give the most of myself. I love kids; if I didn't I probably couldn't do the work. Right now I'm working with second-grade class B, kind of as the teacher's assistant. Pechnikova and I, another student, have put on shows, and I've taught class.

See, I find working with people interesting. First being with them, and then there's wanting to give them something. They give you a lot, too, kids. That's something I've really felt anyway. They teach you kindness and how to get along with others. They're always so great, I mean it always feels so great to be with them, you want to give them something in return. Brighten up their lives. It doesn't always work, of course, like when Svetlana Viktorovna, the class teacher, got sick and we wanted to do a show, well I wanted to, anyway. But the assistant principal wouldn't let us have one of the classrooms. We had everything ready, but there was no classroom, because the school's on a double shift. The third grade got permission to do it late, about five or six o'clock, but the second grade wasn't allowed to for some reason. No explanation, she just said no. Of course, everybody was practically in tears, but what could you do? I did what I could to calm them down. Never mind, they decided to do something for New Year's next year when they're in the third grade.

I love going camping, taking trips to other cities, learning something new. Probably every city is different. Every village, too, and more. Different people, different attitudes toward life maybe, different cultures, different ways of relating. For instance, we noticed that in small towns where everybody knows everybody else people are more charitable somehow. "Charity" has become a fashionable word now, the ability to come to somebody's help and not just a friend or comrade, but even someone you don't know. If you see that somebody needs your help, you should always be willing to help. And I think that this probably means completely without compensation, expecting nothing in return, no reciprocal help. Not just material help. It could be nothing more than a kind word. They say, "Even a cat enjoys a kind word." It seems that we've forgotten this, lost this capacity somehow. We have to learn to simply help someone. I think that word was kind of forgotten, lost maybe. Ten years ago, I remember, I never even saw the word.

I want to graduate with good grades and enter college. A teaching college. I want to be a history teacher. And then after I graduate from college I'll go to work in a school. As soon as I started school I realized that it was very important to me. You know, you have hunches. And I feel like that is where I can do the most good, contribute the way I should. Of course you have to love kids. I mean, they give me a lot, they really do, of course. It's awfully interesting working with them, even second graders. Those kids all have their own personalities. Some are better, some are worse, but they're all very interesting. I don't think they're sorry that I work with them. They're really happy when I come. They always come over and ask when I'll be back.

I want to be a democratic teacher who trusts her students and believes them. I've taught some second-grade classes; I've been working with the same class since September. When you walk into the classroom and thirty pairs of eyes look at you, if you tell them something that isn't true, that itself is probably serious. They hear every word you say. And they believe you, especially in the lower grades.

I don't think teaching is a very easy job, but it's important. A lot depends on the teacher. He's got a big responsibility. Thirty people— what kind of people will they grow up to be? What kind of contribution will they make to society, to their country? Teachers should always recognize the responsibility they have, it should always be at the back of their minds. Because kids are the future. Everybody goes to school, everyone has teachers. The future of this country depends largely on teachers, on their ability to build character, and basically we need as many good educators as we can get, educators who know how to judge kids on their merits.

My mom is a nurse. She graduated from nursing school and now she works at a factory. It's a long way from our home. In this country we have first aid stations at factories. They usually employ a doctor and two or three nurses. Mom is in charge of the first aid station at the Mikromashina plant in Moscow. They produce blowdryers, coffee grinders, and razors. Before, Mom wanted to be a doctor. She worked as a lab assistant, two years I think, at Medical Institute No. 1. She applied to medical school, I don't know, once or twice, but then she decided to become a nurse after all. She probably knows more than any doctor. She knows an awful lot. She always helps everybody, the neighbors and friends. People are constantly coming to her for advice. She knows her job. She's trying to get me interested, even though I don't plan to enter medicine. But she says that everything comes in handy someday. Sometimes I want to go into medicine, probably mostly because of Mom.

My dad's a construction worker for the operational support department of the Ministry of Chemical Industry. He builds apartment buildings for the employees of that ministry. We live in a building the brigade Dad heads built. There are about twenty or thirty people in the brigade, and he's responsible for maintaining discipline, making sure everybody comes to work and all that. And he does construction work himself. He's actually a bricklayer by profession.

What I'd like to say about Mom is that she's easygoing, very kind and calm. I have parents who really try to understand me and are pretty easygoing. Actually . . . Dad's pretty strict. But Mom's easygoing. We don't have any particularly big disagreements. When we had those satellite link-ups* everybody was saying, "My parents don't understand me," and so on, but somehow that's not a problem for me. Of course they worry about

---

*The television "bridges" between Soviet and American audiences.

me, but basically if Mom feels that I'm wrong about something either she or Dad will try to explain why I'm wrong, and then the two of us or the three of us will decide what to do. But we don't have any big conflicts.

My parents have tried to teach me how to live, how to get along with people, and basically how to tell good from bad. And that's very important today, although people have always closed their eyes to . . . well, as they say, the ends justify the means. But isn't that always so? How to judge the world around me, the people around me, probably every parent teaches his child that, but I think I could talk for hours about what my parents have given me, because basically . . . that's the way it works. The first years of our lives—a decade and more—we live with our parents, who teach us everything—how to live, the reason for living, what interests and ideals we should have.

My mom is the person I feel closest to. I can tell her absolutely anything that's on my mind. She's very . . . I think she's what a woman should be. She's easygoing . . . not when she gets home from work, of course. Then she's very tense, because work is tense, but for the most part she's always . . . She's lived a pretty long life and she always helps me, sharing her experience. If I have some conflict I always get her advice. And I feel close to her. There are a lot of school trips, so we're apart almost every vacation, and I miss her very much. And home in general. She's given me a love of home, and you know, I just love being there. I love being with my relatives, with Dad and Mom and Grand-mother. We moved recently. A few years ago Mom probably wouldn't have gotten an apartment. Because an awful lot of housing disappeared. It went to the Executive Committee, and there it was distributed to friends and acquaintances. . . . That doesn't happen anymore.

We didn't wait for an apartment long. My dad's been working for this enterprise that does construction for the Ministry of Chemical Industry. He's worked for about sixteen years now, and for about the past ten I guess we haven't been able to get an apartment, even though there have been a few people who work with him who've managed to get two apartments apiece in a shorter time, six years or so.* They got a two-room apartment first through connections, and then a three-room. Of course before, when I was smaller, it didn't matter so much, but now I'm older, it's probably not so great for a person who's sixteen to have to share a room with her grandmother. The apartment was small. So perestroika's done something good for my family. Mom's so happy now! Before, she says, everything was harder.

---

*Note that Natasha does not consider a ten-year wait for a larger apartment to be a long time. Many people wait far longer than that to get housing.

My grandparents once lived in the country. Then they moved to the city where Grandfather's relatives lived. My Dad is from the Ukraine, Vinnitsa Oblast, a long way away. We went there not too long ago, to the place Dad's from. There were six kids and we often go to visit one or another of his sisters. We drive down to the area he's from. Usually we camp out and travel to Moldavia and the Ukraine. The family—Dad, Mom.

Grandmother got married when she was fourteen. That was common before. Men were given land but women weren't, so people tried to marry off their daughters as soon as possible, because having a daughter around was considered bad and undesirable. Because men were given land, say six hundredths, and women weren't. That was before the Revolution. My grandmother was born in 1901 . . . no, 1903 actually. She's eighty-six. She's had a hard life. Mom's told me about it. But she's a heck of a lady, my grandmother. She considers herself the homemaker. She does everything herself and won't trust anybody else. Sometimes Mom tells her that it's time she took it easy. But she can't sit around doing nothing. She's a country girl, she's always worked. She's used to it. She says, "I can't sit around doing nothing."

I guess you can probably tell that my parents grew up in the period of stagnation. But really they do take an interest in everything that's going on now in this country. There's a big contrast between the past few years and life before. Mom says that when people were growing up they were constantly being told that everything was okay, the country was doing fine, we were ahead in every area. People were kind of indifferent. They put in their time at work and that was that. Now Mom says you can sense a change everywhere. Like at her factory. She's in charge of the first aid station at the factory. They've started holding special events, they opened a gym, and then, something she's particularly interested in, they're conducting check-ups. Of course, I'm no expert, but people have started taking a more responsible attitude toward their work. Before they just came to be checked off on a list, but now they basically have more faith in the doctors.

I really love my school and my class and the kids I go to school with. Our class gets along pretty well. The kids are interesting and you can always be sure they'll be there when you need them. I mean, even when you're sick you wish you were at school. You miss it. Trips are always special occasions. They're work, too, of course, most times, because we seldom go just for the fun of it. In Tashkent, for example, we visited an orphanage and a military hospital for Afghanistan vets and the local Pioneer headquarters. In Tallinn we did work for a museum and met former inmates of the Kola concentration camp. The work has always made us feel good inside.

I usually don't have much free time at all. I'd like to find the time to go spend an hour or two at the library, but no, I've got to do homework. I always come home from school pretty late. At four or five. Relax, walk the dog, and do my homework. Every minute's taken up, but just to have time for myself . . . only when we have vocational skills class, on Thursdays and Sundays. And that's it. I don't have much free time. Vacations are almost always taken up, too. There are always school trips. Leningrad, Volgograd. . . . If you eliminate all those days there's a month left over for summer vacation . . . then there's summer work camp, so about three weeks are left for myself. If there were forty-eight hours in a day instead of twenty-four it might be easier!

PERESTROIKA: A PAINFUL PROCESS

I would like to go back a few years in time, to when Mikhail Sergeyevich first took the post of general secretary. At first everything was quiet and peaceful—that was my impression. I was still a child then, quite young, in fifth or sixth grade. Then he gave a few speeches on television, and I understood very little then. I remember sitting there for more than an hour listening to him, and it seemed very interesting to me. And now it is even more interesting to follow the changes that are taking place here in this country. May God grant him a long life! He began well, of course, but the whole process is quite painful after so many years. It's crucial that later on there will be people just like him to continue on.

I can tell we've got glasnost. Look at how much freedom of speech there is in the press and on TV. Not like before. For instance, I was still little, but for some reason I can remember really well Brezhnev on TV. He always read from a text he had in front of him and we only saw him twice a year. But Mikhail Sergeyevich is always on a trip to some city or other, talking to people. There's always a press conference or meeting. What I mean to say is, he's visible, we already know him. I'm very glad that we now have good relations with a lot of countries like China and America. Things are just more interesting. There's a lot that's new, stuff you didn't know about. Not like before, when everything was going smoothly, no problems.

There are some moments I remember from my childhood. Everything was fine and dandy. I don't know, the newspapers and the way I was in the first and second grades, maybe the third. But now it all seems like a blur. You find some pamphlet now, I don't know, we moved and we found these old newspapers—it was like all the papers said the same thing, only they used different words. Day after day, everything was okay. And all those slogans, like "Life is a thing of beauty and wonder." Who believed it? Maybe the teacher's first assistant and the members of the Komsomol and the Pioneers! It's kind of like that now, too. When people are telling the truth they criticize. They didn't criticize things before because they were afraid, I guess. Probably because it wasn't done and people were afraid, the willingness to take the initiative was literally choked out of them and they didn't have access to much information.

For instance, people have only started talking, you know, openly about the Stalinist purges and that whole time in the past two or three years. Because when people went into battle and were dying they cried "For the motherland, for Stalin!" you know, and what was really going on then? People were just given the bare facts with nothing to back them up, and people probably thought that that's how it was, they probably believed. I think that it's part of man's nature to believe the government.

I don't know whether my parents believed. My grandparents were most affected, of course. Grandmother was affected by the campaign against the kulaks. People used to think that anyone who had a house over two stories tall was a kulak. My grandmother says there were kulaks who had, you know, hired hands. She had a brother who worked and saved up the money he'd earned. He had a cow, no, two cows, two horses, some other stuff she told me about that I don't remember, a two-story house, and seven or eight children, which was normal then. Now people don't have many. Then one day they came and took everything—everything except the wife and kids! He was exiled to Siberia somewhere. She says they did it in front of everybody. Their possessions went into a state fund or a fund for poorer peasants. They say that there were people, well, say somebody who was lazy, and all that stuff went to him. Not all of it, of course, but part. So maybe he didn't do anything and his house and the garden were in bad shape, and maybe there wasn't even a cow. The people who worked had everything confiscated, so of course it was very unfair, and it happened right in front of everybody, too. Those were hard years for peasants, the 1920s and 1930s. My grandmother can't read. She's old and she says that most of them couldn't read. They saw what was going on, but where could they go to complain? In out-of-the-way villages like that very few people could write. Everybody saw what was happening, but they couldn't say anything.

My other grandmother saw Stalin many times, and she even spoke to him, and she says that in those days it was hard to get by. Perhaps I'm about to say something that we're not really allowed to say in the Soviet Union, but she once worked in a secret place near Kirovskaya during the war, and there were two parallel lines in the Metro, and, well, it wasn't exactly a palace, but there was a bomb shelter, and Stalin would go down there surrounded by his guards in his car and that was where he spent his time during air raids. And my grandmother says that she always had the impression he was scared of something. Stalin always looked around and he always had bodyguards. Gorbachev has them too, a few people. But my grandmother says that the people who saw him there were not allowed to talk about where they worked, and she says that it even seems strange to her that she did not end up in that wave of repression. Some of the people who worked there with her did. But she was left alone. Later on she went back to Smolensk, where she was from. But she says that she had the feeling that at any moment somebody was going to come and take her away.

PERESTROIKA, GLASNOST, AND SCHOOL

We have self-administration now at school. Glasnost—yes, of course. Now we're in command. In other words, we're directing the way school is getting run. Mostly the teachers aren't like our bosses anymore, they're not people who tell us what to do, they're people who help us. Everything's just gotten a lot more interesting, classes are a lot more interesting, I guess. We've started saying what we think more. Not to all the teachers, but to most of them. Now we've got a lot of new, young teachers at school who you can pretty much talk to as equals, as friends.

Of course, we're losing a lot of time in history class now, writing outlines so we'll know something about our country. Our teacher lectures; we take notes. We have to write it all out and learn it for the next class. We spend the whole class taking notes. It's not that I want to say anything bad about the teacher; class is very interesting. For four years, from the fourth to the seventh grade, class was conducted on such a primitive level. I mean, we just came to class, opened our books, covered the paragraphs that were in that day's lesson plan, and the teacher asked us questions about them. It didn't spark any interest—and history is such an interesting subject! All the classes were kind of dull. Not like they should have been. Now all that's changed; it's gotten interesting, what with all the information coming out. We're studying modern Soviet history right now. The teacher's telling us so much! The pre-revolutionary period, the Revolution and the first years of Soviet rule, the Civil War . . . It's different. None of that x-to-y stuff. Recently they've started drawing a line connecting history and modern history. We're studying the prerevolutionary period and Stalin's time. We argue and discuss in class. Of course, there's never enough time left for discussion. You want to talk it over and ask questions.

A couple of weeks ago there was a report on the TV show *Up to Sixteen and Older** on a conflict between a history teacher and her tenth-grade class. They told her they wanted to know the whole truth about the time of stagnation and the Stalinist purges and she didn't tell them anything. She said they'd disrupted the class. They told her, "You're our teacher. You know that the things you were telling us were lies." So this conflict arose, and now the kids have had their exams put off two months.

MEN AND WOMEN

What can I say about my future? I'll probably get married. I'll have my home, my hearth; I want everything in the family to go well. In other words, what any woman wishes for! I don't want to lead my life in vain. I want to leave some kind of legacy; I want something good to remain from me.

I probably do have some kind of idea of what I would like my future husband to be. The idea is forming in my head little by little—but we'll see what he turns out to be. It's very complicated to talk about this because I myself still haven't really figured it all out.

Of course, I want him to be a good person. The most important thing is that he be honest, and, of course, have some skills. He should know how to hammer a nail. He should love children. He should be a real person. But who knows what will happen! It seems to me that everybody has to have hope that they'll find that kind of person, because if there's no hope, then why even live? I think that a person lives because, well, every person should dream, should have hope for something, believe in something. And I think one has to have hope about this question as well.

But it seems to me that men nowadays are more like . . . well, in general, the boys in our class—not all of them, but probably more than 50 percent of them—are good guys. They are always ready to help out, and from my own experience I know that when you get sick, they always come visit you at home to see if they can help you with anything. But on the bus to school you come across something totally different! We seem to have so many men who think only about themselves. You get onto public transportation and see a young girl standing with a huge bag,

---

*A popular television program, with news and feature stories, targeted at young adults.

holding on to it as if she were about to fall at any minute, and right next to her some fat, healthy, hefty man sits reading a newspaper and doesn't even seem to have the strength to lift his eyes and take a look at who's standing next to him. It's so insulting sometimes; it happens to me that I can barely stand up, and right next to me some guy who's about twenty is sitting down. So okay, I'm young and I can take it, but what about the old grandmothers? Or a woman who has worked her eight hours and still had to stand for two hours in lines in stores and is only now on her way home? The buses are packed in the evenings; there are so many people. Where I live there isn't a subway yet, only buses. The buses are overcrowded in the mornings and in the evenings, and it's impossible to even get out of the neighborhood. What can you do? You have to fend for yourself somehow!

Of course, they say around here that there's nothing a woman, a Russian woman, can't do, and I think that's true—she is capable of doing everything! Look at what she is already so accustomed to! Everything! She can split wood or stand in a line in a store for three hours. Look at the huge bags they carry around—not just any man could lift those bags! And she can make do in any circumstances, adapt to everything—and she still manages to look more or less attractive. Good God, what she doesn't have to invent; she'll line her eyes with an ordinary colored pencil; she'll use anything whether it's something she's supposed to use or something she shouldn't. It's so hard to live like that! It's terrible! And then they wonder why women can be so evil at work, why they look so bad. They don't want to have to even look at another person, and how can you expect them to, after having to deal with all that—to smile in somebody's face when they have to answer them, or even look at their husband tenderly? I think all this is awful!

Women should at least have time to be able to chat with their girlfriends! It's horrifying to look at the teachers in our school. They spend so much time and energy on the school, and in addition they still have their homes; they have their families. They have to cook, to clean.

Most men aren't capable of everything. These days around here you find quite a few ungentlemanly, indifferent men. Of course, there are plenty of bad women around; I don't mean to deny that, but I simply think that a lot of men are incapable of helping a woman around the house, and they can't go to the stores.

I will re-educate my husband, or at least I'll try to. Perhaps by the time I grow up social consciousness will be somewhat higher, and perhaps then everything won't get dumped on women's shoulders.

It goes without saying that a man should help, but the government should also help us out and make things easier. Because of course the conditions in which women work are not acceptable. Each day she spends only seventeen minutes on educating her children. That's what women are traditionally—homemakers. And the husband should help and make her work easier. Of course it's basically the woman's responsibility, and a man should just help, so that it will be easier for the wife.

I don't know; it just seems to me that a woman should be the one to do the housework. It simply seems that a man often will not be able to do it the way a woman can.

It seems to me that my future doesn't depend totally upon me. Whatever I am able to do is what I'll do. There will be some kind of influence from the outside. Still, for the most part, the future—having a good life or a bad life—depends upon each person. After all, a person has to fight for his happiness. I don't mean to say that nothing bad will happen, that there won't be some kind of pain, but, no matter what, a person has to know how to stand up for himself. I understand that our happiness—the happiness of women—is dependent upon men. But also, in many ways, dependent upon each woman herself, as well as on men. If a man behaves badly toward a woman, doesn't give a damn about her, things will be very bad. Happiness is made up of many different small pieces. Sometimes it comes from circumstances, and sometimes from chance. It seems to me that every woman and every man has to overcome whatever is bad in themselves, whatever negatives there are, in order to have a good character and not be quick-tempered under any circumstances.

Men are somewhat more reserved; men are completely different from us. So I don't know what their happiness depends upon. I don't know how to explain this—they simply are different. Certainly in the sense that what a woman finds interesting is not always interesting to a man. And vice versa. A man won't discuss some outfit or a pair of shoes or a hairstyle, although who knows, perhaps among themselves they do. And women have some kind of weakness. For example, they like to gossip, not because they have evil intentions, of course, but they like to have talks from the heart. It seems to me that that might not be one of the best traits of the female character.

KATYA

"THE IDEALS MY PARENTS AND GRANDPARENTS GREW UP WITH ARE COLLAPSING"

KATYA
Sixteen years old, ninth-grade student

Katya takes care of people. She spends a lot of time looking after her little brother, Andryusha, walks him home from school most days, even if she has to come back later to join her friends. She worries about me, too. If I spend a full day at her school, she always makes sure I've gotten lunch.

She dresses simply when not in her school uniform. Her hair, long, thick, and wavy, is usually pulled back in a ponytail. She wears bangs and not even a trace of makeup.

She takes the interviews quite seriously. She follows events closely, reads newspapers, brings me clippings. There is a lot she reads about that upsets her, and she talks about current events in a rush of words, with an air of great urgency: she is overwhelmed by the number of problems her country faces. I hear this in her voice; I see it in the worried expression on her face when she talks to me.

Dad's the head of a department. He's an engineer and Mom's a senior engineer. Mom isn't really all that happy about being an engineer. She says that engineering is no job for a woman, because when a woman has her kids and family to take care of it's not for her. She leaves for work in the morning and comes back in the evening. The commute on the subway takes a whole hour, and if she has to do any shopping she gets home really late. Six thirty at the earliest. They've got flex time now, so if she's delayed in the morning she stays that much later in the evening.

My dad works an awful lot. He leaves very early and comes home late. Sometimes even after we've gone to bed, but that's just when he's swamped with work. They have lots of Party meetings—he's a Party member. And then there are all kinds of conferences and meetings and they're forever discussing one thing or other, so when he gets home he's really tired and he does something with my brother Andryusha. He and Mom get along really well. Mom does most of the work around the house. She loves to bake and I love to eat what she bakes. Andryusha and I do the cleaning. Dad helps too, of course. He puts nails in the walls and all those jobs men do, like repairs—purely physical work. It's a woman's job to cook, wash, and iron. That's just the way it is in our family. Dad can't cook. Actually, he knows how, but like I said he leaves early and comes back in the evening.

I'm basically very open with Mom and work out any problems I have with her. She really understands me. We usually talk about different things. She's preparing me for adult life. She tells me about a lot of the difficulties I may face, family problems. She's trying to teach me to cook, so that I'll be able to when I have my own family. And then there's the question of what a husband should be like. She says you should have a boy's respect and love, and he should be able to help around the house; that's very important too. That's always helpful. She knows all my friends, and she takes it well, calmly. Basically I tell her everything—what's happening at school, where we're going. I never hide anything from her. She's my best friend in every way.

I love traveling. Ever since the fifth grade I've been going on camping trips and get-togethers with the kids in my class and one of our teachers, Valentina Vladimirovna—she's the one who got us started. Two- or three-day trips to different parts of the country. First we toured the whole area around Moscow when we were in the fourth grade. We saw all those places we've got, the museums near Moscow and all that. Then we've been to Leningrad twice, to Volgograd, Vladimir, the Golden Ring towns—Vladimir, Suzdal, Gus-Khrustalny. This year we visited Minsk and Tashkent. We've done a lot of traveling to different parts of the country like that. We visited Tallinn in the Baltic region.

You learn a lot. Everything about a city is interesting, the culture and all, especially if it's in another republic; everything different is interesting and each ethnic group has its own customs. And then there's the train trip with the other kids from the class. We have such a great time together. Of course we see each other at school, but we go home at the end of the day. On trips we're together all the time. We all became friends a long time ago. I can remember in the sixth grade there was a group of us, boys and girls, we were together all the time. We'd be together during breaks at school, call each other, hang out together, visit each other. Go on trips together—not in separate little groups but all together.

Last year we spent all our time together, this year, too. And we take trips together . . . we take boat trips, and we visited a village. We were always together, this year too. Hikes, trips with the guys. Last spring, before the eighth-grade exams we have to take, the kids from my class, plus this one guy from the tenth grade, we would go out and sit in this little square by the school. We'd go there first thing in the morning, and then after lunch. Exams? Big deal. Go there, cram a little, and everything's fine.

I don't know how things will work out, but I'd like to become a physics teacher. I'll finish college and then go to work. I hope I'll get a job in the field I like best—that would be nice. I'd like to do a lot of things. First of all, I'd like to travel, see different cities in different republics, in Asia, in the Southern republics. I'd like to visit other countries. I'd like to visit America. It's a very interesting country and I'm really curious about it. For some reason more than any other country. We don't know much about America, but it's an exciting country. I think there are probably a lot of interesting things to see there. A beautiful country.

I want to be happy and have a family I can be proud of—a husband, kids. I don't know how my future will turn out . . . I would like to find happiness, a good family, a husband, children. I want things to be good. Sometimes I imagine my future husband. Wise, strong. He would know how to work, and of course he would help out at home. I don't want the kind of husband who comes home in the evening, lounges around on the sofa, and doesn't do anything else. He would definitely have to help around the house and help bring up the children.

THE SOVIET UNION TODAY:
"WE HAVE SO MANY PROBLEMS"

We really do need to reform everything. Lenin once said, "Something has to be done so that the government will be responsible!" Well, not for *every*thing, like it is here, where the State took over everything, and nobody answers for anything, nobody gives a damn, and all that. In other words, the result was terrible—general irresponsibility and total collapse.

We have so many problems in this country right now! The whole system has to be changed. There are problems in the economy and consumer services and industry. Everywhere, in other words! Protecting the environment. Women in the workplace. Services. Industry. . . .

There's the food industry. Of course nothing's available, all the stores are empty. And service? Anybody who has the gall to go someplace and ask a question is asking to be chewed out.

Things are very difficult with furniture. Recently we bought a dresser, and oy, was that a mess! It means you go and register in a store someplace in Tushino, at the other end of Moscow. You have to go there every day and mark your place on the list. My mother has a friend who works in that store, so she marked our place for us on the list. God forbid you miss a day! If you do, that's it. They take you off the list automatically. If you don't come they take note and write that your number was taken off the list. Nobody knows when the shipment will come in or how long you'll have to go and mark off your place on the list. When we bought our kitchen set, we marked our place on the list every day. And it's up to chance who gets what. When we bought the kitchen set there was a wooden set that was really beautiful and we wanted, but they ran out and we ended up with a different kind instead.

And health care! People leave medical institutes completely unprepared to work in hospitals! The service itself is horrible. Hospitals are horrible. Wherever you are there are huge lines. It's better to save money to go to a hospital where you pay, so as not to ruin your health.* You can't imagine what you have to go through there in order to get a set of dentures. But near us there is a dental clinic where you pay, and in one visit they can do everything you need done. And they give you an anesthetic, so you don't suffer. They do very good work there, and they do it quickly, but in a regular clinic you have to keep going, and they can end up ruining your whole mouth! Those are the "qualified" doctors.

My mother had to have one tooth pulled. What's so difficult about that, with these modern operations? But they ruined one of my mother's healthy teeth and left the unhealthy one in her mouth! To make a long story short, they really cheated her there. They even left the bone exposed; I remember how much she suffered. In other words, they say that medicine is . . . they shout, "Free medical care, free medical care!" But who needs that kind of care? Nobody. So let it cost something but at least be decent. So that people don't have to suffer.

There are enormous problems with education, of course. The whole system of education is worthless. The whole program's aimed at the average kid. It doesn't develop anybody's abilities. The better students have to sit in class and be bored because they already understand everything, and the teacher's knocking herself out, explaining it for the

---

*Medical care is free in the Soviet Union and available to all. However, in addition to free clinics and hospitals, there is also a system of clinics and hospitals that charge for their services. Medical care is generally of a much higher quality in these places, and many people prefer them despite the extra expense.

tenth time! The average students kind of understand what's going on, and then there are kids who are completely lost because they missed something.

There's a problem with the uniforms, but there we're getting into industrial problems. I mean, what can kids wear? You can't buy anything now because everything's so expensive and there isn't anything anyway. And if there is, it's very expensive. So you have to wear the uniform, like it or not. It would be okay if the uniform were decent, but it's awful. First of all, you can't pick one out. When you get to the store you can't figure who they were thinking of when they made it. It's all crooked. You can never buy all the pieces in the same size. The jacket is one size, the vest is another, and the skirt's still another. In other words, all different.

We have a whole lot of ministries that don't do anything. They're parasites. They don't do a thing. Just make trouble for people. They really do care more about paperwork than people. Words on some piece of paper, some signature. It can make or break all kinds of stuff. Those ministries have got everybody by the throat. They figured out with machines of some sort that the number of ministries could be reduced to eleven. That's it! In other words, the people there don't do any work, they just sit around. And then it shouldn't always be that if you get a signature, fine, if not, it's all over.

We have a problem with protecting the environment. We need industry that doesn't give off all that waste, because it is really awful the kinds of garbage they are pouring into our rivers. The Aral Sea has already died.* You can already take it right off the map, because it is not a sea anymore, just a big puddle of water. The water receded within a radius of kilometers, and ships are stuck there all rusted over. And not just rivers. Look at the smokestacks and what they give off! And they're even cutting down the trees, tearing down that poor unlucky taiga!†

Ethnic tensions have grown recently. I don't know, but somehow when things get worse in this country ethnic issues make themselves felt more. First of all because people, say, want to buy something, so they go somewhere, to other cities. People get tired of it. Because it's okay when it's just you, but on top of that . . . there are a lot of people from out of town in Moscow, too. Sometimes you get fed up with that, when you can't get anything. People just get so mad. For instance, you'll see a

---

*This refers to one of the worst ecological disasters of modern times in the Soviet Union. The Aral Sea, located in Soviet Central Asia, has almost completely dried up due to rerouting of several rivers feeding into it. The area around the sea is terribly polluted, and the population suffers from serious health problems due to contamination.

†The dense forests of Siberia.

bunch of these old ladies from Central Asia who've got sacks like this and they start buying everything in sight, all this stuff, like they were shopping for the whole village, and you really start to resent it.

The Baltic is more civilized than other parts of the country. And you can tell. Industry's more advanced. We visited Tallinn and there's more of everything in the stores there. Even something as basic as the roads always being clean, having good roads, good highways, whereas here . . . driving conditions in the Baltic republics are the way they should be. The roads are clean. But if you're driving in the Russian Federation or Belorussia, well, the roads are a mess and it's absolutely impossible to use them. We need to improve standards in this country. Somehow things have kind of gotten into a rut. And it seems like if everything would play its role—industry, economics—then progress would be made, and, well, everybody would do their job properly, honestly, conscientiously and everything. That'd be a lot better. Right away you'd see an improvement in standards and the ethnic issue and I don't know what else.

There's an enormous difference between the Baltic republics and Central Asia. We're talking about completely different peoples, first of all, and quite opposite . . . the faiths are different, if you want to get right down to it. The architecture is completely different. And every republic has its own folk crafts. In Tashkent there are all kinds of ceramics, very pretty. Of course, there isn't much in the stores there either, but they've got more than there is in Moscow right now. Everybody is coming to Moscow now to shop, so you can't get anything. As soon as something appears on the shelf it's gone. Nowadays you see more people from other republics and cities than native Muscovites.

Of course we want to live better! Both materially and spiritually!

STALINISM

My grandparents are from the countryside, and when they talk about Stalin, it seems as if everything was fine, prices came down, although it's true that they didn't feel this in the countryside. But at the same time a lot of what they produced was taken from them as taxes, and my grandmother had seven children and she simply could not feed them, they were dying from hunger. But her girlfriend lived in the city and she enjoyed the boons Stalin brought—lower prices for food and transport. She says, "What are you all cursing him for; he was such a great person! He won the war!" All of her feelings stem from the war—that he was victorious.

My grandfather was in a camp, and they received one letter from him. It was clear in that letter that they changed a lot of what he had written and made him rewrite it. And there were whole sections of it crossed out. My grandmother says that people who had relatives in camps had a very hard time living. They were considered enemies of the people, and their children were considered enemies of the people, and they bore the brunt of it all. My grandmother supports what Gorbachev is doing now—that now everybody is finding out what really happened. But there are people who were not at all affected by Stalinism. I even saw a portrait of Stalin in an old woman's house, and in front of it she keeps a vase with cut flowers.

My other grandmother says to me, "Kat, I personally wasn't affected by all of that, and because my husband returned from the war wearing a medal and received special benefits for that, it really helped me live through those times when all of that was taking place." So people have different attitudes to all of it. But of course I feel negatively about that time. Probably nobody really knows what Stalin was like as a person, but as far as his politics are concerned, it's dreadful that there was such a time.

There used to be a blind faith in the Party here. And now that's been destroyed. People simply saw that the Party was not so ideal after all. We became accustomed to seeing everything through rose-colored glasses. Even during Stalinism, when they were arresting everybody, the Party was still always right.

The ideals that my parents and especially my grandparents grew up with are collapsing; a lot of the people they believed in took part in the repression. And it's really hard on my grandparents right now. I see my grandfather; he's really in a bad way, because the people he believed in turned out to be the people who, together with Stalin, were the ones who created all that. In some ways he sometimes even tries to defend them. We try not to talk about these topics with him; he starts to get really nervous. It's really hard now for the people who lived through all of that, now that everything is being redone.

My mother says it's very difficult for her right now, because she studied in the 1950s. She was born in 1945. She says that it was hard even then; there were a lot of things she couldn't understand, some sciences, especially the humanities. She said a lot of ends didn't meet up. She used to think, "Maybe it's just me who's so thick-headed; I just can't understand anything." Because when they would teach them history, they would simply omit certain historical figures, as if they had never existed at all. She says of course it's hard for her, too. A lot of the ideals she was raised with are collapsing.

Sometimes I talk about articles with my parents. My mother says that already toward the end of the 1970s it felt terrible when they began to understand the direction we were headed in. My mother works in a scientific research department and says that there was such a lack of accountability where she worked that whenever she went to turn in her work, in order for somebody to take it any further, they needed a hundred signatures, they had to write and rewrite so many stupid, completely useless pieces of paper. An absolute waste of time.

SOLVING THE PROBLEMS

Perestroika is really necessary. Why, we haven't even begun to touch upon what Lenin wanted to do from the very beginning. Soon after the Revolution, he was shot and injured. Toward the end of his life, when he couldn't even walk, people who paid no attention to him came to power. Stalinism began. And here nobody is responsible for anything, nobody cares about anything, everything belongs to the government. What resulted is terrible, this absolute neglect and total breakdown.

We have to raise the cultural level somehow. During the first few years of Soviet power what kind of culture could there have been? People had never seen a good life. And under Stalin it was like this: It doesn't matter if you live in a hovel, you have to work and die for some kind of "bright future." In other words, people didn't have the conditions to live out their lives decently and allow them to feel good, and useful and needed, but they were supposed to give everything they had to give. . . .

Now we have to restructure everything, our entire way of living. We need more household appliances so people have more free time and can get some rest, unlike what happens so often now, a washing machine breaks and the repairman couldn't care less whether it gets fixed or not. Nobody cares about anything and nobody answers for anything. Everything is done only in the name of quantity. Everything is constantly breaking, washing machines, and mothers have to wash by hand and cook, and there is no time left to rest. All of this has to be changed.

Of course, we did have the Great Patriotic War. It played a very destructive role. People lost everything and they lived in barbaric conditions, in communal apartments with no furniture or anything else. And they tried to do everything for their children. They thought, "Well, I myself had nothing, at least let my child have something," and they gave everything to their children. That of course is also incorrect, because children have to be raised in a realistic way, that is, sometimes you have to discipline the child, so that he will learn how to get along with people, to talk to people, so that he will be able to get along and not be ashamed of himself. But all of that is hard to learn. There is a great lack of general culture here. You go into a store and ask for something, and they will scream at you from head to toe. What kind of cultural level can come from that?

Personally, I feel very positively about Gorbachev. I respect him because, in the first place, he is concerned about the country and is trying to do something so that people begin to live better. He is always traveling around the country, always meeting with simple collective farmers, with ordinary people, and they tell him about their lives, what they are lacking, what needs to be done, and, in relation to everything he hears he sets some kind of goal for himself, for the people. And of course he has done lot in the international arena. Our relations with other peoples have gotten much better. This, I think, is thanks to the peace-loving policies he is pursuing. He understands that we have to have good relationships with other countries. And at least with some countries—not with all—he's been able to establish good relations. He is truly concerned about the fate of the country. When Brezhnev was in power, it didn't feel this way.

Gorbachev's speeches are always interesting. Whenever there is some kind of conference, he always raises interesting questions, and he speaks in an interesting way and finds the path to a solution. And it is so good that he relates to simple people. They count on him to change their lives. He goes out to meet the people.

CAPITALISM AND SOCIALISM; AMERICANS AND SOVIETS

Capitalists are rich people who own factories and have a lot of money and workers. In socialism, as I understand it, a person has a choice about where he wants to work and receives a free education. A factory can belong to one person in capitalism, but in socialism it belongs to the government.

It seems to me that socialism as it is supposed to be hasn't happened here. We haven't even begun to touch on the things Lenin had in mind and the kinds of plans he had. We went in a different direction. To begin with, people have had the desire to work taken out of them. Basically, when they nationalized all of those factories they made a mistake because now people don't really care about them. They should not put everything under state ownership—even Lenin said that. Only the biggest enterprises should be owned by the State, and the smaller ones should be organized as cooperatives. They can give a part of their profits to the government and keep the rest for themselves so that they can expand production and update their technology.

I am for the idea of socialism. It seems to me that people have more
of an opportunity to live well. You won't just lose your job in socialism.
In this sense I support it.

I've heard about the unemployment problem in America. People
can't find any kind of job. Maybe sometimes they don't want to work
because the jobs they are offered require less than what they are qualified to do. That's the way we heard about it—that damned West, unemployment, everything there is bad, a real mess. It seems to me that the
unemployment problem does exist and that that problem really affects
black people, although I've heard that there are rich black people, but
even they have remained in the eyes of many—not everybody, of
course—second-class citizens. They have fewer rights and they live in
poverty.

I also have the impression that Americans are very lively people. It
seems here that they have really dampened people's initiative and people are reserved, or at least they were that way. Things have gotten
better. But when you see Americans you don't get that feeling at all.
They seem like open people who are able to express their opinions
when they are interviewed on the street. And of course you have already
solved a lot of problems there. For example, you can just go to a store
there and buy whatever you need for your home, or anything else,
without a problem. Any kind of food. That takes up a lot of time here,
and that is why people are more tired. Especially now, when you have to
buy something and you have to travel around all of Moscow just to find
it. And then stand in lines—and all of this has to be done after a day at
work.

I think relations between Americans and Soviets have changed. I
think that's great. I'm for better relations. Things are a lot nicer when
we're not at each other's throats, and I think we have to keep it up. Our
countries are a long way from each other, and we simply don't know
anything about each other, so I think it's essential.

SEX

I know of this one girl who had a baby. She and the guy got married.
She's seventeen now and he's in the army. I think that's awfully early.
But these girls that are easy—I don't even know what they want, what
they're thinking—they don't seem to respect themselves. Maybe a guy'll
respect a girl who does those things and maybe he won't, but I don't
know if he'll marry her. She could just as easily cheat on him, and
nobody likes to be cheated on. So what if she's in love? I'm against
getting involved that early. Maybe she's not really in love, maybe she'll

find someone she really loves later on. Of course, there can be true love at fifteen, but that doesn't happen often.

My mom and I have talked, and I don't think there's any need to get involved so soon. In fact, I think that if a boy pressures you, he can't really love you. Just like it's always been, a guy should protect a girl, take care of her, not force her. That's the way I see it. I think that love should be more than just sex. People should have a spiritual bond if they're going to end up living together. Take *Little Vera*. What did they have in common? Nothing. He was an intelligent guy, literate. He even asked her at one point, "Don't you find it boring living this way?" She doesn't understand what he's talking about. She says no. Well, she grew up in that kind of environment, and she has such inane parents, of course there's a lot of that. He already realizes that if they end up living together they won't have any kind of life because they don't have anything in common except sex. That's all. They'll be bored. I don't know. . . . It seems to me that two people should have common interests, some kind of shared values. If they don't have anything in common, well, maybe it'll work, but . . . it still won't be a real family. I think that true love brings people together. Truly together, spiritually and in all kinds of ways.

Mom and I have talked about sex. Mom is good at that. We talked about it when I was little. Sometimes people say, "Later, when you're a little older." That just makes a kid more curious and he gets his information on the street, distorted, and who knows what kind of attitude he'll end up with? My mom's always tried to explain things to me, she's always satisfied my curiosity. I've never had any unanswered questions. And she's never told me that children are found in the cabbage patch or that the stork brings them. My brother knows that women have babies and it doesn't faze him. It was explained to him calmly and he understood. But when people start tiptoeing around and whispering, then of course the reaction is different. If it's naughty you've got to find out. I mean, with us everything has been wrong, off limits, and sometimes the consequences of that ignorance were tragic, when a girl didn't know better and then her mother's having a fit because suddenly she's got a kid. It happens all the time. I read in the newspaper about a girl who was in the tenth grade and her mom wouldn't let her do anything and wouldn't tell her anything. How is she going to turn out when she doesn't know anything? My mom always told me when I had a question that a girl should try to preserve her honor. She pointed me in the right direction. Now she and I talk a lot when the subject comes up, an article in the newspaper or something on TV—they do a lot of stories now about prostitution and that kind of thing. . . .

Somehow we've got to teach guys to show respect for ladies and girls, like on public transportation. After all, everything begins with respect for people, for ladies, with men respecting ladies. Even a little boy, when he's too little to know anything, he should be polite and give up his seat. Even if he's little he can stand. But the way it is now, people will give up their seat for a lady who's pregnant, but if she's older you should hear the squawking. Kids see everything, and then people are surprised that the younger generation is so selfish. I mean, who's to blame? The people who brought them up!

There was this girl on a U.S.–USSR satellite link-up who said she'd had a baby and everybody was okay about it. I don't know how people here would treat somebody like that. It seems like that's the way it should be, that everybody's okay about it. It's perfectly natural. There's nothing weird about it.

It seems to me that women here have a lot of abortions out of ignorance and embarrassment. If anyone found out that would be it. There was a case in Odintsovo, this town near Moscow. My cousin lives there. She has two friends and one of them was raped. The girl's alive, everything's okay, but when people there found out . . . Now the family wants to move away. People look at them funny. Of course it's all . . . I guess it all has to do with sophistication and respect for one another. Respect for people in general. It's all related. The town's small. It probably would have been different in a big city, but in a small town . . . I think that's why there are so many abortions—so that no one will know.

But the subject is becoming more ordinary every day. People are getting used to it. If questions like that were asked now, people would be more open than they were at the time of the satellite link-up. I think it would be easier to talk about it on TV with kids from America or some other country. The first show was broadcast about a year and a half ago. I remember about three years ago it was simply a taboo subject, just bringing it up. . . . And now anything goes. Anything's okay. I think kids now have an easier time talking about it.

Postscript: Summer 1992

In June 1992 I returned to Moscow and met once again with the young people whose narratives are found in this book. Much has changed in their lives during the three years since I last saw them. They have witnessed major social and political upheavals—an attempted military coup thwarted by mass demonstrations, the dissolution of the Soviet Union, increasingly violent interethnic strife, and a rapid decline in the standard of living of the majority of the population, their families included. Together with these momentous changes in their society, they have also experienced extremely important events in their personal lives—the death of a parent; love, marriage, and the prospect of children; for some, the beginning of a higher education, for others, graduation and entry into a rapidly changing world of work. Although they are preoccupied by these immediate concerns, and often told me that they are no longer interested in politics, most of them continue to be acutely aware of current developments in their country and display considerable concern and emotion when discussing them. The general instability engulfing post-Soviet society affects everybody, including these young people, all of whom expressed great uncertainty about the future.

Tanya, now nineteen, has finished her second year at a new experimental pedagogical college, where she is studying to become a primary school teacher. She has one more year of studies to complete her training. Tanya is planning to marry in September 1992. Her fiancé, Seryozha, attends a military school in Moscow, where he is training to become a border guard.

Olya, now twenty, finished her practicum at the vocational school and received her diploma in 1989, but did not go on to work at the base enterprise affiliated with the school, as she was officially required to do. After several attempts to find satisfying work, she took a clerical position at a transportation agency that processes and delivers railway freight shipments to and from the Moscow region. She has been working at the agency for a year and a half.

Lena, now nineteen, has finished one year of studies in the depart-ment of journalism at Moscow State University. Lena took the competitive entrance exams to enter Moscow State immediately after graduating from secondary school, but she was not accepted on her first attempt and had to wait a year until she could try again. In the meantime she took a job as a correspondent for a small newspaper. Her second exams gained her entrance into the correspondence section of the university's department of journalism. Lena continues to work, at a new job in a film studio, and is studying at the same time.

Ilya, now nineteen, has finished his third year of studies in the department of Russian language and literature at Moscow State Univer-sity. In 1991, at eighteen, he married Sasha, a classmate from the uni-versity. Ilya and Sasha are expecting a child in October 1992.

Maxim, now eighteen, finished his course at the culinary school and worked as a cook for almost two years, first in a hotel, then in the cafeteria of a government ministry. He received a deferral from military service, and since that time has spent almost a year without any type of employment.

Yelena, now nineteen, is working at a production training center for students in grades 9–11. She does clerical work at the center and also teaches typing and computer data entry. Yelena has twice tried to be accepted at an institution of higher education, but thus far has not passed the entrance exams. Although she enjoys her work, Yelena wants to com-plete her education and is preparing to take the entrance exams again.

Dima, now twenty-one, is currently living in Canada. After complet-ing two and a half years of military service, he joined an agricultural project organized by a youth agency, designed to interest young people in becoming independent farmers. The project involved an internship with Canadian farm families. Dima decided to stay in Canada when the internship ended: several of the participants in the program, upon re-turning to Moscow, have written to him about the obstacles the project is encountering in its next phase and which may ultimately result in its discontinuation.

Lyosha, now twenty-one, began his military duty upon completing the PTU in 1989, but received an early leave after six months. Currently he is involved in the same agricultural project as Dima. After three months in Canada, Lyosha returned to Moscow, took courses at an agricultural institute, and is now trying to establish a small farm outside the city on land rented from a state farm.

Alexei, now twenty, received his diploma at the PTU where he learned carpentry. He received a medical certificate which excused him from military service. Alexei has worked in various places since graduation. He is currently a co-owner of a small optical cooperative and has become something of an entrepreneur.

Natasha, now nineteen, is studying at the same pedagogical college Tanya attends. She has completed her second year and has one more to finish her course of studies and be certified as a primary school teacher. In March 1992 Natasha married her boyfriend, Andrei. They are expecting a child in November.

Katya, now nineteen, has completed two years of study at the Moscow Aviation Institute, a prestigious school with a variety of departments. She plans to earn a degree in economics, and will begin taking specialized courses in her field in her third year.

Glossary

The reader may wish to consult the definitions below for a better understanding of some terms that occur in the interviews.

Cooperatives. Cooperatives have sprung up since passage of a 1988 law permitting small-group private enterprises in the USSR. They operate in many fields, from restaurants to livestock raising, but are banned from certain sectors, such as the film industry, and have gained little ground in the media more generally. Cooperative tutoring services and private lessons are available, but cooperatives are not allowed to compete with the official state-run ten-year schools. Economically they have been a success: in two years of existence their output reportedly grew to 41 billion rubles, the number of people employed in cooperatives rose to 4.5 million, and they accounted for approximately 5 percent of the gross national product. Nevertheless, cooperatives remain controversial. Official obstacles have periodically blocked their expansion and they have been the target of considerable popular resentment for their high prices and for earning high incomes through "speculation."

Economic Accountability, Cost-accounting *(khozraschet)*. One of the perennial themes of economic reform, *khozraschet* requires enterprises to cover their own operating costs out of gross income rather than rely on state subsidies.

Glasnost (openness). Gorbachev's policy of glasnost was intended to encourage freedom of expression and a general openness in the political, cultural, and intellectual life of the Soviet Union. One of the important accomplishments of glasnost was the suspension of most forms of state censorship. The result has been a revolutionary change in the mass media and other sources of information. In general glasnost has been met with great enthusiasm by the majority of Soviet citizens.

Informal (Unofficial) Groups and Organizations. In a radical break from the past, when all organized activity was Party-controlled, in recent years thousands of unofficial groups and clubs have emerged in every area of Soviet society, even within the Communist Party and the Komsomol. Many of these organizations are of a political nature and resemble parties; many are issue-oriented and focus on questions such as the environment or problems specific to a particular place or population group. In the March 1989 elections to the Congress of People's Deputies and in elections at lower levels, many candidates representing informal groups won their races and are now involved in government.

Informal (Unofficial) Youth Groups. Informal youth groups began to appear in the early 1980s. Members identified themselves by wearing distinctive clothing and hairstyles and adopting names and symbols that often were of Western origin, e.g., *rokery* (hard rock music fans), *panki* (punk rockers), *metallisty* (fans of heavy metal), "hippies," and "pacifists." The appearance of young people wearing chains and young men in earrings and long hair was quite shocking in the conservative Soviet Union and the word *neformaly* (informal) in reference to young people is often used pejoratively.

Land-leasing. For the past sixty years all agriculture and livestock raising in the Soviet Union has been organized on state farms (*sovkhozy*) or collective farms (*kolkhozy*). Individuals could not own or lease land, although every family working on a farm was also entitled to cultivate a small household plot (these account for less than 5 percent of all cultivated land but up to a third of the supply of fruits and vegetables, dairy products, and meat). The legalization of land leases in 1987, intended to encourage private initiative in order to increase productivity, met some resistance from local authorities and distrust from potential farmers who saw the risks involved as too high. After considerable debate, a law was passed in 1990 that allows lifetime leasing of land with the right of inheritance, but it is still illegal to buy or sell land.

Military Service. All young men in the Soviet Union are required to fulfill two years of service in the armed forces (in the navy, three years). If a young man is accepted into an institute of higher education that has a military department, he can fulfill his military service by attending classes there on a weekly basis while continuing his studies. There has been growing resistance to universal military service and there have been proposals to make the Soviet army a volunteer army (so far there is no indication that this will occur). The Soviet army has come under considerable criticism, fueled by revelations about the war in Afghanistan, the questionable behavior of some soldiers there, and its generally poor military performance.

(Official) Youth Organizations. Named for the month in which the 1917 Revolution took place, the **Oktobrists** are the official political organization for children from six to nine years of age. Schoolchildren join the organization almost automatically, and in it they are taught to believe in the ideals of Lenin and the Revolution. The **Young Pioneers**, with a membership of more than 25 million, are the official organization for children from nine to fourteen. Although political education is an important part of Pioneer activities, for many youngsters the Pioneers are primarily a social and recreational organization. Summer camps are run by the Young Pioneers and neighborhood Palaces of Culture run by the organization offer after-school activities. The **Komsomol** (the Young Communist League) is the official organization for young adults from the ages of fourteen to twenty-eight. It has been assigned a fundamental role in the ideological development of Soviet citizens and it has broad access to resources to promote its activity: the Komsomol controls more than two hundred youth and children's newspapers, three publishing houses, and television and radio programs, and is officially represented in various state bodies. Until recently the organization had a membership of almost 35 million. Recruitment began to decline in the 1970s, by which time the organization had lost most of its élan and had become mainly a stepping-stone to university admission or career advancement; Komsomol membership has fallen precipitously in the 1980s and 1990s.

Perestroika (restructuring). Perestroika has become an umbrella term for the comprehensive political, economic, and social reforms initiated by Mikhail Gorbachev since his rise to leadership in March 1985. Gorbachev has always stressed that the goal of his reforms has been renewal of the socialist order and "more socialism." The means proposed to accomplish this include reduction of bureaucracy, the decentralization of economic management, property reforms, the introduction of market mechanisms, and increased local autonomy. Equally fundamental are political democratization and freedom of expression (glasnost). Another important aspect of perestroika is the call for a new world order, particularly improved relations between the Soviet Union and the United States.

Personality Cult/Stalinism. The period of Stalin's rule (from the 1920s to 1953), characterized by brutal repression, a system of labor camps and detention centers, internal exile, mass executions and terror, and by the most extreme adulation of Stalin as a genius and a hero. The Soviet economy boomed during Stalin's rule, and many people still associate that time with visible improvement in the standard of living as well as the Soviet Union's victory in World War II. With glasnost, long-suppressed information about the Stalin period has become public and much of it has been extremely shocking to the general population. Recently published Soviet estimates confirm that up to 20 million people were victims of Stalinist repression.

Stagnation (or the period of stagnation). The period of Leonid Brezhnev's leadership (1964–82), now associated with slowed economic growth, bureaucratization, corruption, general inefficiency, lack of productivity and accountability, and rampant alcoholism. The term "stagnation" has entered everyday speech and may be used to denigrate a person, institution, newspaper, book, or work of art.

Index